D0093012

JAMES MADISON

JAMES MADISON

Richard Brookhiser

BASIC BOOKS
A MEMBER OF THE PERSEUS BOOKS GROUP
New York

Copyright © 2011 by Richard Brookhiser
Published by Basic Books,
A Member of the Perseus Books Group

Books published by Basic Books are available at special discounts for bulk
purchases in the United States by corporations, institutions, and other
organizations. For more information, please contact the Special Markets
Department at the Perseus Books Group, 2300 Chestnut Street, Suite 200,
Philadelphia, PA 19103, or call (800) 810-4145, ext. 5000, or e-mail
special.markets@perseusbooks.com.

A CIP catalog record for this book is available from the Library of Congress.
ISBN: 978-0-465-01983-0
e-book ISBN: 978-0-465-02799-6
10 9 8 7 6 5 4 3 2 1

FOR
Bert and Nina Smiley

CONTENTS

A NOTE ON SPELLING AND USAGE

Eighteenth-century writing had somewhat different rules than today's, and even the well educated followed them rather loosely. Proper names were often spelled whimsically. In his notes on the Constitutional Convention, Madison wrote of Govurneur (Gouverneur) Morris, Oliver Elseworth (Ellsworth), and Roger Sharman (Sherman). William Pierce, meanwhile, wrote of Mr. Maddison.

All spelling and punctuation have been modernized in what follows.

American presidents in Madison's lifetime sent "ministers" abroad, not "ambassadors," and picked "secretaries of departments," not a "cabinet." The newest capital of the United States was called "Washington City," not "Washington." I have sometimes preferred anachronism to quaintness. The Republican Party that Jefferson and Madison founded is the ancestor of today's Democrats; the modern GOP is a different, later organization.

ACKNOWLEDGMENTS

Michael C. Quinn, president of the Montpelier Foundation, and all his colleagues have been of great help. Michael Pack and Tracy Simmons gave me good advice.

The generosity of the John Simon Guggenheim Memorial Foundation helped me complete this book. Akhil Amar, Michael Pack, and Tracy Simmons gave good suggestions and advice.

I would like to thank my editor, Lara Heimert, my agent, Michael Carlisle, and my wife, Jeanne Safer.

Introduction

August 24, 1814, began as a typical summer day in Washington: bright and cloudless, promising heat and humidity as the day wore on. For years, James Madison, the president, had fled high summer in Washington and other low-lying cities for the healthier air of his inland home in the Virginia Piedmont. But this August his presence was required in the capital. America had been at war with Britain for two years. Mr. Madison's war—he had asked Congress to declare it—had been fought along the Canadian border; against Indians on the frontier; on the high seas. Now the war was coming home.

A week earlier, on August 17, twenty British ships carrying 4,500 troops had anchored in the Patuxent River in Maryland, only thirty-five miles away from Washington to the southeast. The president had suggested "pelt[ing] the enemy from the start with light troops." But nothing was done. Instead the British disembarked and made a leisurely stroll up the Maryland countryside, perhaps bound for Baltimore, a booming port, the third-largest city in America. Secretary of War John Armstrong thought so: they would "certainly" not come to Washington, he said; "what the devil will they do here? . . . No, no! Baltimore is the place, sir."

But now the British had made a left turn. Just hours earlier, at midnight, the president had gotten a note from the field: "The enemy are in full march for Washington. . . . Destroy the bridges. . . . Remove the records."

When James Madison had been a congressman, a quarter century earlier, he had helped move the nation's capital from New York to an undeveloped site on the Potomac. The new capital was still hardly more than a small town, stretching from Rock Creek in the west to Capitol Hill in the east: a ragged arc, decorated by a few incongruous public buildings, as if built by ancients or aliens. In the midst of it stood the White House. Madison was the third president to have lived there. John Adams, whom Madison scorned, had spent the dismal last days of his administration in a shell inside a construction site. Thomas Jefferson, whom Madison loved above all men, had run it like a Virginia plantation house, hosting intimate dinners for congressmen and diplomats with good food, excellent wine, and his own sparkling conversation. Madison's White House was grander yet, thanks to his wife, Dolley, who brightened it with banquets and soirees, red velvet curtains and green gilt-edged china, a piano and a macaw.

Now, a little before eight o'clock in the morning on August 24, a message came to this republican palace from Gen. William Winder, commander of the Potomac military district. It was addressed to Armstrong, but the president opened it himself. The general wanted advice, as fast as possible; Madison mounted his horse and left the White House for Winder's headquarters at the Navy Yard.

The Navy Yard was a mile south of town, on the Eastern Branch of the Potomac, now called the Anacostia River. There was a bridge there, about where the Eleventh Street bridge is now. All morning, Madison conferred with officers and cabinet secretaries, who came and went. The three most important represented all the types a president typically finds about him in moments of crisis: those who might help, those who won't, and those who can't.

James Monroe, secretary of state, was a Revolutionary War veteran who had known Madison for decades; he had quarreled with him and reconciled with him. He was the man who had sent the midnight warning about the British march on the capital, and he had thrown himself into the effort to defend it. He had talent and energy, and had decided to serve Madison.

John Armstrong, another veteran of the Revolutionary War, had been appointed secretary of war six months after hostilities had begun, to retrieve the disasters of an incompetent predecessor. In a year and a half on the job, he had cleared out deadwood and promoted fresh faces, but he had also fallen out with the president. He disliked Madison personally and disagreed with him strategically, ignoring Madison's suggestions to hit the enemy as soon as they landed and instead focusing all his attention on Baltimore. Armstrong, too, had talent and energy, and had decided by August 1814 to use neither on Madison's behalf.

The man immediately responsible for the capital's defense was William Winder, a thirty-nine-year-old former lawyer, who had been in the army for only two years. He had received his current assignment in July, largely because he was the nephew of the governor of Maryland. He had been unceasingly busy. "The innumerably multiplied orders, letters, consultations, and demands which crowded upon me . . . can more easily be conceived than described," he wrote. Yet he had accomplished nothing. He had energy, and no talent at all.

At ten o'clock word reached the Navy Yard that the British were making for Bladensburg, Maryland, a village northeast of the capital. There was a gap in the hills there, and a short bridge over the Eastern Branch, five miles up from the Navy Yard, where the stream is narrow. It was the natural route for attacking Washington from the east. Monroe rode off to alert whatever American troops were already there. Winder followed with reinforcements.

Armstrong came to the Navy Yard only after Monroe and Winder left. Madison asked him whether he had any advice to give. He didn't but added that, since the battle would be between American militia and British regulars, "the former would be beaten." Madison suggested that

Armstrong really should take part in the coming engagement ("[I] expressed to him my concern and surprise at the reserve he showed," was how Madison recalled it). Armstrong answered that if Madison "thought it proper," he would go off to Bladensburg, too.

The president, who sensed the importance of the coming engagement even if his secretary of war did not, decided to ride to Bladensburg with his attorney general, Richard Rush. He borrowed a set of pistols and, because his horse suddenly went lame, a second mount, and set off.

James Madison was sixty-three years old. He had never heard a shot fired in anger. He was a small man—just over five feet tall, just over a hundred pounds—and a sickly one: all his life, he was subject to what he called bilious attacks (upset stomach and bowels) and, less often, "attacks resembling epilepsy, and suspending the intellectual functions." He had talent and energy in spades: he was smarter than Monroe, Armstrong, and Winder put together; smarter than Jefferson, perhaps even smarter than Adams. Over a lifetime of public service he had put his mind—forget his shoulder—to the wheel, reading, writing, speaking, and thinking, driving himself so hard that he often undermined his already weak constitution.

But Madison was not a warrior. Two years earlier, the day war was declared, he had made himself ridiculous by visiting the War and Navy Departments in "a little round hat and huge cockade"—a crude attempt to become a military leader by dressing like one. It is arguable (and some of his contemporaries did argue it: Madison, said Rep. John Calhoun, lacked "commanding talents") that he was not by nature an executive. But that morning he was the chief executive and commander in chief. War was five miles away, and he rode to meet it.

He and Rush took the road that is still called Bladensburg Road, overtaking American units as they went. After an hour in the saddle, they came down a hill, alongside an orchard, and toward the bridge that led over the Eastern Branch to Bladensburg's main (and only) street and its brick houses. An American horseman waved them back. The president and the attorney general had ridden ahead of their own front line; the British were already entering the town from the opposite direction. Winder, Monroe, and Armstrong were posted on the hill they had just descended, to the rear. Madison and Rush rode back toward them.

It was now about one o'clock. There were 7,000 Americans on or near the field, a mixture of militia and regulars, plus 500 sailors who were still marching with cannon from the Navy Yard—more than enough to beat back the British, if they were well-positioned and well-led. If the Americans crumbled here, however, there was nothing to stop the enemy from taking the capital—and perhaps the president and his cabinet as well. The Americans had been arranged in three lines, two close to the Bladensburg bridge, a third a mile farther back. Monroe had taken charge, altering some of the dispositions at the last minute, not to advantage (he pulled troops from the orchard and into fields, where they had no cover). Winder was frantic, unable to make decisions or give orders. Madison asked Armstrong whether he had made any decisions or given any orders. The secretary of war answered that he had not. "I remarked," wrote Madison, "that he might offer some advice." (Armstrong was not the only passive-aggressive personality outside Bladensburg that morning.)

Madison and Armstrong rode up to Winder for a last-minute consultation. Muskets and artillery were already firing back and forth across the stream. Spooked, the president's borrowed horse reared and plunged so that Madison could not take part in the conversation. When the secretary of war and the general were done speaking, Madison asked Armstrong whether he had offered any advice. Armstrong replied that he hadn't and that "the arrangements . . . appeared to be as good as circumstances admitted."

What John Armstrong said was true. The American arrangements for the Battle of Bladensburg were as good as the circumstances, which included the abilities and deficiencies of the commanders, and the abilities and deficiencies of the man who had given them their jobs, and kept

them there, admitted. The charm was wound up. Now the battle for the
capital would play itself out.

T he courage James Madison showed on the morning of the Battle of
    Bladensburg is what first prompted me to write about him. It was
moral courage even more than physical. He did not put on a hat and a
cockade, he put himself at the point of contact. On a bad day that was
likely to get worse, he chose to see what was happening and to face the
consequences of his actions.

But the War of 1812 is not what people most associate with Madison.
He is most famous for his role in producing the Constitution. Madison
was called the Father of the Constitution during his lifetime, and he has
borne the title ever since.

It is a misleading title if taken too literally. Madison was only one of
seven Virginia delegates to the Constitutional Convention of 1787, one
of fifty-five overall, and did not get exactly the document he wanted. As
the convention wrapped up, he worried, in a letter to his friend Jefferson
in Paris, that the Constitution might not "*answer* its *national object* nor
prevent the local *mischiefs* which every where *excite disgust*." (The words
italicized here were written in cipher—a practice Madison and Jefferson
used to guard their thoughts from prying foreigners—or Americans.)

Other men besides Madison made essential contributions to the Constitution, to the fight for ratification, and to its first and most important
amendments. The document was written in its final form by Gouverneur
Morris, the peg-legged delegate from Pennsylvania ("a better choice" for
a draftsman, said Madison, "could not have been made"). Some of Madison's greatest writing went into his arguments explaining and praising
the Constitution in *The Federalist*, but the impresario of that project was
Alexander Hamilton, who picked the authors (Madison and John Jay, in
addition to himself) and wrote three-fifths of the eighty-five papers. The
strongest argument for ratifying the Constitution was the approval of

George Washington, signaled by his presence at the convention and his quiet support afterward. Madison understood that Washington was the heavyweight champion of American public life, which is why he stuck by him, like a trainer, from the planning stages of the convention through the early days of Washington's presidency. Finally, the resistance of the Constitution's opponents (such as Madison's enemy, Patrick Henry) obliged the document's supporters to offer something that they, as authors, had neglected to provide—a Bill of Rights.

But only Madison played a central role at every stage in the Constitution's birth. He was present before, during, and after the creation. He was a delegate to the Annapolis Convention of 1786, which called for the convention in Philadelphia a year later. When the Philadelphia convention met in 1787, he arrived (the first out-of-towner to show up) with an agenda in mind. He never missed a session, and he spoke more often than any other delegate, except the flashy Morris and James Wilson, another Pennsylvanian. "He always comes forward," wrote delegate William Pierce of Georgia, "the best informed man [on] any point in debate." Thanks to *The Federalist*, published in New York, Madison was a player in the fight for ratification in that state, and he led the pro-Constitution forces in Virginia. Political reality and Jefferson's urging persuaded Madison to accept the idea of a Bill of Rights, and as a member of the First Congress he threw himself into that project with characteristic energy, sorting the proposals of earnest idealists and secret saboteurs into something like the first ten amendments we have today (plus the Twenty-Seventh Amendment, which regulates congressional pay raises, proposed in 1789 but not ratified until 1992).

Madison was also the first historian of the Constitutional Convention. As he helped shape the document, he worked to shape the future's view of it. Every day the convention met, he posted himself in front of the head table in Independence Hall. "In this favorable position for hearing all that passed, I noted . . . what was read from the Chair or spoken by the members, and losing not a moment unnecessarily between the adjournment and reassembling of the Convention I was enabled to write out my daily notes." Madison's notes, the most complete set left by any delegate, have been grist for historians ever since.

Madison earned his paternity of the Constitution. He was a devoted and anxious parent, for he believed "the happiness of a people great even in its infancy, and possibly the cause of Liberty throughout the world," was "staked" on what he and his colleagues had made.

The Constitution was not the only subject that engrossed Madison's relentless mind, however, and the late 1780s were not his only active years. He was a precocious young man, and like many hypochondriacs he lived to be a very old one, and he devoted his long adulthood to analyzing an array of issues, all related to the cause of liberty. What was the basis of religious liberty? How did public opinion sustain liberty? How did war and slavery threaten it?

In 1776, age twenty-five, Madison fought to amend the Virginia Declaration of Rights, from guaranteeing "fullest toleration" of religion to "free exercise." Madison's change of wording grounded religious liberty in nature, not the permission of the state. Toleration is a gift; truly free men exercise their rights. The Virginia Declaration of Rights was a statement of principles; Madison's principle of "free exercise" was not enacted into law until the Virginia Statute for Religious Freedom, written by Jefferson, was passed ten years later. Jefferson was so proud of this law that he mentioned it on his tombstone. But it was Madison who pushed Jefferson's law through the Virginia Assembly. "I flatter myself," Madison wrote Jefferson after he had succeeded, that "[we have] extinguished forever the ambitious hope of making laws for the human mind."

In 1791, after the Constitution was ratified, Madison sat down to rethink some of the most important debates he had just won. In *The Federalist* he had argued that the very size of the United States and the complexity of its new federal system would buttress liberty, since malign factions would find it hard to seize power. But now he decided that another guarantee was necessary: enlightened public opinion, which would spot threats to liberty and unite "with a holy zeal" to repel them. In a new series of essays published, like those of *The Federalist*, in the newspapers, he teased out the consequences of this idea. Drowning in poll data, we understand the power of public opinion, though we often doubt how enlightened it is. But in the early 1790s, regularly consulting public opinion was a new concept. Many of Madison's colleagues, including Washington and Hamilton, had little use for it. They thought the people should rule when they voted, then let the victors do their best until the next election. But Madison glimpsed our world before it existed.

Madison was consumed with questions of war and peace. The Bastille fell during his first year in the First Congress, and the wars touched off by the French Revolution continued through the War of 1812. The United States began its national life in the shadow of a world war, as violent as World Wars I and II, longer than both of them put together, and as ideological as the Cold War. Would war advance the cause of liberty or destroy it? It was ironic that Madison had asked for war in 1812 and found himself on a battlefield two years later, for he feared war as the enemy of liberty and had tried, first as Jefferson's secretary of state, then as president, to avoid it. Surely, he believed, trade was a more powerful weapon than arms. Yet when he felt America's honor was compromised, he chose to fight. Both of his attitudes—a disposition to pacifism and a touchiness about America's pride and its position in the world—wind through later American history.

In his long retirement, almost twenty years, Madison grappled with the questions of slavery and union. He heard the coming of the Civil War decades before Fort Sumter. His solutions to the problem of slavery were worthless, a pathetic case of intellectual and moral failure. His position on the problem of union would help solve the problem of slavery.

But Madison is more than the Father of the Constitution, or of other intellectual constructs. He is the Father of Politics. He lived in his head, but his head was always concerned with making his cherished thoughts real. In a free country the road to reality runs through politics. Madison spent as much time politicking as thinking, and he was equally good at both.

He did what came naturally to him: preparing, persuading, setting agendas, conducting committee work, legislative maneuvering. He grew up in a family as large as an oyster bed: good training for a future law-maker. He worked at what did not come naturally to him: public speaking, campaigning. His voice was both harsh and weak; time and again, the notetakers at debates he participated in left blanks in his remarks or simply gave up, because Madison "could not be distinctly heard." Yet, when circumstances required it, he debated Patrick Henry; he debated James Monroe in the open air in a snowstorm so bitter he got frostbite on his nose (he won both debates).

When he found a political chore he absolutely could not do, he was not too proud to work with men or women who could. Dolley Madison was more than a hostess, she was a political wife, America's first: half a campaign tag team, and often the better half. Likewise, Madison worked with Washington, profiting from his charisma and his judgment, and with Hamilton, profiting from his dash (when Madison was not alarmed by it). He worked with Jefferson, visionary philosopher and politician par excellence, for forty years. He consented to learn something about money from his younger colleague Albert Gallatin, a Swiss immigrant who spoke with a French accent but knew more about America's finances than most natives. Madison was a great man who was not afraid of assisting or de-ferring to other great men (another legacy of his tight-knit family). He also worked with the less-than-great: hatchet men and gossips, snoops and spies; on one occasion he turned a blind eye to a mob. They do the work of politics too; they are part of the game.

Politics has its own institutions, and Madison invented a few that have lasted as long as the Constitution. In the early 1790s he helped found America's first political party, the Republicans, who later changed their name to the Democrats (the modern GOP is an unrelated organization). Today's Democrats hold Jefferson/Jackson Day Dinners to commemorate their origins, though they might better call them Jefferson/Madison Day Dinners, since their party began in 1791, when Madison joined Jefferson on a trip through New York and New England, supposedly collecting biological specimens for the American Philosophical Society, but actually collecting allies for themselves.

Madison helped found the first party newspaper, the *National Gazette*, which dissected issues and personalities and ground ideological axes. (*The Nation*, *The New Republic*, *National Review*, FoxNews, and MSNBC perform the same tasks today.) He recruited the paper's first editor, Philip Freneau, an old college chum who wrote poetry. Jefferson gave Freneau a nominal job as a translator in the State Department, and in his free time Freneau smacked Hamilton and Washington in prose. Madison's interest in publicity flowed naturally from his interest in public opinion. Such a powerful force could not be allowed to develop randomly or to be molded by liberty's enemies. If enlightened public opinion was a bulwark of freedom, then leaders must labor ceaselessly to enlighten or manipulate it.

Madison was a cogwheel in one of the first American political machines, the Virginia Dynasty. America revolted against George III and the House of Hanover, but the dynastic temptation remained strong. John Adams, second president and the only founder president with sons, saw his eldest, John Quincy Adams, become the sixth president. But the Adamses were unpopular one-termers. Between them stretched the Virginia Dynasty: two terms of Jefferson, two terms of Madison, two terms of Monroe—twenty-four years of government by neighbors, and ideological soul mates.

One of the iron laws of politics is that what goes around comes around. Throughout his career, Madison was beset by enemies and supposed friends, wielding the same dark arts that he himself practiced. Fortunately for him, he was generally skillful enough to beat them back.

But another iron law of politics is that you can't win them all. Heroes can aspire to perfection, especially if they die young, through the purity of an action, or a stance. But the long haul of politics takes at least some of the shine off almost everyone. Madison had an unusually good record when it came to winning elections; not quite so good when it came to sizing up issues and men. The years would see many achievements, as well as rigidities and blunders, from demonizing people and countries to mishandling his own associates.

We pay much less attention to James Madison, Father of Politics, than to James Madison, Father of the Constitution. That is because politics embarrasses us. Politics is the spectacle on television and YouTube, the daily perp walk on the Huffington Post and the Drudge Report. Surely our founders and framers left us something better, more solid, more inspiring than that? They did. But they all knew—and Madison understood better than any of them—that ideals come to life in dozens of political transactions every day. Some of those transactions aren't pretty. You can understand this and try to work with this knowledge, or you can look away. But ignoring politics will not make it stop. It will simply go on without you—and sooner or later will happen to you.

Dolley Payne Todd, in the first excitement of meeting a possible suitor, her future husband, told a friend "the great little Madison" had asked "to see me this evening." All his life, Madison's acquaintances rang the changes on this contrast: he was a mighty figure, and a little guy. The contrast has a moral dimension, too. James Madison was a great man who helped build a republic. He was also an ambitious and sometimes small-bore man who stumped, spoke, counted votes, pulled wires, scratched backs, and stabbed them. He was not afraid of the contrast, for his deepest thinking told him that the builders of liberty had to know and sometimes use the materials of passion and self-advancement.

If war is the continuation of politics by other means, it makes sense to introduce Madison on a battlefield, even a dubious one. Americans ignore him there, too, because we divide our wars into two categories—those we look back on as stirring (Washington's crossing, Pickett's charge, D-Day) and those we ignore as unseemly, or botched, or both. But our present experience of Afghanistan and Iraq may illuminate the War of 1812. There were miscalculations and disasters in Mr. Madison's war. But there were also moments of valor, discipline, and learning from mistakes—even at Bladensburg.

But Madison rode to Bladensburg more than sixty years into his life, forty years into his career. Let us begin at the beginning.

CHAPTER ONE

Youth, Revolution

John Maddison, an English ship's carpenter, came to Virginia in 1653. By taking advantage of a bounty system that awarded fifty acres for every friend, relative, or contract laborer a Virginian brought over, John died thirty years later owning 1,900 acres of Tidewater land. His son, also named John, increased the acreage and became a county sheriff.

A son of the second John, Ambrose, dropped one of the D's from his surname and in about 1730 moved to the Piedmont, a belt of rolling, fertile soil above the fall line. He built a house in Orange County southeast of the Blue Ridge Mountains, and there he and the next few generations of Madisons stayed.

In 1749 Ambrose's eldest son, James, married Nelly Conway, daughter of another wealthy landowner. On a March midnight in 1751, she gave birth to their first child, James Jr.

Disease swept colonial Virginians away, but if spouses died, they remarried and started over. By this means, young James Madison was born into an ever-spreading thicket of cousins and in-laws, some of them famous—he was related to Edmund Pendleton, who would sign the Declaration of Independence—most of them not known at all, except in Virginia, which was the only world most Virginians knew. Everybody in the plantation gentry in which young James Madison grew up knew everybody else, and everybody was related to almost everybody else.

Madison's extended family was large; his immediate family was close, and he would stay close to it all his life.

James Madison Sr. was a local grandee, a justice of the peace, and a vestryman of his Anglican parish (vestrymen in colonial Virginia were responsible for poor relief, and for enforcing Sabbath observance). He was an economic powerhouse, too, a successful planter and entrepreneur who owned more than 3,000 acres and dozens of slaves.

When young James was nine years old, his father built a new house, later christened Montpelier (the son remembered helping to carry furniture into it); a smithy off the north corner of the building served the local farmers.* Young James would make Montpelier grander, but it was impressive enough when it was new, with a sweeping mountain vista off the front porch.

Young James was conscious of his father's status—and his own. He was known, and thought of himself, as Junior. In 1772, answering a letter that William Bradford, a college friend, had sent him at home, he added in a postscript that, although Bradford's letter had been correctly addressed, "the addition of Junr. to my name would not be improper." The neighbors also knew which Madison was which. In 1775, when Orange County rallied its militia to resist Virginia's colonial overlords, both Madisons became colonels (James Sr. organized the militia and James Jr. drilled with it, though neither of them ever fought). But until the day James Sr. died, in 1801, his eldest son was known in the county as "the young colonel."

James's mother was a quieter, yet in some ways even greater presence in his life. All we know of Nelly Conway Madison is that she raised her children and lived at Montpelier a very long time. She was nineteen when

---

* The name did not come until the 1790s, and Madison always spelled it with two L's.

she bore James Jr.; she lived to be ninety-seven. When James Madison was a former president, living in retirement at home, every day he and his wife visited Mrs. Madison in her room. It had some of the character of a state visit.

Madison had eleven siblings, six of whom survived childhood. When he came home to Montpelier after college, he wrote his friend Bradford that he was teaching "my brothers and sisters in some of the first rudiments of literature" (Virginians typically began their educations at home). When he wrote this, his charges were twelve, ten, eight, and four years old. Madison would soon become interested in politics; we do not know if he made the connection, but herding small children is good training for certain aspects of legislative work.

As Madison aged, he had both good and bad relations with his three brothers. He came to rely on Ambrose, the middle one, as a surrogate manager of both family affairs and local political business, while he served in the state capital or Congress. But his oldest brother, Francis, withdrew from the rest of the family in young adulthood, and his youngest, William, became estranged over time. The mixture of closeness and coldness is another pattern that repeats itself in political bodies and alliances, even among "friends."

Growing up in a family as tightly woven as the Madisons, you either run away to sea or learn to play well with others. James Madison made some gestures at independence, and would find ways to maintain a cordon of personal space even at Montpelier, but he clearly chose the latter path.

M adison found a second family in his youth, which he kept close by for the rest of his life: books. In 1762, age eleven, he was sent seventy miles away to Caroline County to study with Donald Robertson, a Scottish schoolmaster. Madison came home for vacations but boarded with Robertson for five years. After two more years studying at home with the local minister, Madison left Virginia in 1769 to attend the College of New Jersey at Princeton, run by another Scotsman, Rev. John Witherspoon.

Scottish teachers were popular in mid-eighteenth-century America because they were sparks from a furnace of intellectual life. Scotland was a poor, small country, but it was unusually literate, and its universities and the men who graduated from them provided the best education in the English-speaking world.

Madison's home had a typical plantation library, good enough in its way, but Robertson and Witherspoon gave him the opportunity to delve. For Madison, books were as powerful and compelling as people: he questioned them; if they could not give him answers, he sought out new ones. (A decade after he left college he made this request of Thomas Jefferson: "If you meet with *Graecorum Respublicae ab Ubbone Emmio descriptae*, Lugd. Batavorum [Leiden] 1632, pray get it for me.") As Madison read, he wrote down his own thoughts, first by copying thoughts he liked into a commonplace book—"The Talent for insinuating is more useful than that of persuading. The former is often successful, the latter very seldom" (Cardinal de Retz, a seventeenth-century French politician). As he grew older, he wrote essays that digested what he had learned. Writing extended Madison's bookish discussions—it was a form of talking with himself.

All his life, Madison was reserved and awkward in the presence of strangers, a trait that probably encouraged, and was in turn fostered by, his bookishness. But his years at Princeton showed the mirror image of his shyness: once he settled in to a place or a relationship, he settled in very comfortably. The best-known story of Madison's college days is a solemn tribute paid him by Witherspoon, who said he "never knew" his brilliant student "to do, or to say, an improper thing." One of the people Witherspoon said this to in later years was Thomas Jefferson, who liked to tease Madison with it. In fact, Madison did and said a number of improper things while he was at Princeton, writing abusive poems about students who belonged to the other of the college's two debating societies.

Madison's squibs are filled with talk about whoring, pimping, chamber pots and other sophomoric paraphernalia.

> *Come, noble Whigs* [Madison's society], *disdain these sons*
> *Of screech owls, monkeys and baboons.*

Madison gave up versifying, for which he had no talent, but all his life he kept up his naughty talk, in private. "[He is] full of anecdote," wrote one diplomat years later, "sometimes . . . of a loose description." Yet Witherspoon's testimony to Madison's propriety was true as far as Witherspoon was concerned. Madison could please his academic mentor, then turn around and be one of the boys. Only someone like Jefferson, who knew both sides of him, could laugh at the contrast. Madison's willingness to be the straight man of Jefferson's jokes showed his ability to please his knowing friend, too.

Madison's learning was not directed toward any of the ordinary professions. After graduating in 1771—he went through college in only two years—he stayed on in Princeton for a year, pursuing "miscellaneous studies" with Witherspoon. He learned some Hebrew,* a prerequisite for the ministry, though he seems to have had no intention of preaching. He read law books, though he never practiced law. His learning was focused on men and society—he never warmed to math or science, and even *belles lettres* fell by the wayside—but what role was he planning, as he entered his twenties, to play?

After returning home in 1772, Madison wrote Bradford that he did not expect "a long or healthy life." "You hurt your constitution by too close application to study," Bradford told him in reply, though he tried to cheer Madison up: the poet Alexander Pope was sickly, "yet you see he lived longer than the generality of mankind do."

---

* He already knew Latin, Greek, French, and Italian.

Madison would suffer bouts of ill health, often after bouts of hard work, for the rest of his days. But there was something afflicting him besides illness: he did not know what to do. "I am too dull and infirm now to look out for any extraordinary things in this world," he complained. The thought also ran backward: his uncertainty about what might be "extraordinary," and thus engaging, made him feel dull and infirm.

Only two years later, in 1774, a new subject—in ordinary life, not books—riveted his attention: the religious persecution of Virginia's Baptists. The established religion of the Virginia colony was Anglican (hence the political powers and responsibilities that Madison's father derived from being a vestryman). Beginning in midcentury, there had been a surge in the number of Baptists, a low-church Protestant sect that disdained Anglicanism's hierarchies and sacraments. Virginia's Anglicans reacted with bullying zeal. Madison had a stronger name for it: "that diabolical Hell-conceived principle of persecution."

The hellish principle was at work only thirty miles from Montpelier. "There are at this time," he wrote his friend Bradford early in 1774, "in the adjacent county [Culpeper] five or six well meaning men in close jail for publishing their religious sentiments." The Culpeper County jail was a bad place to be. One Baptist minister who had been held there a few years earlier left an account of his treatment. "When I have been engaged in preaching the gospel of my dear Redeemer" through the bars of the cell window, his Anglican tormentors "got a table, bench or something else, stood upon it, and made their water right in my face." Madison's letter to Bradford stormed on: "I have neither patience to hear, talk or think of anything relative to this matter, for I have squabbled and scolded, abused and ridiculed so long about it, to so little purpose, that I am without common patience."

Madison does not say with whom he had been squabbling: Anglican friends or relatives? His father the vestryman? (That might explain his passion.) No matter: when it came to religious freedom, Madison was forthright and tireless. "Religious bondage," he told Bradford, "shackles and debilitates the mind." He had spent his greatest exertions over the past decade on improving his mind; he could not bear that his efforts, or anyone's, might be controlled or frustrated.

What was Madison's religious faith? He had grown up among believing Christians. Robertson, his first teacher, had been licensed to preach, and Witherspoon, his last, was a minister. In 1774 one of his cousins, also named James Madison, was in England being ordained. Yet Madison hardly ever wrote or spoke of his beliefs, then or later. Did he have faith? Had he lost it? The most he ever said, in a wintry letter at the end of his life, was that "the mind prefers" the idea of an infinitely good, if invisible, God. "In this . . . belief all philosophical reasoning on the subject must perhaps terminate."

In 1774, Madison found another consuming subject—not local, but international in scope. Britain's American empire was in crisis. Britain had defended its colonies, including Virginia, against France in a series of wars throughout the eighteenth century. The last one, the French and Indian War, had ended only eleven years earlier, when Madison was twelve (several of his neighbors had fought in it). Britain's arms had been victorious, but Britain's debts were huge, and its efforts to induce its colonies to help pay them struck Americans as both onerous and tyrannical. Americans were happy to be British subjects, but they did not want to be taxed for the privilege, and they did not want their right to set their own taxes to be superseded by London.

In the spring of 1774, Madison went to Philadelphia to visit Bradford, who was the son of a printer there, just as American disaffection came to a head. The city was in ferment. Benjamin Franklin, scientist, politician, and Philadelphia's (and America's) most famous man, had been accused by a royal committee in London of encouraging political protests in Massachusetts. Franklin's supporters burned an image of his accuser using an electric starter.

Yet more incendiary news arrived during Madison's stay: Parliament had closed the port of Boston and put Massachusetts under military rule.

The Virginia legislature voted to take a day of prayer and fasting in sympathy with Massachusetts; the colonial governor, a royal appointee, dissolved it.

Madison left no records of his thoughts on these events—he was staying with his habitual correspondent, Bradford—but when he returned home in the summer he joined in the patriotic upheaval. Virginians elected a convention to meet in Williamsburg, the capital, in place of their legislature, and similar bodies sprang up throughout the colonies. They were protorevolutionary institutions, outside the law, but in Virginia they were run by the local gentry, who felt as threatened by London's behavior as radical Bostonians. In the fall these conventions sent delegates to a Continental Congress in Philadelphia, to coordinate American strategy. Meanwhile, local radical organizations sprang up as well, to oversee retaliatory boycotts against Britain. In December 1774, Orange County elected a Committee of Safety, chaired by Madison's father; Madison, age twenty-three, was the junior member. "There is something at hand," Madison wrote Bradford, back in Philadelphia, "that shall greatly augment the history of the world."

In the spring of 1775, a British attempt to sweep up radical leaders and weapons in the countryside around Boston led to the battles of Lexington and Concord. Madison's Committee of Safety called the fighting "a hostile attack on this and every other colony, and a sufficient warrant to use violence." After a year of further battles, it became clear that the colonies were contending not with a rogue ministry or an unfeeling Parliament, but with Britain itself.

In April 1776, Madison was elected, along with one of his uncles, to represent Orange County at the Virginia convention in Williamsburg. On May 15, the convention took a momentous step. It voted unanimously to ask the Continental Congress to declare American independence. At the same time, it appointed a committee to draft a Declaration of Rights for an independent Virginia. Madison was one of more than thirty men tapped for the job. His first important political task coincided with a transformative moment in Virginia history.

Madison's most notable colleague on the drafting committee was George Mason, a fifty-year-old Potomac planter: brilliant, self-taught, reclusive, and gruff, like a badger with genius. Mason did not enjoy the collaborative process: the committee, he wrote a friend, was stuffed with "useless members," who would generate "a thousand ridiculous and impracticable proposals." So he took the drafting of the Declaration of Rights into his own hands. He did a splendid job, crafting sentences that would find their way, almost verbatim, into both the Declaration of Independence ("all men are born equally free and independent, and have certain inherent natural rights . . . among which are the enjoyment of life and liberty . . . and pursuing and obtaining happiness") and the Bill of Rights ("excessive bail ought not to be required, nor excessive fines imposed, nor cruel and unusual punishments inflicted").

Madison, half Mason's age, improved his language, proposing a crucial change to the clause on religious liberty. Mason's draft, reflecting a hundred years of liberal thought going back to John Locke, called for "the fullest toleration in the exercise of religion." Yet this did not seem liberal enough for Madison. Toleration implies those who tolerate: superiors who grant freedom to others. But who can be trusted to pass such judgments, even if the judgment is to live and let live? Judges may change their minds. The Anglican establishment of Virginia, compared with established churches in other colonies, had been fairly tolerant—except when it hadn't, and then it made water in Baptists' faces. So Madison prepared an amendment. "All men are equally entitled to the full and free exercise" of religion. No one could be said to allow men to worship as they wished; they worshipped as they wished because it was their right as men. Madison's language shifted the ground of religious liberty from a tolerant society or state, to human nature, and lifted the Declaration of Rights from an event in Virginia history to a landmark of world intellectual history.

But Madison also added a phrase that doomed his amendment: "No man or class of men ought, on account of religion to be invested with peculiar emoluments [payments]." This alarmed Anglicanism's die-hard defenders, because Virginia supported the Anglican Church financially. They might swallow toleration of other faiths, even full and free exercise, but they could not risk the salaries of their rectors. Their treasure was laid up in their stipends. When Madison's amendment died on the floor, he came back with another: "all men are equally entitled to . . . the free exercise of religion, according to the dictates of conscience," with no mention of emoluments. Mason approved Madison's changes, and on June 12 they passed, along with the rest of the Declaration of Rights.

Madison moved neither of his amendments himself. Conscious perhaps of his inexperience, he got Patrick Henry, America's greatest orator, to introduce his first amendment. When it failed, Madison turned to his cousin Edmund Pendleton, a stalwart Anglican layman, to introduce the second. If Pendleton endorsed it, Anglicans concluded, it must not be bad.

The young Madison knew how to find allies, and how to change plans in midstream. He was applying theory to politics; he was also showing precocious skill at how to work a committee.

The convention—renamed the Virginia Assembly after a summer recess—sat until December. In the spring of 1777, Madison experienced a rare event in his life: he lost an election, which would have sent him back to Williamsburg for another term in the new legislature. Elections in Virginia were festivals; eligible voters, plus hangers-on, converged on the county seat, where candidates, as Madison wrote afterward, "were in the practice . . . of giving them treats, particularly of intoxicating drinks. . . . No candidate who neglected these attentions could be elected. His forbearance would have been ascribed to a mean parsimony, or to a proud disrespect." Madison, however, favored "a more chaste mode of conducting elections," refusing to buy rounds. But Charles Porter, a tavern keeper, did—and won. Madison's loss still rankled forty years later, when he wrote down these recollections. He was not cheap or disrespectful, but he had shown a little too much pride in his notions of how things should be done.

However much the young politician still had to learn about voters, he had impressed the political elite of his state. In November 1777, the legislature picked him to fill a vacancy on the Governor's Council, an eight-man group that advised the governor on all executive decisions. Two years later, the legislature chose him again, this time to be one of Virginia's delegates to Congress, a choice the legislature repeated twice until he hit Congress's term limit (no delegate could serve more than three years out of six).

Madison's service in Williamsburg (1778 to 1779) and in the nation's capital (1780 to 1783) spanned the grim middle and endgame of the Revolution. The bright ideals and the brave victories of the early years (matched, it is true, by disastrous defeats) had given way to a long strategic slog, a struggle for professionalism in the army, and an even harder struggle against incompetence and disorganization in government. It wasn't so much that individual revolutionary politicians were incapable (though many of them were) as that the political systems they had cobbled together so often failed them. Madison's work in the government of the largest and most eminent state, and in Congress, gave him a close-up view of the country's political problems.

Madison approached his jobs in what had already become his characteristic style. In public he could be quiet and unprepossessing. When he was thirty years old, one of his peers assumed that he had just graduated from college. He waited months before giving his maiden speech in Congress; one foreign diplomat thought he had been silent for two years.

"They say he is clever," wrote a congressman's wife, a Virginian no less, but "he has nothing engaging or even bearable in his manners. [He is] the most unsociable creature in existence."

Madison shone in the daily drudgery of work. The Virginia Governor's Council met six days a week. During his first, seven-month session, from January to July 1778, Madison missed only seven days. In the three and a half years he spent in Congress—most of that time in Philadelphia—he missed hardly any days. Bachelorhood helped him compile these almost-perfect attendance records; so did being the son of a wealthy father who managed the family business back home, and loaned him money whenever he needed it. But Madison made the most of the opportunities his situation in life gave him. He wanted to work, and the more he did, the more he was given.

During these years, Madison learned still more about working with, and sometimes around, others. Losing a vote was not the same as losing the argument, because if you could then write the guidelines for implementing the decision, you could nudge it in a better direction. Benjamin Franklin, America's minister to France since 1778, was the star of the diplomatic corps, but he had enemies, who accused him of being lazy, high-living, and careless about corruption and spies. Perhaps those qualities made him the perfect minister to France. Madison called him "the venerable philosopher" and backed him to the hilt. When Congress voted, over Madison's objections, to send a new envoy to France to act as a spur and a corrective to Franklin, Madison managed to downgrade the envoy's title and to serve on the committees that defined his mission.

Madison backed France as strongly as he backed Franklin. France had allied with America in 1778 to injure its ancient enemy Britain; it devoted cash, supplies, ships, troops, and officers to the struggle. The Frenchman all Americans, including Madison, fell in love with was the young Marquis de Lafayette, whose ardor for liberty suggested that old Europe was somehow in step with the new republic. Madison's gratitude to France may have been augmented by knowing the language (one of his early tasks on the Governor's Council was drafting its correspondence in French, until the members broke down and hired a translator). Madison valued the French alliance, and his fond memories of it would influence him for the rest of his life. Some Americans were more wary; John Adams, a congressman turned diplomat, warned against falling under the sway of another superpower. Madison found Adams touchy and pompous—another opinion he would hold for years. Madison's criticisms of Adams were as true as those made by Franklin's enemies, but, in the case of Adams, Madison saw no compensating virtues.

Even when victory was by no means ensured, Madison was thinking, beyond independence, of new territories to the south (Florida) and west (Louisiana). In 1780 he drafted a congressional letter to John Jay, America's minister to Madrid, instructing him to ask that Americans have the freedom to navigate the Mississippi River, which Spain then controlled. Spain, like France, was an enemy of Britain, and therefore a friend of the United States, but Spain also had a vast empire on our borders and was naturally cautious about letting its new ally grow. Madison told Jay that America's claims were supported by "clear indications of nature and providence, and the general good of mankind." When Madison appealed to nature in support of religious liberty, he wrote nobly; when he appealed to it to justify national interest, his words rang like tin. He couldn't hear the difference; he would pursue American expansion with single-minded zeal for decades.

Both on the Governor's Council and in Congress, Madison was forced to confront the shortcomings of the new American government. Reacting against their imperial overlords, Americans had hedged their own government with restrictions. The Articles of Confederation, the first American constitution, written in 1777 and finally ratified in 1781, established a "perpetual union" but defined it as a "league of friendship" among the thirteen states, which retained their "sovereignty, freedom and independence." There were no national courts and no chief executive: the "president" at that time was merely the presiding officer of Congress, who had hardly any power. Congress consisted of one house, and each state could send as many as seven delegates to it, but states cast only one vote apiece. The largest (Virginia) was thus equal to the smallest (Delaware). Major decisions—declaring war, signing treaties—needed the approval of nine states. Changing the Articles of Confederation had to be a unanimous decision. But perhaps the most serious consequence of ongoing state sovereignty was that Congress had no power to tax: it could requisition money from the states, but states did not have to pay. As a result, the United States was perennially broke. Its debts, to friendly countries and foreign bankers, were not paid. More seriously, neither were its soldiers.

In his second year as a congressman, Madison considered some rough and ready solutions. Congress, he wrote a friend, should be "arm[ed] with coercive powers." He meant it quite literally: "a small detachment" of the army could get money from balky states, or "two or three" warships could "make it their interest to yield prompt obedience." Amusingly, Madison called the contributions that would be extorted by such means "voluntary."

Over time, he would modify some of these notions, though not all of them. He could learn from experience as well as from reading and thinking, and both his thoughts and his tactics could be supple. But there were also dogmatic impulses in him, and when they surfaced, they could take people who did not know him very well by surprise.

The most important thing Madison took from his war years was the friendship of other men. The Revolution drew the Virginian onto a larger stage, with greater actors. William Bradford, his Princeton friend, was a good man who became a colonel in the army, and later, U.S. attorney general. But during the war, Madison met world-changing figures, some of whom would be in his life for the next fifty years.

The first Virginia governor he counseled was Patrick Henry. Those who heard Henry speak instantly appreciated his great qualities—eloquence,

obviously, but also wit and passion. Those who worked in harness with
him, as Madison now did, learned that he could be vain, lazy, impulsive.
They erred, however, if they underestimated him. Madison would test
his mettle many times.

The second governor Madison served, elected in June 1779, was
Thomas Jefferson. Madison and Jefferson worked together for six
months; the two men were together again in 1783, working in Congress.
When they were apart, they wrote.

Jefferson, eight years older than Madison, was a planter in Albemarle
County. His home, Monticello, was a day's ride from Montpelier. Like
Madison, he was a liberal aristocrat, devoted to reform and independence. He was as learned as Madison, and as bookish. During their time
together in 1783, the two Virginians happily drew up a list of books for
a congressional library: more than 1,400 volumes, everything from Aris-
totle to Voltaire. But Congress wouldn't make the investment.

Madison and Jefferson were as bound by their differences as by their
similarities. Jefferson had a gift of seeing views and making leaps. He was
a prophet; he was also a bluejay, snatching at every shiny idea that caught
his eye. He expressed his thoughts in crystal-clear words; the words in
turn brightened the thoughts. His "Summary View of the Rights of
British North America" (1774) had contained some of the most ringing
political prose ever written by an American ("The God who gave us life,
gave us liberty at the same time: the hand of force may destroy, but cannot disjoin them"), until he topped it, two years later, with the Declaration of Independence. Mason's Declaration of Rights inspired him, but
Jefferson exceeded his model. Those were command performances; Jefferson could also toss an immortal phrase without warning into his ordinary correspondence. Madison thrilled at the contact.

Shortly after the war, when Jefferson was in France, he asked Madison
to send him the measurements of American animals, to refute French
scientists who asserted that species shrank in the New World. Madison
sent him the measurements of a weasel and a mole. A novelist would

never dare to concoct such an assignment, which seems too obviously symbolic of the friendship: Jefferson the scientist patriot, earthbound Madison. Yet those were the animals Madison measured. The man who had never had an older brother found one in Jefferson, along with unfailing stimulus and inspiration.

What did Jefferson get from Madison? Early on Jefferson appreciated and praised Madison's sound judgment and good heart. Madison was certainly good to his friends: affable, considerate, loyal. There was something selfish in Jefferson's appreciation of this goodness: Madison was no trouble, and he knew his place. There were no quarrels, no fireworks. But one function of Madison's place was to give Jefferson the benefit of his judgment. Madison was often more practical, sometimes more temperate, and Jefferson knew he needed access to these qualities. Moles know their way around.

The two men shared one emotional bond: pain. In January 1783, Madison fell in love with Catherine (Kitty) Floyd, the daughter of a New York congressman who roomed, with his family, in the same Philadelphia boardinghouse as Madison did. She was pretty, she played the harpsichord; she was fifteen, going on sixteen—not too young for marriage in that fast-blooming, still patriarchal time. Jefferson watched the romance sympathetically. "It would give me a neighbor," he wrote Madison, meaning Kitty, "whose worth I rate high." "Your inference on that subject," Madison wrote back, "was not groundless." The courtship continued through the spring. Then, in July, disaster. Kitty Floyd broke it off; she would marry a medical student, twelve years closer to her own age. Years later, Madison blotted out his copy of the letter he had sent Jefferson describing this fall from grace. Jefferson bucked him up: "Firmness of mind and unintermitting occupations will not long leave you in pain. . . . Of all machines ours [he meant the human heart] is the most complicated and inexplicable." Jefferson knew what he was talking about: his adored wife, Martha, had died the year before, of complications from her seventh pregnancy. He had found distraction and hope in his young friend's coming marriage; now he could offer him consolation.

The war thrust Madison together with George Washington, commander in chief. Until the Revolution, Washington had been a kind of ideal Virginian—a wealthy, largely self-made planter, a solid politician, a heroic veteran of the French and Indian War. Since taking command of America's armies in 1775, he had become something else—an American, almost the personification of America. He had not won all his battles, but he had won enough of them to keep the cause going. Even more impressive, he had done so with unfailing deference to the powers of Congress and the states, and the norms of American liberty. There was no visual mass media to broadcast his image, but enough Americans saw him and described him in letters and newspapers that the whole country knew he looked the part. "There is not a king in Europe," gushed Benjamin Rush, a signer of the Declaration of Independence, "that would not look like a valet de chambre by his side."

As a freshman politician, nineteen years Washington's junior, Madison could at first serve him only from afar, as an admiring commissary. In 1778, the Governor's Council, noting "the great fatigues" to which Washington was exposed, decided to send him "a stock of good rum, wine [and] sugar." Two years later, a congressional committee Madison sat on sent Washington a dozen boxes of lemons and two casks of wine. "As for our illustrious general," wrote Madison, "the rich Madeira should flow in copious streams." He would not buy a round for voters, but he would treat George Washington.

They finally met in person in the winter of 1781–1782, when the commander in chief came to Philadelphia to plan the war's endgame with Congress. The battle of Yorktown had been won in October 1781, but peace still had to be negotiated, and the enemy, who still occupied important cities, watched in the meantime.

Washington was always on the lookout for talented acolytes, and in Madison he found devotion, hard work, and (in time) good advice. The younger man provided a fourth gift, which he unwittingly revealed in a discussion of his hero decades after he had died. "The story so often repeated of [Washington] never laughing," Madison told a historian, "is wholly untrue; no man seemed more to enjoy gay conversation, though he took little part in it himself. He was particularly pleased with the jokes, good humor and hilarity of his companions." Men with the weight of history on their shoulders need relief. Men who do not talk readily like it when others keep the ball rolling. And who, in private anyway, was more "full of anecdote" than Madison? Did he try out his anecdotes "of loose description" on Washington? History is silent.

All Americans thought of Washington as their political father: the first reference to him as "father of his country" appeared in an almanac in 1778. Madison's filial admiration for Washington was what almost any revolutionary, especially of his generation, would feel. But Madison would have more opportunities than most to serve his idol.

Madison met a brilliant younger colleague in November 1782, when Alexander Hamilton took his seat as a congressman from New York. He was almost as different from Madison as it was possible to be. Hamilton was an immigrant, born and raised in the Caribbean; illegitimate (his parents had two sons, but no marriage certificate); orphaned (his father abandoned the family, his mother died); a dropout (island patrons sent him to King's College, now Columbia University, to be educated, but he quit as soon as the Revolution began); and a veteran (captain of artillery, colonel on Washington's staff). Though he was six years younger than Madison, by 1782 Hamilton already had a job as a New York lawyer, a wife—the former Elizabeth Schuyler, a lovely heiress—and a son. Hamilton gave his first speech in Congress the day after he arrived: he never hesitated to speak, in private or in public. A French diplomat summed up the contrasting personae of the two men this way: "Mr. Hamilton has the determined air of a republican—Mr. Madison the meditative air of a politician."

For all that, both Madison and Hamilton were patriotic, political, and sharp as nails. Hamilton's education had been more scattershot than Madison's, but he had a powerful mind that gripped the topics it took up and a will to turn his knowledge into action.

What drew them together was the issue of money and reform. Madison had a politician's view of Congress's poverty and impotence. Hamilton, from the vantage of his military career, had seen the damage, in erratic supplies and unpaid troops. The problem was getting worse, not better. As the war wound down and peace negotiators met in Paris, the shortsighted saw less need for fiscal reform. The army was still in the field, however, ready to fight if the peace negotiations failed, and yet the soldiers and officers were still unpaid. In November 1782, a possible reform measure—an amendment to the Articles of Confederation, allowing Congress to collect imposts, or tariffs—failed when Rhode Island refused to support it, depriving the amendment of the necessary unanimity. Madison and Hamilton, the brand-new member, were appointed to a committee to give Congress's answer to Rhode Island. Hamilton wrote the statement: it is "pernicious to leave any government in a situation of responsibility disproportioned to its power." But Rhode Island would not budge. In December, Madison was dismayed when Virginia withdrew its approval of the impost amendment. As a Virginian, Madison was particularly dismayed: "the most intelligent members" of Congress, he wrote, feared for "the character" and "the duration" of the country.

Madison and Hamilton agreed on the problem and the need for change. They were soon working so closely that friends of theirs would write letters of common interest to one, asking him to show them to the other; when one of the pair answered, he might say that the reply "contains both of our ideas." But they disagreed in their strategies for change.

Madison tried to find some way to thread the needle of Congress. In January 1783, Congress received a petition from a delegation of army officers who declared, "We have borne all that men can bear." A Grand Committee of one congressman from each state (Madison and Hamilton representing Virginia and New York) met with the officers, then proposed that Congress ask the states for the power to collect revenue for its own purposes—what was called "general funds." Madison tried to make the change seem less sweeping with a parliamentary maneuver, dividing the question in two: Should Congress have general funds? And should Congress itself, rather than the states, collect them? Defenders of the status quo might approve taxes for the benefit of Congress if they did not have to swallow congressional tax collectors. Hamilton upset these calculations by making what Madison called an "imprudent and injurious" speech on the first motion, in which he envisaged "the energy of the federal government . . . pervading and uniting the states." Madison was trying to calm those who feared a stronger Congress; Hamilton proclaimed that was exactly what he wanted. Two enemies of reform told Madison, with a wink and a nod, that "Mr. Hamilton had let out the secret."

Little did they know what else Hamilton was up to. While Madison labored in Congress, Hamilton wrote Washington, his former boss, describing the financial and political impasse, and predicting that Congress would do nothing about it. The solution he proposed was for Washington to make himself the spokesman of the army's discontents and to "guide the torrent." The army should force Congress to reform itself, but Washington should lead the army so that force did not get out of hand.

Washington had no intention of pursuing such a confrontational course. He had spent his years as commander in chief serving Congress; he would not end his tenure by bullying it. When some of his comrades at army headquarters, in Newburgh, New York, tried to rally the officer corps to action in March 1783, Washington put them in their place with a gravely impassioned speech, mixing dignity and fellow-feeling: "You will give one more distinguished proof of unexampled patriotism and patient virtue, rising superior to the pressure of the most complicated sufferings." Shamed and inspired, the officers backed down.

Meanwhile, Madison's efforts to relieve their suffering sputtered. He moved a compromise revenue plan in April, calling for a 5 percent impost, limited to twenty-five years; the states, not Congress, would collect the money, and all the states would have to approve. Hamilton, disgusted with the plan's feebleness, voted against it, with Madison accusing him of "rigid adherence" to his own ideas, "which he supposed more perfect."

After tension and near-tragedy, farce. In June 1783, some three hundred soldiers camped near Philadelphia marched into town, surrounded the statehouse where Congress was meeting, and drunkenly demanded their back pay. Hamilton, the former officer, tried in vain to disperse them. Congress fled to Princeton, where Madison was forced to share a room and a bed with fellow Virginian Joseph Jones, who was six feet tall. The states never approved the impost; the army went home with IOUs. America had won its independence, but it was starting life as a deadbeat.

Madison had moved to the center of national affairs. He was learning politics in the arena; he knew the movers and shakers, and he knew how to make moves of his own. America had won its liberty. How to secure it was the next problem.

CHAPTER TWO

The Constitution

I n September 1783, America and Britain signed the treaty ending the
Revolutionary War. Madison's term in Congress ended two months
later, allowing him to return to Orange County for the first time in almost three years.

His time away from home encouraged him, if not to move, at least to
think of buying land out of state. He took a trip to central New York
with the Franco-American hero Lafayette to look at land freed by the
war from the Iroquois Indians (most of whom had sided with the
British), and he bought 1,000 acres in partnership with James Monroe,
a young Virginia congressman. The land lust that most Virginians felt,
and the wanderlust that sent many of them to Kentucky and beyond,
fluttered in Madison.

But politics kept him anchored to Virginia. Except for one brief
period, he would hold elected or appointed office until his mid-sixties.
When one job ended, he moved to another. Pursuing a political career
required a political base. This was his county, and his state.

Thanks to term limits, Madison could not be sent back to Congress
for another three years. So in the spring of 1784, his neighbors elected
him to the Virginia House of Delegates, the lower house of the Virginia
Assembly, which met in the new state capital of Richmond.

He did not neglect the relations he had formed during the Revolution. The closest, and the most important, was the one conducted at the longest distance, with Thomas Jefferson. In the summer of 1784, Jefferson left America for Paris, where he would serve as a diplomat until the fall of 1789. Keeping in touch with him was not easy. Transatlantic communication in the eighteenth century was almost whimsical in its slowness. Correspondence had to be carried by travelers or friendly captains; there could be all sorts of delays before ships sailed, and Atlantic crossings could take from a few weeks to a few months. Madison began one letter to Jefferson in June 1786, saying that he had just gotten a letter Jefferson had sent him the preceding October. "I began to fear it had miscarried." Eighteenth-century letter writers on opposite sides of the Atlantic began to fear that their letters were lost only after seven or eight months had passed. They lacked the blessings of Twitter and Skype; what they got in return was leisure to think.

"Seven o'clock, and retired to my fireside, I have determined to enter into conversation with you," Jefferson began one letter to Madison in October 1785. Distance did not lessen their intimacy: Jefferson wanted his far-off friend to hear his voice; he wanted to see his friend listening. Something had upset the American abroad, and he needed to hash it out. Jefferson was in Fontainebleau, a town forty miles from Paris where the king of France hunted, and where the court attended him when he did so. Jefferson had gone for a walk, "to take a view of the place," and had fallen into conversation with a woman laborer who showed him a hillside path. She told Jefferson she had two children (she made no mention of a husband) and she earned eight sous, or four pennies, a day—when she could find work, which was not always. As she and Jefferson parted ways, he gave her twenty-four sous, at which she burst into tears. "She probably never before received so great an aid." This led Jefferson into "a train of reflections" on the cause of his guide's plight—the unequal distribution of property.

"The earth is given as a common stock for man to labor and live on. If for the encouragement of industry we allow it to be appropriated"—

that is, owned by individuals—"we must take care that other employ-ment be provided to those" who own no land at all. "If we do not, the fundamental right to labor the earth returns to the unemployed." How would Jefferson encourage a distribution of property that would not leave his guide weeping over a twenty-four-sou tip? He made two suggestions: abolishing feudal forms of inheritance that steered an estate to one heir, and progressive taxation. Abolishing feudal forms was advice aimed at France; Virginia had already abolished primogeniture and thus, Jefferson believed, mammoth estates like the king's at Fontainebleau. But Jeffer-son's letter implied two far more radical ideas. Property is only a second-ary right, since society allows it "for the encouragement of industry," and the right to earn a living—"to labor the earth"—precedes it. Such thoughts would call all Virginian, and American, society into question. Jefferson was grappling with a deep political subject—the intersection of work and rights—and he sent his thoughts to Madison because Madi-son was smart enough to follow him, and bold enough not to dismiss him out of hand.

Madison's answer shows how he handled such starbursts. He started with praise—Jefferson's reflections would be "a valuable lesson" to law-makers everywhere. Then he tried to slow his friend down. He did not even address Jefferson's suggested solutions because he saw a larger prob-lem: overpopulation. Let land "be shared . . . ever so wisely," there would nonetheless be "a great surplus of inhabitants." Madison described the lives that surplus people led: as "idle" landowners, makers of luxury items, servants, soldiers, merchants, and sailors. He admitted that sailors would exist in any country with seacoasts, and he dismissed merchants as not numerous enough to worry about. All the others, he assumed, were per-nicious, and he hoped that "simplicity of manners" and "juster govern-ment" would thin their ranks. If people did not live luxuriously, there would be no idlers, no servants to serve them, and no makers of luxuries to cater to them; if the government was neither bellicose nor oppressive, it would not need soldiers. Virginia planters had luxuries and servants, of course, but far fewer than aristocrats in Europe. Madison had his own sweeping thoughts, dismissing whole classes of people, but they were extrapolations from life as he knew it; he used them to deflect Jefferson from thoughts that might upset that life.

Madison ended his letter on a safer subject, with his measurements of the weasel.

But Jefferson could not leave the earth and its owners alone. Three years later he wrote Madison from Paris, attacking the subject from a different direction.

"I set out on this ground, which I suppose to be self-evident, that the earth belongs in usufruct to the living; that the dead have neither powers nor rights over it." This, with its echo of the Declaration ("self-evident") was Jefferson at his most terse. Except for the phrase, "in usufruct"—a legalism meaning the right to use property for a certain time—Jefferson's words could be chiseled in stone, or shouted on the hustings.

Jefferson then tried to give his insight some concrete shape, by turning to the actuarial tables. When a man became an adult at age twenty-one, he could expect to live for thirty-four more years, according to contemporary calculations. Jefferson proposed to make that span of time a yardstick for financial obligation. No generation "can validly engage debts beyond what they may pay in their own time, that is to say, within thirty-four years of the date of the engagement." Virginia planters had good reason to worry about the debts they had engaged, as tobacco prices sank throughout the late eighteenth century. But Jefferson wanted to apply his thirty-four-year sunset rule to laws, too. "No society can make a perpetual constitution, or even a perpetual law. . . . If it be enforced longer, it is an act of force, and not of right."

"Turn this subject in your mind, my dear Sir," Jefferson concluded. "At first it may be laughed at, as the dream of a theorist; but examination will prove it to be solid and salutary." Jefferson feared his thoughts were laughable, but he was also compelled by them. He put himself in Madison's hands.

Madison's answer to these suggestions was wiser than his reply to Jefferson's earlier letter, but it followed the same trajectory of praise and criticism. Jefferson had made "many interesting suggestions" and seen "sublime truths . . . through the medium of philosophy." But Madison would also consider them with "the naked eye of the ordinary politician."

He raised three objections. First, constitutions were strengthened by their "antiquity"; scrapping them every thirty-four years would make them flimsy. Second, the past is not only a burden, for the dead pass on improvements as well as debts. (Madison did not specify any, but it is easy to think of ways that even the earth itself is improved: roads and bridges built, trees planted.) Third, if people expect a clean sweep every thirty-four years, they will game the system in the run-up to every deadline.

Instead, Madison proposed an alternative way to think of time and rights: "tacit assent . . . may be inferred where no positive dissent appears." If men continue to obey an old law, they have given it their consent, as much as if they had voted for it themselves.

Then he raised his most important objection to Jefferson's scheme of generational autonomy. The continuity of laws and debts is not the only thing sustained by "tacit assent." Majority rule depends on it, too. "On what [other] principle does the voice of the majority bind the minority?" How could there be any laws if every law had to be passed unanimously, and repassed in every generation?

These exchanges were not "merely" theoretical. Nor should they be scored as if Jefferson and Madison were playing a tennis match, in which we root for either the poet or the realist. Jefferson and Madison were revolutionary politicians trying to define the freedom they had helped win. Jefferson was searching for freedom's furthest ramifications; Madison was helping him test what was right or practical.

M uch of Madison's correspondence with Jefferson was quite practical—news flashes, gossip—keeping his friend in touch with Virginia politics, especially when it touched on Jefferson personally.

Both men had a stake in religious freedom in Virginia. In 1779 Jefferson, just as he was about to become governor, had offered a bill whose key provision declared "that no man shall be compelled to frequent or support any religious worship, place, or ministry whatsoever." Jefferson's bill would have extended Madison's language on "free exercise" in the Declaration of Rights and given it the force of law.

After the Revolution, Virginians took up the politics of religion once again. In 1784 Patrick Henry called for a tax to support religious instruction. His bill appeared to have something for everyone—Virginians could earmark their taxes for the church of their choice—but Madison was determined to stop it anyway. He had opposed "emoluments" for the Anglican Church in 1776; he did not want them given to every church now.

His first move was to get Henry out of the assembly, by kicking him upstairs to the governorship.* His second move was to stir up opposition to Henry's bill. In the summer of 1785, Madison wrote "A Memorial and Remonstrance Against Religious Assessments," which was circulated throughout the state. (He did not sign it, because he wanted the support of Henry's allies on other matters. No point in burning bridges.) He employed a range of voices, from pious to alarmist. Madison the theologian explained that Christianity "disavows a dependence on the powers of this world." It would be un-Christian, then, for the state to subsidize churches. Madison the rabble-rouser warned that "the same authority which can force a citizen to contribute three pence . . . may force him to conform . . . in all cases whatsoever." Churches that accepted state help today would be smothered by state control tomorrow.

Recounting the story in a letter to Jefferson, Madison wrote that his polemics "produced all the effect that could have been wished." When the legislature met in the fall of 1785, "the table was loaded with petitions and remonstrances from all parts" of the state.

Henry's bill died; in its place, the legislature took up Jefferson's old bill for religious freedom. But before victory, maneuvering. Jefferson had written a philosophical preamble, in his most sweeping style: "Well aware

---

* The assembly chose the governor.

that the Almighty God hath created the mind free," it began. But the
state senate objected to some phrases about the supremacy of reason.
After some back-and-forth, Madison, in the House of Delegates, accepted a few cuts. "They did not affect the substance," he told the bill's
author, "though they somewhat defaced the composition." But Madison
did not want "to run further risks, especially as it was getting late in the
session and the house growing thin." Only after all the votes were taken
and victory was achieved could Madison wax philosophic himself. "I flatter myself [we] have in this country extinguished forever the ambitious
hope of making laws for the human mind."

The distant friends were establishing a template for their relationship—
Jefferson the philosopher and strategist, Madison the reality check and
right-hand man. As time passed, they would, like an old couple, occasionally switch roles—Jefferson pulling wires, while Madison stayed on
the sidelines, if not in the clouds. But the template would serve them for
years.

George Washington was separated from Madison by an obstacle as
great as the Atlantic Ocean—his eminence as a hero. Yet Madison
managed to cross that barrier. One of his earliest tasks after he reentered
the assembly in 1784 was to find some way for Virginia to thank the
great man for "his unremitted zeal" in the cause of liberty. A committee,
on which Madison sat, resolved to commission a statue "of the finest
marble, and best workmanship." In Paris Jefferson got the great French
sculptor Jean-Antoine Houdon to do the job, and the statue Houdon
carved is a masterpiece of calm, self-contained grandeur: an image of
fame and force of personality, controlled by republican will. Madison
was at Mount Vernon when Houdon visited to observe his subject, and
he wrote the inscription for the pedestal.*

---

* The statue stands in the rotunda of the state capitol in Richmond.

Madison's entrée to Washington's affections came not from statuary, however, but from inland navigation. Washington was obsessed with connecting the Potomac and the Ohio Rivers by canals and portages. The stakes were huge: the furs and crops of middle America could reach the outside world cheaply only via water—up the St. Lawrence past Montreal, or down the Mississippi through New Orleans. Why not convey them, thought Washington, on the Potomac?

He was personally invested in the project, as the owner of thousands of acres of western land that would attract renters or buyers only if the Potomac were developed. He would reap a double benefit if Alexandria, next door to Mount Vernon, became a major port. But he believed America's investment in inland navigation was even greater. Settlers were already streaming west over the Appalachians. If their business went through British Montreal or Spanish New Orleans, why should they stay loyal to the United States?

In November 1784 Washington went to Richmond to lobby the assembly for improvements to the Potomac. A bill was introduced, sponsored by Joseph Jones, the six-footer with whom Madison had shared a bed when Congress was crammed into Princeton. But after Jones left the legislature to take a seat on the Governor's Council, Madison took over management of the bill.

Developing the Potomac was not in fact dear to Madison's heart. His preferred method of opening the interior to trade was to wrest control of the Mississippi from Spain, a dream he believed blessed by both demography and providence. "Nature has given the use of the Mississippi to those who may settle on its waters," he wrote Lafayette, in the holier-than-thou tone that the subject of expansion often drew from him. But drawing closer to George Washington was even dearer to Madison's heart, and so he took on the Potomac project.

The father of his country and the delegate from Orange County worked well together. Washington supplied prestige and persuasion; Madison got the legislative work done. "Your own judgment in this business will be the best guide," Washington acknowledged in a letter to his

young partner. As a result of their labors, the Potomac River Company
was chartered in the spring of 1785, with Washington as president. Madison's first visit to Mount Vernon followed in the fall. After he left, Washington extended an open-ended invitation to further collaboration: "if
anything should occur that is interesting, and your leisure will permit it,
I should be glad to hear from you on the subject." He signed this letter,
"Affectionately."

One bit of business arose immediately. At Madison's urging the assembly had given Washington fifty shares in the Potomac River Company, valued at more than $22,000. But such a direct benefit struck
Washington as unseemly. Madison drafted a letter for him, asking the
assembly to give the profits of his shares to charity. Then Madison served
on the committee that made the necessary changes to the gift, and that
praised Washington for this "fresh and endearing proof" of his disinterestedness. It was not the last time Madison would act as Washington's
ghostwriter or draft the responses to his own ghostwritten words.

When he was in Congress, Madison had tried to give it more power
by amending the Articles of Confederation; hotter heads, including his colleague Alexander Hamilton, had tried to use the army to force
the process. Both efforts had failed. But by the mid-1780s, the two men
were looking at regulating interstate commerce as another route to
change.

The Articles of Confederation allowed each state to levy its own tariffs
and tolls, which restrained trade and generated bad feeling. Some states
shared navigable rivers: the Potomac flowed between Virginia and Maryland, the Susquehanna from Pennsylvania through Maryland. Who
would collect the tolls, and who would pay for maintenance? Other states
had no ports—cargo bound for New Jersey came through Philadelphia
and New York—which left them at the mercy of their neighbors.

In March 1785 there had been a conference on the subject of Potomac
navigation in Alexandria. Madison was supposed to attend for Virginia

but didn't, because Governor Henry, suspicious of interstate ventures, had not announced where or when the meeting was (two other Virginia delegates made it only by chance). Washington, the champion of Potomac navigation, invited the conferees to meet at Mount Vernon, where they agreed to ban interstate tolls and share expenses for lighthouses. At year's end, Virginia called for a follow-up meeting of commissioners from all the states to consider commercial issues.

The meeting was scheduled in Annapolis, Maryland, the first Monday of September 1786, but it got off to a weak start. When Madison, who was one of Virginia's commissioners, arrived in Annapolis (this time he knew the time and place), only two other commissioners were in town. A week later, there were only twelve, from five states.

But one of them was Hamilton, who was eager to put the occasion to good use. Madison and Hamilton, so close when they had been working side by side in Congress, had hardly been in touch since the war. Now, as they met again, the Virginian saw that the New Yorker's aggressive temperament had not changed.

The commissioners decided they were not numerous enough to do more than write a report calling for yet another meeting. The assignment was given to Edmund Randolph, a rising statesman: member of one of Virginia's first families, cousin of Jefferson, soon to become governor. But Hamilton produced a draft of his own in two days.

In his report, Hamilton flayed the shortcomings of the Articles and requested a meeting the following year, to consider "measures . . . to cement the union of the states." Madison knew this was too blunt, and he may have guessed that Randolph was irked at being preempted. "You had better yield to this man," he warned Hamilton, "otherwise all Virginia will be against you." Hamilton modified his language just enough—the final report asked for a meeting to "render the constitution . . . adequate to the exigencies of the union"—and the commissioners unanimously called for a convention in Philadelphia in May 1787. Then, fearing that more cooks would spoil their broth, they adjourned—

so quickly that commissioners going home passed others still struggling to arrive.

No one had asked the Annapolis convention to call for full-scale political reform. In stretching their mandate and then getting out of town, Madison and Hamilton had pulled a fast one—a clever and opportunistic maneuver. But the intent of their maneuver was to appeal to the public: first to the nation's political class (the report went to all thirteen states and to Congress) and, through them, to the people. Madison's only quibble with Hamilton was that he had appealed too boldly.

Madison worked in solitude, as well as with his friends. He read up on the experiences of other countries and reflected on his own, and he wrote essays—memos to himself—digesting and arranging what he had learned.

Jefferson had sent him more than two hundred books from Paris—Madison called them his "literary cargo"—which he spent the spring and summer of 1786 studying. Most of the books were the work of historians, from Demosthenes to recent European writers. This reading generated an essay, "Of Ancient and Modern Confederacies," which he would use over the next few years as a briefing paper for debates or published essays. He covered Greece, the Holy Roman Empire, Switzerland, and Holland. Ancient Greece had been divided into city-states that at different times formed defensive leagues. The Holy Roman Empire—modern Germany, plus a few neighbors—was a collection of countries, still hanging together from the Middle Ages; Switzerland and Holland were unions of semi-autonomous provinces. Everywhere Madison found strife and disorder. The cause of all these confederacies' problems was the absence of compelling and legitimate authority. The lack "of subjection in the members to the general authority," he wrote about one of his Greek case studies, "ruined the whole body." Chaos led to collapse, or to bullying by the stronger members, or to foreign conquest.

The following winter, after Madison had had time to reflect on his handiwork at Annapolis, he wrote another essay, "Vices of the Political System of the United States." Here, he was writing from the news, and his own observation. The states acted against each other, and acted on their own. (He had the cheek to cite Virginia and Maryland's agreement over navigating the Potomac as an instance of the latter.) The states could not act together on matters of "common interest": his examples of neglected projects included canals and national colleges. Congress's laws were dead letters because Congress had no power to enforce them. Here Madison allowed himself a joke: if state laws were mere recommendations, "what probability would exist that they would be carried into execution?"

Madison was short on solutions. Prudence, religion, and character (by which he meant concern for reputation) were not enough to ensure that rulers or people would behave well. But he was already considering another incentive to good conduct. He would bring it forward soon enough.

As one of Virginia's representatives in Annapolis, Madison had called for a convention in Philadelphia. As a member of the Virginia Assembly in Richmond, he wrote a bill to approve the recommendation he had made. By playing different positions in quick succession, Madison could execute double plays with himself.

With Madison's input, the assembly picked a slate for Philadelphia that included Edmund Randolph, now governor, Patrick Henry, George Mason, and Madison. The most important man in Virginia and America, George Washington, headed the list.

Henry, the partisan of states' rights, refused to go. "I smelt a rat," he explained. More important, Washington did not want to go either. He offered various reasons: He had earned his ease. His health was bothering him (he had rheumatism in his shoulder). There was also the awkward question of what to do about the Society of the Cincinnati, an organization of Revolutionary War officers that would be meeting in Philadelphia at the same time. The society had been criticized as a nest of would-be aristocrats (its membership was supposed to be hereditary), and Washington refused to attend their meeting until the controversy was resolved. But he worried that if he went to Philadelphia for the convention, he might offend the Cincinnati.

Madison spent all winter and spring wooing him. He wooed him with tact. When he wrote Washington in December 1786 to tell him that he was on the list of delegates, he underplayed his own role in putting Washington there. "It was the opinion of every judicious friend whom I consulted that your name could not be spared. . . . In these sentiments," he added, "I own I fully concurred."

He wooed Washington with lobbying. Madison's three-year time-out mandated by congressional term limits had ended at the end of 1786, and in January 1787 he went back to Congress, which was now sitting in New York City. On his way, he stopped at Mount Vernon to strategize with his host. He wooed Washington, perhaps most effectively, with vote counts. In February, a week after arriving in Congress, he wrote Washington to tell him that all the middle states were sending delegates, "except Maryland which it is said means to do it." A month later, he reported that New Hampshire, Massachusetts, New York, South Carolina, and Georgia "have come into the measure." He discussed who their delegates would be ("Col. Hamilton" was one of three New Yorkers). It is astonishing how many people, otherwise intelligent but amateurs in politics, do not understand the importance of counting votes ahead of time. Yet vote counts answer the first questions any politician asks: Who will be in the room? Which side are they on? Madison was supplying Washington this information.

Washington needed the information because his reputation was at stake. He had become the nation's idol by winning a war for independence, then going home. The legend of Cincinnatus, the Roman who returned to his plow after saving his country, had been reenacted in modern life (Houdon's statue would show Washington, sword set aside, standing by a plow). If he came out of retirement to reenter politics now, he would need unimpeachable justifications—and he required a reasonable chance of success. If the friends of reform were up for a real fight, then Washington would join it.

Several of Washington's friends were advising him to do just that, including Henry Knox, his old commander of artillery, and Hamilton. But Madison was his in-state adviser, with his finger on the pulse of Richmond, and of Congress. "I will hope for the best," Washington wrote Governor Randolph in April, having decided to go to Philadelphia.

The convention was called to meet on May 14. Madison was in Philadelphia on the 3rd, the first out-of-stater to arrive. He took a room at a boardinghouse he had used as a congressman, a block from the statehouse (now Independence Hall) where the convention would sit, and made reservations for his fellow Virginians. When Washington arrived on the 13th to a hero's welcome, he was whisked away to the home of Robert Morris, richest man in America. But that was only down the street. Madison wanted all the Virginians together so they could plan their agenda, which he intended to be the convention's agenda.

The convention did not have a quorum until the 25th; "these delays," wrote Washington, "sour the temper of the punctual members." (Rhode Island never sent a delegation, all the New Yorkers except Hamilton walked out early, and New Hampshire came late, so there were never more than eleven states represented at a time.) But Madison and his fellow Virginians put the days of delay to good use.

An ambitious delegate had to come to Philadelphia with a plan, or at least a goal, if he hoped to have an impact. Of the fifty-five men who would attend the convention during the spring and summer, there were a few ciphers, a few chronic absentees, and a few bores and blowhards. But more than half the delegates were proud, powerful, intelligent men, committed to a range of jostling interests. A man would have to know what he wanted, and push for it, if he hoped to get it from his peers.

Madison knew what he wanted, and on May 29, Governor Randolph told the convention what it was. The convention had already held two housekeeping sessions, unanimously choosing Washington as presiding officer, and establishing its rules, the most important of which forbade "licentious publications of their proceedings" (there was to be no transparency in Philadelphia). On day three, Randolph, as Madison put it, "opened the main business."

After reviewing the defects of the existing government, Randolph offered fifteen resolutions, which became known as the Virginia plan. The first was a feint: "the Articles of Confederation ought to be . . . corrected and enlarged." The next fourteen went far beyond correction and enlargement.

The Virginia plan called for a national government of multiple branches—a two-house legislature, an executive, and a judiciary. There was also a "council of revision," composed mainly of judges, which could require the legislature and the executive to reconfirm certain decisions, though it could not block them permanently. (Almost no one liked this idea, and it soon fell by the wayside.)

The most striking features of the plan were the scope of the new national government and the source of its power. The national legislature would hold sway over American political life. It could make laws "in all cases to which the separate states are incompetent" and could veto any state law. The new national government would rest on popular choice. The lower house of the legislature was to be elected "by the people," in a proportional vote based on the population or wealth of their states. The lower house then chose the upper house. The whole legislature would then choose the executive and the judiciary. The new constitution was to be ratified, not by the state legislatures that had sent delegations to Philadelphia, but by state conventions "expressly chosen by the people."

If the Virginia plan passed, the days of state hegemony, enshrined by the Articles of Confederation, would be over. After the delegates had had

a night to think about Randolph's proposals, Charles Pinckney of South
Carolina asked, not unreasonably, "whether he meant to abolish the state
governments altogether."

I t is impossible to say for sure who contributed what to the Virginia
plan, but its congruence with themes Madison had been developing
in his memos to himself, and in letters to friends, shows his dominating
influence. In a letter to Washington a month earlier, he had outlined the
three branches of government, popular ratification, and the national veto
over state laws, which he called "absolutely necessary." Without the veto,
every power given to the national government "will be evaded and defeated. The states will continue to invade the national jurisdiction . . .
and to harass each other with rival and spiteful measures." Just as it was
characteristic of Madison to work through others (in this case Randolph),
it was characteristic of him to do their work for them ahead of time.

Over the next six weeks, as the convention debated the Virginia plan,
he justified it using other fruits of his preconvention homework. Madison
was a republican who believed in majority rule. "The majority . . . are
the safest guardians both of public good and of private rights," he had
written in one memo to himself, and he said so again and again during
the convention: the Virginia plan was "consistent with the democratic
form of government"; if the delegates had "justice and the majority of
the people on their side," they "had nothing to fear."

Yet republican government had its problems, which Madison, as a state
legislator and congressman, knew all too well: factionalism and bullying
at the state level (the travails of Virginia's Baptists), impotence and cross-
purposes at the national level (unpaid bills, restraints on interstate commerce). Why was the Virginia plan the best way to solve them? Because,
as Madison argued on June 6, the plan expanded the arena of political
contention. This was the idea he had discovered during his year of reading and writing.

Under the status quo of the Articles, republican government in America existed only within each of the thirteen states. Their joint forum, Congress, was a league of equals, in which the representatives of Delaware (population 59,000) stood toe to toe with the representatives of Massachusetts (population 379,000), Pennsylvania (population 434,000), and Virginia (population 747,000).

The Virginia plan would extend majority rule over the whole country or, as Madison said on June 6, "enlarge the sphere" of government. A national government elected on republican principles, he argued two days later, could "control the centrifugal tendency of the states," which would otherwise "continually fly out of their proper orbits." It would also be powerful enough to defend "the weaker party" within any state against persecution. It would not become tyrannical itself because of the very size and variety of the electorate that had chosen it. "So great a number of interests and parties" would ensure that a vicious majority could never coalesce nationwide.

Enlarging the sphere of government for the sake of republican government was a new idea. Most republics in history had been small (Greek or Italian city-states, Swiss cantons); the largest, the Roman Republic, had been undermined by the Caesars and transformed into an empire. But Madison knew from his reading that leagues and confederacies, even those made up of small republics, had not been stable either. America was already large, and since it was determined not to have emperors—the man presiding over the Philadelphia convention had proved that point by going home to his plow—Madison was willing to consider the possibilities of large republics.

Once Edmund Randolph laid out the Virginia plan, Madison led the struggle for it. Although he was content to let Randolph take the first step and the credit, he was willing and able to shoulder the burdens of small-group infighting. He wielded his reading like a weapon. In one speech he cited "the intrigues practiced among the Amphyctionic confederates, first by the kings of Persia, and afterwards fatally by Philip of

Macedon; among the Achaeans, first by Macedon and afterwards no less
fatally by Rome; among the Swiss by Austria, France and the lesser neighboring powers; among the members of the Germanic body by France,
England, Spain and Russia; and in the Belgic republic [Holland] by all
the great neighboring powers." (This was Madison's own account of his
erudition; he seemed quite proud of himself.) On another occasion, he
corrected a fellow delegate, Oliver Ellsworth of Connecticut, on the history of proportional representation. "Passing over the German system in
which the King of Prussia has nine [votes]," Madison reminded Ellsworth
of the Lycian confederacy, "in which the component members had votes
proportioned to their importance, and which Montesquieu recommends
as the fittest model for that form of government." Ellsworth, one hopes,
took note.

Madison was no orator; there was not an ounce of melodrama in him,
scarcely of drama. But he did remind his colleagues of the stakes. "We
were now digesting a plan," he said late in June, which "would decide
for ever the fate of Republican government."

Perhaps his greatest strength was persistence. He attended every session
of the convention—the delegates met six days a week at ten in the morning, adjourning in midafternoon—and spoke at almost all of them,
sometimes as often as three or four times in one day. William Pierce of
Georgia, the only delegate to leave sketches of his colleagues, credited
Madison with "a spirit of industry and application . . . he always comes
forward the best informed man [on] any point in debate." (He is "a gentleman of great modesty," Pierce added, "with a remarkable sweet temper." Even while correcting Ellsworth, Madison praised him for his "able
and close reasoning.")

During the Philadelphia convention, Madison had several allies. Washington and Hamilton he knew coming into the convention. A new supporter was one of the Pennsylvania delegates, Gouverneur Morris (no
relation to Robert, though they were business partners). Despite a peg
leg and a withered arm, souvenirs of various accidents, he was a forceful

and compelling presence. "Every species of talent," wrote Pierce, made him "conspicuous and flourishing in public debate." He also flourished in private conversation, as the ladies of Philadelphia could attest.

But these were, for various reasons, erratic allies. Morris came on strong as the summer progressed, but he skipped three weeks of June ("fickle and inconstant," Pierce also wrote of him). Hamilton gave a long, powerful speech in mid-June, of such an extreme nationalist tendency— he recommended an executive elected for life and dismissed the Virginia plan as not radical enough ("pork still, with a little change of the sauce")—that its only effect was to make Randolph's resolutions seem moderate by comparison. Lacking Madison's patience, Hamilton missed all of July and all but one session in August. "I am sorry you went away. I wish you were back," Washington wrote him forlornly.

Washington himself loomed over the proceedings in impartial silence, less like a god on Mount Olympus than the mountain itself. Whatever he may have said offstage—and he may not have said much, for he could be remarkably tight-lipped in private—his role as presiding officer imposed public silence on him.

Only James Wilson of Pennsylvania—a Scottish tutor turned lawyer and businessman (and who was in the process, even as the convention met, of turning bankrupt)—joined Madison at every session, speaking even more often and generally taking the same side. "No man," wrote Pierce, "is more clear, copious and comprehensive than Mr. Wilson."

Madison might have had a dozen allies or none, for his task was in fact hopeless. Almost everyone at Philadelphia wanted change, but the small states—a shifting coalition whose core was Connecticut, New York, New Jersey, and Delaware—were determined to fight a system of national proportional representation, in which they feared being swallowed up. They counterattacked on June 15, with a set of nine resolutions proposed by William Paterson of New Jersey (population 184,000). The New Jersey plan called for a strengthened Articles of Confederation: the states would retain equal representation in a one-house Congress, which was given the power to levy taxes, regulate commerce, and pick a national executive. New York (population 340,000) threw its weight to the small states because its governor, George Clinton, anticipated booming revenues from the port of New York, which he wanted controlled by him, not by the United States. He had made sure that New York's delegation contained two of his allies—Robert Yates, a state judge, and John Lansing, mayor of Albany—who would outvote Hamilton. Lansing now told the convention that the New Jersey plan "sustains the sovereignty of the states," while the Virginia plan "destroys it." After the New Jersey plan was offered, John Dickinson of Delaware chided Madison privately, "You see the consequence of pushing things too far."

Other states were less concerned with the structure of government than with their own particular interests. Connecticut (population 238,000) was a small state. South Carolina (population 249,000) was larger and expected to grow. But more than 40 percent of South Carolina's people were slaves—the highest percentage of any state. Slavery was an interest that cut across the large state/small state divide. If slaves were counted in the representation, every slaveholding state, whether large or small, would benefit. (Slaves, of course, would not vote, but would only swell the power of their masters.)

Both Connecticut and South Carolina were represented by hard bargainers. Roger Sherman of Connecticut had taught himself to be a lawyer; one fellow Yankee called him "cunning as the Devil . . . you may as well catch an eel by the tail." John Rutledge of South Carolina had learned law at the Middle Temple in London; a foreign diplomat called him "the proudest and most imperious man in the United States." If the devil and the aristocrat made a deal between themselves, and the small states, they might catch the whole convention by the tail.

Madison was aware of the power of slavery as an issue, and he offered a deal of his own that would save the underlying shape of the Virginia plan. At the end of June, in the same speech in which he corrected Oliver Ellsworth, Madison admitted that "the great division of interests in the

United States . . . lay between the northern and the southern." Perhaps proportional representation in one house of the legislature could be based on total population, slaves included, while in the other it would be based on the number of free inhabitants only. "By this arrangement the southern [side] would have the advantage in one house, and the northern in the other."

But he did not find enough takers. After weeks of increasingly stubborn debate on the issue of representation, the convention on July 2 chose a committee of eleven (one from every state then present) to offer a compromise. Madison opposed the committee to the last, saying that in Congress "he had rarely seen any other effect than delay" from such bodies. He had certainly seen no good effects from committees on which he had not served. Neither he nor Wilson was picked to serve on this one, though Sherman and Rutledge were.

After a two-day break to celebrate the Fourth of July, the committee presented its compromise: one house of the legislature would be based on proportional representation, with each slave counted as three-fifths of a free inhabitant; in the other house, each state would have an equal vote. Slave states and small states alike managed to win special status. Days of wrangling followed, but by July 16 the compromise had been ratified.*

The next morning, delegates from the large states held an informal caucus before the convention opened. Some of them (including Madison? the record does not say) suggested that they offer their own plan of government to America, but most resignedly accepted what had been done. "The time was wasted in vague conversation," wrote Madison. It was a typical losers' confab, directionless and dispirited.

Madison was the most dispirited of all. He took the survival of state equality in one house as an unmitigated defeat, an intrusion into his plan of all the weaknesses of leagues and confederacies. He had studied history

---

* South Carolina, which had helped give birth to the measure, voted against it in a last-ditch effort to have slaves counted equally with free inhabitants.

so thoroughly and reasoned from it so closely, how could he now accept his colleagues' mistake?

So Madison would not get what he wanted. But that is a common result in politics. One common response is to complain, and Madison did plenty of that, nursing his dissatisfaction through the hot weeks of July and August, on into September, when he grumbled, in a letter to Jefferson, that "the *plan should* it *be adopted* will neither effectually *answer* its *national object* nor prevent the local *mischiefs* which every where *excite disgusts* against the *state governments.*"

Another possible response to disappointment is to keep going. Maybe something can be saved from the wreck. Maybe the wheel will turn in your favor. Maybe, in response to further thoughts or further developments, you will change your mind.

Madison kept going, even as he kept complaining. His perfect attendance record remained unblemished, even though he began to feel ill. The new legislature, after the compromise of July 16, suffered other changes from Madison's original plan. It lost its power to veto state laws and to make laws "in all cases" where the states were incompetent (though since the legislature had changed its composition, that was no longer, from Madison's point of view, such a bad thing).

Madison's principle of majority rule won a belated victory at the end of August, when the convention agreed that its handiwork should be ratified by a convention in each state, not by state legislatures. "The people," said Madison, were "the fountain of all power, and by resorting to them, all difficulties were got over. They could alter constitutions as they pleased."

Throughout these debates, Madison persisted in a task he had begun in May: writing notes of every day's deliberations. The convention had a secretary, William Jackson, one of Hamilton's comrades from Washington's wartime staff. But he recorded only motions and votes. Madison had a more ambitious aim and a motive unique to him. "The curiosity I had felt during my researches into the history of . . . confederacies . . . and the deficiency I found in the means of satisfying it . . . determined me to preserve, as far as I could, the most exact account of what might pass in [this] convention." The frustrated historian wanted to create the perfect research tool.

So Madison posted himself every morning in front of the head table, where the presiding officer sat. "In this favorable position for hearing all that passed," he noted everything in his own private shorthand; then "losing not a moment unnecessarily between the adjournment and re-assembling of the convention," he fleshed out his notes. Practice, and in-creasing familiarity with the thought patterns of the major players, made his job easier. He checked a few speeches with the authors, including one "very extravagant" effort of Gouverneur Morris's. "When the thing *stared him in the face* (this was Mr. Morris's exact expression) . . . he laughed and said, 'Yes, it is all right.'"

A few other delegates also took notes. Robert Yates of New York kept the next most complete set, but his record broke off in early July, when the states' rights New Yorkers went home, even more disgusted with the victories that Madison had won than Madison was by the defeats he had suffered. Madison's record stands alone for completeness.

But Madison was not only serving the muse of history. Information is power, and though he honored the convention's secrecy pledge by keep-ing his notes unpublished as long as he lived, he would honor his political alliances by sharing selected information with chosen friends. No one has suggested that Madison distorted his own record; he did not believe in altering the past to control the present. But he did believe in revealing bits and pieces of the past to affect political dynamics, and he had taken care to amass the largest supply of bits and pieces concerning this epochal event.

Madison and his allies enjoyed a last hurrah as the convention wound itself up in early September. Madison, Hamilton (truant no more), and Gouverneur Morris were appointed to a Committee of

Style to produce the final version of the document. Morris did all the work, spinning the preamble out of his head, and smoothing and trimming the rest. "A better choice," wrote Madison decades later, "could not have been made." On the last day, September 17, Washington broke his silence to suggest a minor revision; it passed without objection. This was also his indirect seal of approval: nothing else needs to be changed; we have done the best we could. Hamilton applied his own quirky seal of approval. "No man's ideas were more remote from the plan" than mine, he said. "But is it possible to deliberate between anarchy and convulsion on one side, and the chance of good . . . on the other?" If even I am getting on board, it's time everyone else did, too. He signed for himself, the defection of Lansing and Yates having left him stateless; thirty-eight other delegates, representing all eleven states present, joined him.*

The Constitution then went to the country. Madison's work on it was less than half done.

---

* John Dickinson, who had gone home sick, asked a colleague to sign for him.

CHAPTER THREE

The Federalist,
The Bill of Rights

M adison was still a delegate to the Congress he had been laboring to supplant. As soon as the Philadelphia convention adjourned in September 1787, he returned to New York and his double duties—as a legislator, and a lobbyist for change.

One fire had to be put out immediately. The convention had asked that the Constitution be "laid before" Congress, then "submitted" to the states. But some in Congress proposed submitting it with amendments. This was a mischievous suggestion. The Constitution, "when altered," wrote Madison, "would instantly become the mere act of Congress," rather than the special creation of the convention. It would then require the approval of all thirteen states, like any other amendment to the Articles of Confederation. Besides Madison, there were ten other signers of the Constitution in Congress, almost a third of the total membership, enough to make sure that amendments would not happen. But even a debate would suggest controversy before the ratification process began. Madison and his allies managed to send the Constitution along from New York on September 28 without comment, pro or con, and with none of their deliberations on the record.

The Constitution declared (Article VII) that it would go into effect after nine states had ratified it; the Philadelphia convention had wanted to avoid the veto of lone holdouts, which had doomed every previous attempt to alter the Articles of Confederation. Within four months, five states (Delaware, Pennsylvania, New Jersey, Georgia, and Connecticut) would ratify. But for the new government to succeed, it was essential that the Constitution be embraced by all three of the largest states—Virginia and Massachusetts, as well as Pennsylvania—plus New York, thanks to its pivotal location.

There was early trouble in Virginia. Two of its delegates to the convention had refused to sign. George Mason, the prickly theorist, had become more and more unhappy as the summer wore on: he feared the power of the president and the Senate, predicting that the new government would end in monarchy or aristocracy. He also wondered why the document had no bill of rights, a question that would resonate over the months to come. He "would sooner chop off his right hand," he said, "than put it to the Constitution as it now stands." Mason's stand ended his long friendship with George Washington, and it provoked Madison to sour mirth. In a letter to Paris filling Jefferson in, Madison reviewed Mason's objections, then added that since he was "now under the necessity of justifying his refusal to sign, he will of course muster every possible one."

Edmund Randolph, the governor and the proposer of the Virginia plan, was the second of Virginia's non-signers. He had a host of objections: he didn't like the Senate trying presidential impeachments, or the president's power to pardon traitors, or Congress's power to set its own pay—and he asked for another convention to revise the Constitution they had just spent four months writing. But Madison judged him less stubborn than Mason and therefore handled him with flattery. He urged Randolph to remember his prominence and the responsibility that went with it. "There are subjects to which the capacities of the bulk of mankind are unequal, and on which they must . . . follow the judgment of others not their own." Randolph should be a leader of popular thought, and Madison would lead him to that thought.

The situation in New York, the host state of Congress, was even worse than in Virginia, for New York's governor, George Clinton, was a firm and energetic anti. Clinton's best-known portrait, a posthumous image by Ezra Ames, shows a jowly red face run to beef. But in 1787, Clinton was at the top of his game, beginning the eleventh of what would be twenty-one years as governor. His base, the Dutch farmers of upstate, was suspicious of change; self-interest encouraged him to hope that New York could enjoy its growing prosperity as a semi-sovereign state. He and his precocious nineteen-year-old nephew, DeWitt Clinton, wrote anti-Constitution essays for the newspapers (New York City had five at that time).

The ablest critique came from Clinton's lieutenant, Robert Yates, in a series of essays that invoked the highest authorities. Yates wrote under the pen name Brutus, which referred not to Caesar's assassin but to his sixth-century BC namesake, who had founded the Roman Republic. Brutus's first piece, which appeared on October 18, appealed to an equally great figure of the modern world, the early eighteenth-century French political philosopher Montesquieu, whom Americans considered an oracle. "A free republic cannot succeed over a country of such immense extent" as the United States, wrote Brutus, then quoted Montesquieu for confirmation: "It is natural to a republic to have only a small territory. . . . The interest of the public is easier perceived, better understood, and more within the reach of every citizen." Madison, reading Brutus hot off the press, fretted that he wrote so well.

The Constitution needed its own New York media campaign. Alexander Hamilton decided to organize it. Journalism was in his blood. As a teenager, he had written poems and a description of a hurricane for a newspaper in his native Caribbean. As a student at King's College, he had published two prorevolution pamphlets that ran to 50,000 words. He now reached for one of his wartime pseudonyms, Publius, another of the Roman republic's founders. (American opinion writers used so many classical pseudonyms that their bylines read like the dramatis personae of a history play.)

Hamilton's leadoff essay, called "The Federalist," first appeared on October 27 (seeking market saturation, Hamilton arranged for each essay to run in different newspapers on different days). It began with a noble appeal to debate at the highest level. "The people of this country" will "decide the important question, whether societies of men are really capable or not of establishing good government from reflection and choice, or whether they are forever destined to depend for their political constitutions on accident and force. . . . My arguments will be open to all and may be judged of by all."

For all his energy, Hamilton needed help. He enlisted John Jay, an older man, grave and sensitive, who had been a diplomat under the Articles of Confederation. (Madison thought Jay had not pushed Spain hard enough to open the Mississippi.) He also asked Gouverneur Morris and William Duer, another New Yorker with Caribbean connections. Morris declined, and Hamilton decided that Duer's contributions were not good enough to be included in the burgeoning series. So after nine essays, five by Hamilton and four by Jay, Publius was reinforced by Madison. And when Jay came down with rheumatoid arthritis in early November 1787, Publius became a two-man operation.

There is no record of how Hamilton and Madison made their arrangement, since they were living in the same city, around the corner from each other, and had no need to correspond. Friends sent ideas to one man assuming he would easily share them with the other, as had happened in Philadelphia in 1783. Years later Madison recalled their close quarters and their frantic pace. "In the beginning it was the practice of the writers . . . to communicate each to the other their respective papers before they were sent to the press. This was rendered so inconvenient, by the shortness" of their deadlines "that it was dispensed with." After Madison joined the project, the essays appeared four times a week, at 2,000 words each. "It frequently happened that whilst the printer was putting into type the [first] parts of a number, the following parts were under the pen, and to be furnished in time for the press." Madison's first essay appeared on November 22. In a little over three months, he would write twenty-eight more.*

Many of the founders were occasional or even full-time journalists— John Dickinson, John Adams, Samuel Adams (a newspaper publisher as well as a writer). Thomas Paine was so eloquent he almost rose to the level of a founder by his journalism alone. Benjamin Franklin was the greatest of all American journalists. But journalism was a new task for Madison. His "Memorial and Remonstrance Against Religious Assessments" had been distributed far and wide in Virginia, but it was a one-shot. Now he was grinding it out in the press alongside peers and hacks. Madison recalled, he and Hamilton were helped by all the intellectual preparation they had done for the convention. But preparation carries you only so far. You still have to get the words out, in good order and on time. This would not be the last time in the ratification fight that Madison would step up to some brand-new task because the struggle required it.

How do his contributions to *The Federalist* work? Occasionally Madison reveals the humor he usually reserved for intimates. His funniest bit is a set piece in #38, comparing the authors of the Constitution, and their critics, to doctors. (Only a chronically ill man could have written with such attention to medical detail.) "A patient who finds his disorder daily growing worse . . . calls in such [physicians] as he judges most capable of administering relief." They prescribe a remedy that will improve "his constitution" (nice touch). "The prescription is no sooner made known however, than a number of persons interpose, and . . . assure the patient that the prescription will be poison. . . . Might not the patient reasonably demand before he ventured to follow this advice, that the authors of it should at least agree among themselves, on some other remedy to be

* Douglass Adair sorted through the competing claims of authors and their partisans, deciding that Hamilton wrote fifty-one papers, Madison twenty-nine, and Jay five. Computer analysis of stylistic traits seems to confirm this count. Yet #63, Madison's twenty-ninth, sounds like Hamilton to me—the insistent use of "I," a certain dark, relentless tone.

substituted? And if he found them differing as much from one another, as from his first counsellors, would he not act prudently, in trying the experiment unanimously recommended by the latter?" Madison uses a universal human situation to illustrate one of the strengths of his side: the Constitution's supporters had fought their battles ahead of time, and agreed on one document, whereas their critics were all over the map. This was true, and also a sly way of blunting the sharpest criticisms (critics might disagree among themselves, but maybe one of them was right).

Occasionally Madison holds his arguments together with tacks and twine. In #40, he claims "that the great principles of the constitution" are "the expansion of principles . . . found in the articles of confederation." Since the Constitution was a thorough repudiation of the Articles, this sinks to the level of a lie.

Number 54 is a slippery effort to justify the three-fifths rule for counting slaves in one house of the legislature. New York was a slave state, but the local political elite, including Jay, Hamilton, and Governor Clinton, had founded the Society for Promoting the Manumission of Slaves in 1785; the tide of opinion in the state was slowly shifting and had to be addressed. Since Publius was supposed to be a New Yorker, Madison pretends to speak for "one of our southern brethren." Br'er Southerner says that since slaves are chattel, they are "irrational animals, which fall under the legal denomination of property." On the other hand, since they cannot be wantonly killed and are responsible for any crimes they commit, they are also "moral person[s]" under the law. The three-fifths rule simply reflects their mixed character. Switching back to his "own" voice—that is, the voice of the pretend New Yorker—Madison admits that the southerner's argument is "a little strained," yet claims to be persuaded by it. Madison's bad faith as a writer matches his bad argument.

Some of Madison's most telling points—shrewdly observed, sharply phrased—are made in passing. He sweeps to his goals but sends out ripples as he goes. "A nation of philosophers is as little to be expected as the philosophical race of kings wished for by Plato." "If men were angels, no government would be necessary. If angels were to govern men, neither external nor internal controls on government would be necessary." "In all very numerous assemblies, of whatever characters composed, passion never fails to wrest the scepter from reason. Had every Athenian citizen been a Socrates, every Athenian assembly would still have been a mob."

At least once, he rises to real eloquence. In an answer to Brutus's critique of large republics, Madison makes a counterargument, and it is a strong one. But for a moment he invites the reader to step back and look at the entire situation, with hope instead of fear. "Why is the experiment of an extended republic to be rejected merely because it may comprise what is new? Is it not the glory of the people of America, that whilst they have paid a decent regard to the opinions of former times and other nations, they have not suffered a blind veneration for antiquity, for custom, or for names, to overrule the suggestions of their own good sense, the knowledge of their own situation, and the lessons of their own experience? To this manly spirit, posterity will be indebted for the possession, and the world for the example of the numerous innovations displayed on the American theatre, in favour of private rights and public happiness." There is an echo of Jefferson in "decent regard" and a slower-paced but perhaps equally powerful echo of his freshness and hope.

What are Madison's actual arguments? He refutes Brutus and Montesquieu by repeating the argument he had made in June at the convention in support of the Virginia plan. Then he spoke of enlarging the sphere of government; now he writes of extending it. "Extend[ing] the sphere" of a republic is "a republican remedy for the diseases [of] republican government." Large republics are stronger than small ones, because unjust majorities will find it harder to connive at long range and will face more opposition from the "greater variety of parties and interests" present in large electorates.

But Madison offers new thoughts on extending the sphere, in response to the changes made in the Virginia plan at Philadelphia. Then he had been oppressed by the survival of state equality in one house of the legislature. Now in #39 he takes a different tone. The House of Representatives, he explains, is based on proportional representation and majority rule, the original ideals of the Virginia plan. But in the Senate, each state is represented equally by two senators. He calls the first system *national*—based on the will of the people. The second system he calls *federal*—the states retain their identity, and a share of their power. "The proposed constitution," he concludes, "is in strictness neither a national nor a federal constitution, but a composition [mixture] of both."

All this was rather dry, but Madison was working toward a great point. He had written that extending the sphere of government would frustrate unjust majorities. What about unjust government? Is it enough, he asks in #48, to rely on "parchment barriers against the encroaching spirit of power?" Any ruler, or body of rulers, will aggrandize himself or itself if given the chance—even elected rulers. Madison quotes a line of Jefferson's, written several years earlier: "An *elective despotism* was not the government we fought for."

In #51 Madison reveals his solution. "The interior structure" of government must be arranged so that its "constituent parts" may "keep . . . each other in their proper places"—its constituent parts and its constituent personnel. "Ambition must be made to counteract ambition. The interest of the man must be connected with the constitutional rights of [his] place." Extending the sphere was a remedy that applied to the government as well as to the nation. The more moving parts government had—state versus national, House versus Senate, Congress versus president versus courts—the less likely would any one of them, or all of them together, be able to oppress.

What didn't Madison write about, and did it matter? He focused on the nature and structure of government, particularly as it applied to Congress. But everything in *The Federalist* on the presidency—(e.g., "Energy in the executive is a leading character in the definition of good government")—would be written by Hamilton. When Hamilton considered the extended sphere of the republic, he thought less of its political structure than of its economic potential, "the veins of commerce in every part" being replenished by "the commodities of every part." He already had his eye on American prosperity and on the president—or the presidential adviser—who could foster it.

Years later, Madison claimed that even then there was "a known difference" in their ideas. True, or true only in memory? Madison and Hamilton were working intimately, even wearyingly together. Sometimes colleagues are so busy, or so excited to be in harness, that they ignore how different they really are.

Early on Madison sensed that *The Federalist* would be useful outside New York. Before he had written a single essay, he sent the first seven to Washington, suggesting that they be reprinted in Richmond. Washington would arrange it. In March 1788, Madison abruptly sent himself back to Virginia for the next test of strength.

M adison had profited from his ubiquity, shuttling between state, national, and constitutional politics. But maybe his enemies could profit by it, too, catching him out of position.

In February 1788, Massachusetts ratified the constitution, becoming the sixth state to do so and the second of the large states. Virginia, the largest, had scheduled its ratifying convention for Richmond in June, with the election of delegates taking place in March. Madison did not want to serve. He was suffering from bilious attacks (they found their way into *Federalist* #19, where the Holy Roman Empire is described as "agitated with unceasing fermentations in its own bowels"), which made all-day coach rides humiliating as well as uncomfortable—he had to make frequent stops for relief. Madison also wondered whether a delegate to the Constitutional Convention ought to sit in judgment on his own handiwork.

A string of letters from home changed his mind. Governor Randolph wrote to tell him that George Mason was running for a seat in the ratifying convention, not in his home county, which was staunchly pro-Constitution, but from another county down the Potomac. (Would-be delegates were allowed to shop for friendly constituencies.) Meanwhile, Madison also learned that he was being lied about in Orange County. "You will be greatly surprised," wrote the justice of peace there, "to hear . . . that you are opposed to the system, and I was told the other day that you were writing a piece against it." Distorting a politician's views was a common tactic: a Baltimore newspaper had likewise reported that John Jay opposed the Constitution. Madison's father, who rarely talked shop with his son, told him that the local Baptists were lining up against the Constitution, since it made no mention of freedom of religion. "I think you had better come in as early in March as you can."

Madison was also summoned by the father of his country. Washington, who had heeded Madison's coaxing to go to Philadelphia, now returned the favor by commanding him to go to Richmond. "The consciousness of having discharged that duty which we owe to our country is superior to all other considerations." It was like being addressed by Houdon's statue.

Opponents of the Constitution were much concerned with the lack of a bill of rights. The idea of including one had not even been raised in Philadelphia until the last week of the convention, when Mason asked for a committee to draw one up; he thought it would take only "a few hours." Roger Sherman answered that state bills of rights were still in force, hence a national bill of rights was not necessary; the convention voted not to bother.

But once the Constitution was given to the world, the issue would not die. Bills of rights had been a feature of Anglo-American political life since the Magna Carta, the charter of freedoms issued by King John in 1215. James Wilson tried to address the Constitution's lack of one at the Pennsylvania ratifying convention in November 1787. The Magna Carta and other English bills of rights were carved, he said, from a background of royal power. But under the Constitution, power "remains in the people at large, and by this Constitution they do not part with it." There was no reason to guard against the abuse of powers the people had not surrendered.

But Brutus in New York had already anticipated Wilson's argument. He pointed to Article I, Section 9, which indeed guarded against certain abuses: the writ of habeas corpus (no arrests without reason) was secured; bills of attainder (convictions by legislative act, without trial) were forbidden, along with ex post facto laws (criminalizing acts that were legal at the time they were committed). If arguments like Wilson's were correct, "what propriety is there in these exceptions?" But if the three rights discussed in Article I, Section 9 deserved special protection, why not others?

One complaint was addressed directly to Madison. In December 1787, Jefferson sent him his reaction to the Constitution. Although Jefferson found much to like, first on his list of dislikes was the lack of a bill of rights. "A bill of rights is what the people are entitled to against every government on earth . . . and what no just government should refuse." Jefferson expressed himself with his habitual sweep, but this time he was not singing some new song of his own, but defending an established feature of Anglo-American political life.

By February 1788, Madison had decided that he must run for a seat in the Virginia ratifying convention. He left New York on March 4, stopping at Mount Vernon on his way home. He also stopped to confer with John Leland, a Baptist missionary who had led the church's revival in Virginia. Leland could tell Madison his flock's concerns for the security of religious liberty, and he knew from Madison's record that they would be taken seriously.

In the national debate over a bill of rights, Mason, Wilson, and Brutus were weighty figures; weightier still were Madison's most intimate intellectual partner in Paris and the facts on the ground in his own state.

Madison got home on March 23, two days before Election Day in Orange County. On the 25th, he did something as new for him as writing a *Federalist* paper. He explained in a letter to his former landlady in Philadelphia: "For the first time in my life" Madison mounted "the rostrum before a large body of the people, and . . . launch[ed] into a harangue of some length in the open air and on a very windy day." Madison won the vote handily; in last place came Charles Porter, the man who had beaten him eleven years ago by treating voters to drinks.

The Virginia ratifying convention met in Richmond on June 2. By then, two more states had ratified, Maryland in April and South Carolina in May, bringing the total to eight—one short of success.

Almost everybody in Virginia's political class came to Richmond, 170 delegates in all; too many for the statehouse, they could be accommodated only in a huge new school auditorium across the street. Governor Randolph, as Madison had hoped, had come around to support the Constitution. Among the younger men in attendance were John Marshall (for) and James Monroe (against).

The most compelling presence was Patrick Henry. Fifty-two years old, he had been an American hero since his blazing oration against the Stamp Act in 1765, in which he supposedly said, "If this be treason, make the most of it!" Jefferson, who disliked him every bit as much as Madison did, nonetheless acknowledged that he spoke "as Homer wrote." There was no higher praise of verbal skill in the eighteenth century—Homer's poetry and Henry's speeches were forces of nature.

Henry opposed the Constitution now from a sincere fear that the power of his state and the rights of individuals were at risk, and from a canny sense that many Virginians—his once and future public—shared that fear.

Henry would hold the floor in Richmond almost one-quarter of the time the ratifying convention sat (the Virginians met for three and a half weeks, six days a week, for six or seven hours a day). Madison could not go head to head with Henry as an orator. We owe our record of what was said at the ratifying convention to David Robertson, an attorney who took notes in shorthand and published them shortly afterward (there was no secrecy pledge in Richmond). Time and again, he noted Madison's shortcomings as a speaker: "he spoke so low that his exordium could not be heard distinctly"; "here Mr. Madison made some other observations, but spoke so very low, that his meaning could not be comprehended."

But Madison scored points by sticking to the point. On the second day of the ratifying convention, George Mason moved that the Constitution be debated clause by clause. This was a godsend for Madison, for no one was as immersed in the document's ins and outs as he. Repeatedly he called Henry and other opponents to order. "I hope that gentlemen, in displaying their abilities on this occasion . . . will condescend to prove and demonstrate. . . . Let us not rest satisfied with general assertions of dangers, without examination." Madison's thoroughness inspired one commentator to poetry.

> *Madison among the rest,*
> *Pouring from his narrow chest,*
> *More than Greek or Roman sense,*
> *Boundless tides of eloquence.*

His was the eloquence of the well-informed.

Madison's unprepossessing appearance and manner made his expertise all the more effective. Men who were not threatened by him could allow themselves to be persuaded.

The delegates tussled over two great Virginians who were not there—Jefferson in France, and Washington at Mount Vernon—each side hoping to enlist an absent hero in its ranks. Henry began it, invoking "an illustrious citizen of Virginia, who is now in Paris. . . . Living in splendor and dissipation* he thinks yet of bills of rights. . . . Let us follow [his] sage advice." Madison was not Jefferson's only correspondent, and Henry had gotten ahold of one of his doubting letters to someone else.

Madison leapt to counterattack. "Is it come to this then, that we are . . . to introduce the opinions of respectable men not within these walls?" He then did it himself. "Could we not adduce a character equally great on our side?" (Washington, of course.) Back to Jefferson. "I wish his name had never been mentioned. . . . I know that the delicacy of his

---

* Surely Henry meant to say "living *in the midst of* splendor and dissipation."

feelings will be wounded when he will see in print what has and may be said concerning him." Madison managed to make Henry seem prying, and to pry into Washington's thoughts at the same time.

Madison addressed the missing bill of rights directly. He deployed one of his favorite arguments—the importance of structure and extended spheres. These were the only effective guardians of freedom. "If there were a majority of one sect, a bill of rights would be a poor protection for liberty." The "multiplicity of sects which pervades America . . . is the best and only security" for the right to worship. Madison also suggested that a bill of rights could be dangerous. "If an enumeration be made of our rights, will it not be implied, that every thing omitted [from the list] is given to the general government?" His was a subtle argument, but the legal mind and the appetite for power being what they are, it was not a baseless one.

Such arguments only moved Henry to scorn. A "bill of rights may be summed up in a few words." Why not write them down? "Is it because it will consume too much paper?"

Madison could see that the pressure for a bill of rights was irresistible. When Massachusetts had ratified in February, it had recommended amendments for later adoption. South Carolina in April had done the same, and the Constitution itself (Article V) made provision for amendments. Agreeing to propose a bill of rights now seemed like a way to compromise pros and antis.

The question then became when amendments should be offered. Henry was determined to propose them now—in a second convention, if possible, as conditions of Virginia's ratification if necessary. He scoffed at the idea of leaving amendments until after the Constitution went into effect: "You agree to bind yourselves hand and foot—For the sake of what?—Of being unbound. You go into a dungeon—For what? To get out."

Madison knew that Henry was being disingenuous. Conditional ratification would raise a storm of legal challenges, revisions to other states' ratifications, and arguments about those revisions. In the whirlwind, the

Constitution would go down. Conditional ratification was in fact rejection. The most Madison would offer in Richmond was the possibility of adding a bill of rights later. Doing so "can produce no danger, and may gratify some gentlemen's wishes."

Madison made that remark late in the session of June 24. There was a wild coda. Henry rose to speak one more time and all hell broke loose. "A storm suddenly arose. It grew dark. The doors came to with a rebound like a peal of musketry. The windows rattled; the huge wooden structure rocked. . . . The members rushed from their seats with precipitation and confusion."

The next day, storm over, they voted. Henry moved previous amendments. He lost, 88–80. Next came a vote to ratify, with recommended amendments. It passed 89–79. Technically Virginia's ratification was not decisive: New Hampshire had become the ninth, and vital, state to approve the Constitution on June 21 (though the news would not reach Virginia for days). But the vote in Richmond gave the new government America's greatest state, and the nursery of some of its greatest talents.

After the vote, Washington, assuming a maternal role, invited Madison to unwind at Mount Vernon. "Moderate exercise, and books occasionally, with the mind unbent, will be your best restoratives."

A month later, at New York's ratifying convention, in the Hudson River town of Poughkeepsie, the other two authors of *The Federalist*, Hamilton and Jay, beat George Clinton and his allies 30–27.

Madison's work still was not done.

There was no question who would be the first president under the new Constitution. All George Washington had to do to win was not announce that he would not serve. A southern president meant a northern vice president, and the most eminent northerner was the patriot and diplomat John Adams. (Madison still disliked him, writing in cipher to Jefferson of his "*extravagant self-importance*.")

But every other elective office was up for grabs. Washington wanted Madison to be one of Virginia's senators. Patrick Henry had accepted his defeat in Richmond with apparent good grace, but no one who knew him believed he would not try to fight again another day.

So it proved. According to Article I, Section 3 of the Constitution, senators were to be chosen by state legislatures. Since the Senate was starting from scratch, each state got to pick two. Early in November 1788, Virginia's legislature, dominated by Henry, voted for two opponents of the Constitution to represent the state; Madison finished third, respectably but still out of the running.

That left a shot at the House of Representatives, but Henry had thought of that, too. Virginia was to have ten representatives in the First Congress. Henry made sure to put Orange County in a hatchet-shaped district stretching from the Blue Ridge to Fredericksburg, along with seven other counties, most of which had opposed the Constitution. He also imposed a residency requirement on congressional candidates, so that Madison had no choice but to run there. The requirement was unconstitutional—Article I, Section 2 said only that a representative must live in his state—but it would not be challenged and overturned for years.

Madison's enemies came up with a strong opponent—his investment partner, James Monroe. Seven years younger than Madison, Monroe was tall, handsome, earnest, vigorous. He had crossed the Delaware with Washington and survived a bullet in his lungs at the Battle of Trenton; after leaving the army, he had read law with Jefferson. Jefferson loved Madison, but he loved his other protégé, too. At one point he dreamed of both men moving next to him at Monticello. With such neighbors, he wrote Madison, "I could . . . lay myself up for the residue of life, quitting all its contentions."

But Monroe had a contentious side: he resented Washington for what turned out to be an unsatisfactory assignment during the Revolution, and he was miffed at not having been sent to the Constitutional Convention, for which he blamed Madison, among others. When Madison's enemies approached him to run, "he resisted for a time," according to one relative. A short time.

The central issue of the election was how and when to amend the brand-new Constitution. Virginia's vote for ratification had been accompanied with a list of forty proposed amendments, New York's with a list of twenty-three. Patrick Henry and George Clinton wanted these amendments to be laid before a second convention, one of two avenues for change provided by the new Constitution (Article V). But Madison knew what Henry was really up to. A second convention, especially one so soon in the Constitution's life, might be as freewheeling as the first, and so long as it was a real option, the new government would be in limbo. "The secret wish of his heart," Madison wrote Governor Randolph, is "the destruction of the whole system."

Under the pressure of events, Madison had come to see a bill of rights, shepherded through Congress, as a necessary compromise, even a good thing. Back in the summer, Jefferson had sent him a bulletin from his Paris observation post. "I sincerely rejoice at . . . our new constitution," he began cheerily. "It is a good canvas, on which some strokes only want retouching." First of these was a bill of rights, which "the general voice from north to south" demanded. Madison's answer in the fall showed signs of weariness: why was his friend simultaneously so upbeat and so nagging? Madison admitted that a bill of rights was "anxiously desired by others," though not by him. He called it a "parchment barrier," repeating the phrase from *Federalist* #48, and reminded Jefferson that Virginia's Declaration of Rights had been "violated in every instance where it has been opposed to a popular current." But ultimately he found a reason to yield. The political truths declared in a bill of rights, he wrote at the end of his letter to Jefferson, "acquire by degrees the character of fundamental maxims of free government, and as they become incorporated with the national sentiment, counteract the impulses of interest and passion." A bill of rights might be of use, because people would come to think of it in capital letters, as the Bill of Rights. Jefferson accepted Madison's conversion and fixed it with an amateur architect's metaphor. "A brace the more will often keep up the building which would have fallen" without it.

Now Madison had to win his election. Once again he was in New York, serving in the soon-to-be-dead Congress. The election for the new Congress was scheduled for February 2, 1789, the very worst time of year for relocating and campaigning. He wrote Governor Randolph that he "despised" vote-getting, Washington that he had "extreme distaste" for it. His body expressed his thoughts, afflicting him with hemorrhoids. Nevertheless, he traveled south, spending the week before Christmas at Mount Vernon. (By now, Madison's friends were sending their letters to him there.) He arrived home before the new year.

The weather for the next five weeks was vile: rain, hail, ice, sleet, and snow, accompanied by hard frost. Madison stumped his district, writing letters, meeting with supporters, and debating Monroe. Years later he recalled one appearance in Culpeper County, the largest in the district and a stronghold of opposition to the Constitution. The two candidates spoke in front of a German Lutheran church while the congregation, standing in the snow listening, "seemed to consider it a sort of fight, of which they were required to be spectators." Afterward Madison had a twelve-mile ride home, which left his nose frostbitten.

Madison told the story of the debate with the humor of reminiscence. But the Lutherans and other religious minorities in his district understood the issues and took them very seriously.

The Monroe campaign accused Madison of opposing any amendments, on the grounds that the Constitution was perfect. Early in January he wrote a letter defending himself to the Reverend George Eve, a Baptist minister. Madison explained that although he had opposed prior amendments, now that the Constitution was safely ratified, the First Congress should protect "essential rights, particularly the rights of conscience in the fullest latitude." Later in the month, Eve defended Madison at a public meeting in Culpeper, recalling "the many important services which [he] had rendered . . . in particular the act for establishing religious liberty." Madison had changed his mind on the bill of rights, but he had never changed it on religious liberty. Voters will forgive a politician for tacking this way and that so long as his course is clear. His good deeds rose up to help him.

Even good deeds he had never done. In a letter, reprinted in several newspapers, Madison claimed that he not only supported a bill of rights now but had been an "unsuccessful advocate" of one at the Constitutional Convention. So unsuccessful that he had not recorded his advocacy in his notes. He favored amendments—to the Constitution, and to his record.

When the vote was held, Madison beat Monroe by 1,308 votes to 972. The Baptists and the Lutherans in the snow had rallied to him, along with his Orange County base. He sent the results to Jefferson, adding, with the grace of a smart winner, that his friendship with Monroe had not experienced "the smallest diminution." As a winner, he could afford to be gracious; as a smart winner, he put it on record.

George Washington took the oath of office on a balcony of Federal Hall on Wall Street in New York City on April 30, 1789. The House had been meeting in the same building, in a two-story chamber on the ground floor, since the beginning of the month. Madison left no descriptions of the drama, the anxiety, or the hoopla of the new system going into effect, perhaps because he was so used to being at the center of things.

He was too busy to do much observing. He had stopped at Mount Vernon on his way back to New York in late February to help Washington write his inaugural address. David Humphreys, a former colonel on Washington's staff who was writing a biography of him, had produced a monster, a seventy-three-page draft. Madison wrote a more wieldy version, in six paragraphs. After Washington gave the speech in Federal Hall, Madison wrote the House's response, and Washington's answer to the House's response. The observant and the envious noticed Madison's access. Sen. William Maclay of Pennsylvania, who kept a diary, wrote that

Madison was "deep" in the president's "business. . . . The creatures that surround him would place a crown on his head, that they may have the handling of its jewels."

Congress had plenty of business of its own. It had to construct a government, filling in the outlines of the Constitution, and then govern. One item of business Madison insisted on putting on its agenda was a bill of rights. He wanted the bill fashioned by Congress, where he could influence the process, and he wanted it done quickly to mollify the Constitution's critics. In May he managed to table a petition from his own state calling for a second convention. The next month he presented his own list of amendments in the House.

Madison had to contend with two sorts of skeptic—those who wanted to do nothing, and those who wanted to undo everything. The do-nothings argued, not unreasonably, that the government was brand-new; how could they fix problems before they arose? Radical amenders were hostile to the government itself: many of Virginia's forty proposed amendments were structural, altering the power to levy taxes, make treaties, and regulate trade. Madison made it clear that he was interested only in "the security of rights," not in "reconsider[ing] the whole structure of the government."

His amendments included a Jeffersonian preamble about the source of rights and the ends of government; some fussing with the number of constituents each congressman represented and congressional pay; and versions of what would become the first ten amendments.

Madison drew on centuries of Anglo-American precedent. The rights to petition and to trial by jury went back to the Magna Carta. The English Bill of Rights, proclaimed in 1689 after the ouster of James II, forbade excessive bail and fines, and cruel and unusual punishment, and upheld a rather specialized form of the right to bear arms: "Protestants may have arms for their defense" (the deposed king was Catholic). Many other guarantees were to be found in the Virginia Declaration of Rights, including the one Madison had rewritten: "all men are equally entitled to the free exercise of religion."

The most unusual of Madison's amendments was his fifth, which responded to the new, multilayer structure of the Constitution: having secured elsewhere rights of conscience, freedom of the press, and trial by jury, he proposed that no state should violate these rights. As the debate in the House wore on, he would call this amendment the "the most valuable . . . on the whole list." He had not forgotten the misbehavior of his own state, its Declaration of Rights notwithstanding.

He repeated on the House floor the concession he had finally made to Jefferson in favor of "paper barriers": "they have a tendency to impress some degree of respect for them, to establish the public opinion in their favor, and [to] rouse the attention of the whole community." His do-nothing colleagues, being pragmatists, could be appealed to on pragmatic grounds, and so he argued that adding a bill of rights would show a "spirit of deference and concession" to those who wanted one. Advocates of structural change were impossible to satisfy—Rep. Aedanus Burke of South Carolina called Madison's amendments "frothy and full of wind"—but happily they were a small minority in Congress.

Madison's handiwork went to a select committee in July, then before the full House for eleven days of debate in August, and finally in late August to the Senate (which met in its own chamber on the second floor of Federal Hall). New York sweltered; the "political thermometer," wrote one congressman, was equally high. Some politicians, intent on other issues, wondered why they were wasting time on amendments. "They were treated contemptuously" when they were first debated in the Senate, wrote Sen. Maclay. But in the grind of politics, the amendments moved on.

Madison's prohibition on state infringements of rights fell by the wayside; it would be a century and a half before the judiciary wondered whether the states should be held to the same standard as the federal government. His preamble disappeared, too; Roger Sherman, now a Connecticut congressman, said it would "injure the beauty" of the existing preamble, Gouverneur Morris's lithe little essay.

The most striking change in Madison's original list was a matter of copyediting: Madison had proposed shoehorning his amendments into the existing articles of the Constitution wherever they were relevant, but his colleagues decided to list them as new articles at the end.

In late September 1789, House and Senate agreed on a final version and sent twelve amendments to the states.

The first amendment on Congress's list was a formula for modifying the number of constituents each congressman represented, to better regulate the size of the House. It never passed, and later Congress addressed the issue by legislation. The second amendment, regulating congressional pay raises, was slow to catch on: it was not approved until 1992, by which time it was the Twenty-Seventh, not the Second Amendment.

So the Bill of Rights, Amendments Three through Twelve, became, once ratified, Amendments One through Ten. Their distinct position, and their number, echoing an even more famous set of ten laws, boosted their stature and made Madison, their sponsor, a secular Moses.

The Bill of Rights also fulfilled its immediate political task. Madison predicted that it would "kill the opposition" to the Constitution. He was right. Three states ratified them by the end of the year; five more would do so early in 1790. Any pressure for a second convention collapsed. Virginia gave its assent in December 1791, making the Bill of Rights valid. But Patrick Henry had given up long before. "Virginia has been outwitted," he complained.

W̶hen we celebrate the Constitution, we tend to focus on the Constitutional Convention. Howard Chandler Christy's twenty-by-thirty-foot painting *The Signing of the Constitution* hangs in a stairway of the House, as bright and extroverted as an eighteenth-century fashion show: look at the cool, gold moiré coats of Charles Pinckney and Daniel of St. Thomas Jenifer, stage right and stage left; Washington, hovering over the action in sleek black, is cooler yet. Signers' Hall, in the National

Constitution Center in Philadelphia, lets us stroll among forty-two life-size bronze statues of delegates: the thirty-nine signers, plus the three last-day holdouts (Mason, Randolph, and Elbridge Gerry of Massachusetts). The *New York Times* described Madison's statue as "pensive," Hamilton's as "brash" and "handsome." Perhaps the first and most monumental celebration of the convention was Madison's notes. The convention takes obvious precedence in the story of the Constitution: it is where the words lawyers and judges quote were written, where the men we honor as framers signed their names.

But producing the Constitution took more than five months in Philadelphia; it also took three years in Annapolis and New York and Richmond. At every major stage—the Annapolis convention, the Philadelphia convention, writing *The Federalist* and fighting for ratification, writing the Bill of Rights—Madison was a major player. He dealt with all the other major players—Washington and Hamilton, Morris and Wilson; he kept Jefferson informed and on board, and fended off Brutus and Henry. Sometimes he was wrong or stubborn; these are flyspecks against his patience and energy, learning and savvy.

He lost arguments and he changed his mind. That is because the Constitution was produced by politics as well as theory. Several times in *The Federalist* Madison speaks of theorists, always scornfully ("an ingenious theorist" might plan a constitution "in his closet, or in his imagination").* He was one, more than he knew, but he also knew that a man in public life had to be more than that. In #53, discussing foreign policy, he said the best way for congressmen to acquire the necessary knowledge was by "practical attention . . . during the period of actual service." This was true of many other kinds of knowledge as well.

Once the Constitution was done, it entered the realm of politics. Disagreements about it would destroy many of Madison's friendships; they

---

* See also #10 M 164 and #53 M 308.

would in his lifetime inflame the country to madness, including blood-shed, and threaten worse—secession, civil war. Disagreements would propel Madison to the heights of power (which is one reason he helped foment these disagreements).

All that was to come. By the fall of 1789 Madison had done a great thing. If he was not quite the Father of the Constitution—success has a thousand fathers—he was its midwife.

CHAPTER FOUR

The First Political Party

In 1789 James Madison was on top of the political world. He was the acknowledged leader of the House of Representatives. Rep. Fisher Ames, a sharp young congressman from Massachusetts, not easily impressed, described Madison a month after meeting him as "a man of sense, reading, address, and integrity. . . . He is our first man." Madison himself complained of his eminence, on the grounds that hardly any of his colleagues were capable of sharing "the drudgery of business" with him, but that was a backhanded way of boasting. How much more pleasant to direct business oneself.

The president of the United States was Madison's friend and partner, and Madison served him as more than a ghostwriter. When, early on in Washington's presidency, Vice President John Adams and the Senate wanted to saddle him with a title, something sonorous and ridiculous like "His Highness the President of the United States of America and Protector of the Rights of the Same," Madison steered Congress away from the blunder: such "splendid tinsel," he argued, "would disgrace the manly shoulders of our chief." He also beat back an attempt to trim Washington's freedom of action. The Constitution (Article II, Section 2) empowered the president to nominate executive officers "by and with the advice and consent" of the Senate. Then, argued Rep. Theodorick

Bland, a fellow Virginian, the president needed the advice and consent of the Senate to dismiss them, too. But that, said Madison, would "destroy . . . responsibility." If the Senate took a hand in dismissals, appointees would no longer be answerable to the president, and he would not be answerable for their misconduct. Madison defended Washington's dignity and his power.

Another friend and partner of Madison's filled one of the new government's highest positions. Alexander Hamilton lived and worked on Wall Street, a block and half from Federal Hall, where Congress met. Madison roomed at a boardinghouse on Maiden Lane, a few blocks north. Decades later an old lady would remember having seen the two men "talk together" that inaugural summer, "and then turn, and laugh, and play with a monkey that was climbing in a neighbor's yard."

One thing they must have talked about was Hamilton's ambition to be the nation's first treasury secretary. It was a role he had been preparing for since his days as a merchant's clerk in the islands.

In one of his partly coded letters to Jefferson, Madison speculated about possible treasury secretaries, all New Yorkers: Robert Livingston, a Hudson River grandee and judge who had administered the oath of office to Washington; *Federalist* coauthor John Jay (maybe Madison put Jay on the short list because he wanted him away from diplomacy). But "*Hamilton . . . is perhaps best qualified* for that *species of business* and *on that account would be preferred* by those *who know him personally.*"

Washington knew Hamilton personally and offered him the job. Hamilton began to work at the Treasury in September. He took the job on the assumption that he would have Madison's "personal goodwill" and "firm support. . . . I do not believe I should have accepted under a different supposition."

Madison labored to give an even higher position in the administration to his dearest friend, Thomas Jefferson, who was coming home from France in the fall of 1789. During this leave of absence, he would tend to his estate and return his maturing daughters to America, far from

French men and French nuns (Martha, the eldest, had said she wanted to take the veil). But Washington and Madison wanted Jefferson to stay on as secretary of state. Jefferson had the necessary diplomatic experience, and he would maintain the government's regional balance: Hamilton and Jay, who had become first chief justice of the Supreme Court, were New Yorkers; Adams and Henry Knox, the secretary of war, were from Massachusetts. Washington and Jefferson (and the new attorney general, Edmund Randolph) would represent Virginia.

But Jefferson did not want to serve. This was in part a pose—Jefferson playing the role of Cincinnatus. It was also a deeply felt desire to remove himself from the scrum of politics. Jefferson was a very private public man, much more so even than Madison. His estate, Monticello, was a hilltop aerie, and when he found the world beating a path to its door, he built a second, even more remote estate at Poplar Forest. He needed to be asked, and asked again.

But Washington would not do all the asking. The man who had answered his country's call to preside over everything from festivity to disaster expected his peers to do the same.

So Madison played the matchmaker, floating the offer to Jefferson, ignoring his refusals, waiting in New York to meet him off the boat, then following him, after he landed instead in Norfolk, to Monticello. After a couple more months and a couple more letters, Jefferson agreed in February 1790 to join the Washington administration as secretary of state.

We look back at certain past moments as idylls of unity. They may feel that way even to the people involved in them: we have won, or we are about to begin; we are all pulling together. But politics never rests, even among friends and allies. Even when they agree, there are still slight shades of difference that may deepen over time. New or ignored questions arise on which they differ greatly. And there is always ambition. Washington was president, with the approval of everybody. But there would come a time when someone else would be president. Who would that be? The second tier could not all occupy the office together.

Washington's team was no sooner assembled than it began to pull apart. The two causes were Alexander Hamilton and world politics.

The House had asked Hamilton, as soon as he stepped into his job, to come up with a plan for balancing the nation's books. He responded in mid-January 1790, with the Report on Public Credit, 20,000 words with eleven appendices, which was read aloud to the House in one day. Madison wrote Jefferson at Monticello that it was "too voluminous" to be sent by mail.

Hamilton's report addressed the new nation's very real debt crisis. Although the United States was not quite a deadbeat nation—its creditworthiness on the bourses of Amsterdam and Antwerp, the financial nerve centers of the world, had risen since the ratification of the Constitution—it was still struggling to pay its Revolutionary War debts. Some states, particularly South Carolina and Massachusetts, were even worse off than the country as a whole (Massachusetts's efforts to tax its way out of debt had driven its farmers to rebellion). Other states had addressed their debts by shifty means—North Carolina had simply written off the bulk of its debt; Rhode Island had been making ends meet by printing paper money.

Most American IOUs had changed hands since the war's end—a problem that seemed, to many, moral, not economic. Everyone agreed that the country's debts to its veterans were debts of honor. But was a merchant, who had accepted a soldier's back-pay certificate at a discounted price, owed the same consideration? What about a speculator, who had bought the discounted certificate from the merchant, or directly from the soldier?

Hamilton proposed that the Treasury assume all government debts—the United States' and those of the states—and pay them back at common rates, not discriminating between original holders and later purchasers. He supported assumption on the grounds of order: "colli-

sion," "confusion," and "interfering regulations" would result if the federal and state governments scrambled to settle their obligations separately
but simultaneously. He opposed discrimination because investors would
not tolerate it. Who in the future would ever pay a decent price for a
U.S. bond if the new government began its life by picking and choosing
whose debts it would honor, and whose it would shortchange? Hamilton
knew, from experience as well as study, how investors thought and markets worked.

The Report on Credit caused a storm of speculation. If the United
States was really about to pay what it owed, now was the time to snap
up IOUs while they were still undervalued. Investors got busy. "I call not
at a single house," wrote Sen. Maclay in his diary, "but traces of speculation in certificates appear." Speculators ranged beyond the drawing rooms
of New York into the hinterlands, where they trolled for clueless debt
holders: "two expresses with very large sums of money," Maclay noted,
were said to be "on their way for North Carolina."

The report also caused a storm of criticism: Hamilton's character,
Maclay added, was "damn[ed] forever." Hamilton had kept his own
counsel during the weeks he devised his plan, but Maclay and others were
convinced that heavy bettors had inside information. For their part, speculators tried to read Hamilton's silences for clues.

Early in February Madison began unfolding his own views in the
House. Hamilton's old ally joined his critics. Madison backed discrimination, having heard the same tales of shyster speculators as Maclay: they
were "exploring the interior and distant parts of the union," he wrote Jefferson, "to take advantage of the ignorance of [original] holders."

He revealed his views of assumption at the end of the month. "We
must go much further" than Hamilton's plan, Madison told the House.
He proposed a form of super-assumption, arguing that states that had
already paid off their debts be compensated for what they had done. In
effect, their debts would be paid twice—once by the states themselves,
then again by the federal government to the states.

Madison was giving moral answers to economic questions: all states had borne an equivalent share of the revolutionary struggle, so pay them all, but some individual debt holders had done less than others, so pay them less. Hamilton was giving moral answers, too, but his were drawn from the practices of commerce and banking as they had developed over time.

Discrimination, for all the passions it roused, was voted down at the end of February—enough congressmen shared Hamilton's knowledge of the way the world worked, or had speculated in government paper themselves. But the debate on assumption, lengthened by Madison's resistance, dragged on through the spring. Madison's super-assumption proposal "hangs heavy on us," Fisher Ames complained in March. "If he is a friend" of assumption, "he is more troublesome than a declared foe."

But assumption was not the only game in Congress, and Madison and Hamilton were not the only players. Another question of equal importance arose as summer approached, and it seemed that both might be resolved together.

New York City had invested a lot of money in being the nation's capital, hiring Pierre L'Enfant, the French engineer and architect, to redesign Federal Hall. But other localities wanted the privilege. Philadelphia, the former capital, was still the country's largest city. George Washington wanted a site on the Potomac. Southerners might find it onerous to bring their slaves to a free city (Philadelphia) or a slave city with a Manumission Society (New York).

The liveliest account of what happened next is by Jefferson. On his way to the president's house on Broadway one day, Jefferson ran into Hamilton, "somber, haggard and dejected." "Even his dress [was] uncouth and neglected," Jefferson wrote. If Congress did not pass assumption, Hamilton told Jefferson, he might as well resign. The secretary of state offered "to bring Mr. Madison and Col. Hamilton to a friendly discussion of the subject" at dinner at his lodgings on Maiden Lane (which was also Madison's street). When the two guests arrived, Jefferson told them he did not understand the topic himself but "encouraged them to consider the thing together."

The result of their considering was that Madison, while continuing to vote against Hamilton's plan for assumption, would stop fighting it, thus allowing it to pass. In return, the capital would move to the Potomac, after a temporary relocation in Philadelphia (which Hamilton would use as bait to bring Pennsylvania's congressional delegation into the bargain).

Neither Madison nor Hamilton ever described the dinner, and neither had Jefferson's appetite for hoarding nuggets of anecdote and gossip. Jefferson wrote down this little nugget two years after the fact. One detail—Hamilton, the careful parvenu, being badly dressed—seems unlikely, and another—Jefferson, not understanding an important question—seems impossible. Washington's preference for a Potomac site, certain to have been a factor in everyone's calculations, is concealed. Jefferson also omitted to mention a key side arrangement: Hamilton pledged that Virginia would get a better deal on those of its war debts that were still unpaid. Yet, since events worked out as if Jefferson's dinner-table deal had been struck—Congress voted to move the capital to Philadelphia, then to the Potomac, and Hamilton's version of assumption squeaked through at last—something like it must have happened.

The fights over Hamilton's first financial plans were momentous—the federal government took a step toward solvency and hideous D.C. summers—but they were politics as usual. Hamilton had won something, but so had Madison: Virginia was in a better position fiscally and, with the future capital in or near it, geographically.

More fights were coming. In December 1790, Congress returned to Philadelphia, not to Independence Hall, but to the new county courthouse, renamed Congress Hall, next door. There Hamilton unfolded his next plan: a national bank, with a capital of $10 million.

There were a few banks in the United States already, including the Bank of New York, which Hamilton had helped set up a few years earlier, but their combined capital was only $2 million. Hamilton wanted a new bank to inject liquidity into a cash-starved economy and to draw Americans, both high rollers and ordinary people, more deeply into saving and investing. His Report on Public Credit had responded to an immediate problem. His proposal for a national bank was meant to push the country into a new financial world.

One-fifth of the money for the new bank would come from government deposits of customs duties and tax receipts; the rest would be supplied by selling shares to private investors. The constitutional justification for Hamilton's bank came from Article I, Section 8, which gave Congress the power "to borrow Money on the credit of the United States." When Congress needed to borrow, the bank would supply the loans.

Once again, Madison opposed him. He did not see the need for a bank, though his objections on this score were a bit hazy: the government, he said, could raise money from individuals and existing banks, and by collecting its taxes "a little in advance."

He had a more powerful objection, however: Hamilton's bank was unconstitutional. The power to borrow could not be construed into the power to charter a bank to make loans. Madison made an early argument for strict construction, attacking "the diffuse and ductile terms which had been found requisite to cover the stretch of power" in Hamilton's bill.

There was an objection to Madison's objection, and the bank's supporters made it. Article I, Section 8, a long enumeration of Congress's powers, included one last power: "to make all Laws which shall be necessary and proper" for executing everything that had gone before. *The Federalist* #44 had elaborated: "whenever the end is required, the means are authorized; wherever a general power to do a thing is given, every particular power necessary for doing it, is included." The author of #44, as it happened, was James Madison. In the debate over Hamilton's bank, Rep. Elias Boudinot even quoted #44, assuming that it had been written by Hamilton.

Madison defended himself against himself. Hamilton's bank was not a particular power necessary for accomplishing a general power but a stretch to a stretch to another stretch. "Mark the reasoning on which the validity of the bill depends. To borrow money is made the *end* and accumulation . . . of capital, *implied* as the *means*. The accumulation of capital . . . is then the *end*, and a bank *implied* as the *means*. The bank is then the *end*, and a charter of incorporation . . . *implied* as the *means*. If implications, thus remote and thus multiplied, can be linked together, a chain may be formed that will reach every object of legislation."

Congress rejected Madison's reasoning and passed a bank bill in February 1791. But there was another hurdle yet: the president's veto. Washington had not yet exercised his veto power. Jefferson and Attorney General Randolph urged him to do it now. Washington talked the bank bill over with Madison, "listen[ing] favorably as I thought to my views," and asking Madison to prepare a veto message. But he also asked Hamilton for his opinion, which Hamilton gave in a 15,000-word essay finished in an all-night session. At the end of February, Washington signed the bill.

This time Hamilton had gotten all he wanted, Madison and Jefferson nothing. Was this to be the shape of politics as usual in the new administration?

The other force tugging at Washington's team was the domestic politics of world politics.

Britain and France, the world's superpowers, had been fighting on and off for a century; the American Revolution was only one episode in their Hundred Years' War. If they fought again, America might stay out of it but could not hope to remain unaffected.

Madison was a Francophile going back to his days in the Continental Congress. He was also, and would remain all his days, an Anglophobe. He resented Britain as a Virginian and as a republican. Virginia had not suffered as badly during the Revolution as New York or the Carolinas, but the last year of combat had been humiliating. Benedict Arnold and

Cornwallis had raided the state at will, chasing the government into the mountains and plundering Monticello. Ideologically, Britain was a force for ill in the world—the more ill, because of all the good it had once done. The nursery of rights and self-government was a bastion of monarchy and privilege.

Yet, despite recent history, most of America's commerce was with Britain and its empire; Americans imported manufactured goods from Britain, and sent crops and raw materials to Britain and the British West Indies. Britain often seemed not to appreciate this business, trying to keep America's ships out of the West Indies, though colonial governors made ad hoc arrangements to let them in. American merchants went where the biggest markets were regardless of British manners.

Madison had a plan for bringing American commerce in line with his predilections, which he offered to the House in the spring of 1789. Britain's share of America's trade, he said, was "unnatural," an artifact of habit and common language. Congress should "turn the tide to a more favorable direction" and steer trade to our ally, France. Madison proposed to accomplish this with a scale of duties, based on the tonnage of ships: American ships would pay least; ships of countries with whom we had commercial treaties (such as France) would pay more; ships of "other powers" (Britain) would pay most. After this regulatory push, Americans would make as much money from France as they had from Britain.

Madison got this bill through the House, but the Senate, where commercial interests were stronger, balked and it died.

Madison's notions of a potential trade bonanza with France were fantastic. The year before, France's ambassador had asked him what French products Americans needed. Madison answered that, for woolens, hardware, and leather, Britain had "greatly the advantage." But wine, brandy, oil, fruit, silk, cambric, lawn, glass, kid gloves, and ribbons "may be best obtained from France." This was trade policy through the prism of a planter's dinner table and wardrobe, failing to take into account what planters needed to outfit their slaves and their draft animals, to say nothing of what ordinary Americans consumed.

If Madison's trade policy had no basis in economic reality, then it had to be justified by realpolitik—by America's power to change the policies of other countries. If America slapped duties on Britain, then it might lower its duties in return and learn, as Madison told the House, that "advantages are to be gained by . . . reciprocity." He would have twenty-five years to test the effectiveness of this line of action.

Madison's tonnage bill bemused Hamilton, who had studied trade firsthand by ticking off bills of lading in a Caribbean port. Trade went where there was demand. "Mr. Madison," he said, "is a clever man," but "very little acquainted with the world." Hamilton offered this judgment to George Beckwith, a British spymaster during the Revolution who had come to New York in 1789 to sound out the new government (Britain had not yet sent an ambassador). "We think in English," Hamilton assured Beckwith, stressing the common history, commercial and otherwise, that Madison disdained. Hamilton showed his own unworldliness in being so open with a British agent. Americans had much to learn about great power politics.

G reat power politics moved to a new level of tension in the summer of 1789. Three months after Washington's inauguration, the Bastille fell. Louis XVI's ministers had been trying to reform France's finances (which had been strained, in part, by its support of the American Revolution). Now reform had provoked a new revolution.

Lafayette seemed to be the man of the hour, commanding a new patriotic militia. He supported a constitutional monarchy and consulted with Jefferson on a French bill of rights. France saw America as a model, Jefferson wrote Madison; our authority "has been treated like that of the bible, open to explanation but not to question."

A few Americans were not so hopeful. Hamilton, an old friend of Lafayette's from Washington's staff, sent him a cautionary letter warning him of "the vehement character of your people." Gouverneur Morris, who had arrived in Paris on a long business trip just as Jefferson was leaving, had similar fears: France's leaders "want an American constitution" without "reflecting that they have not American citizens to support it."

America's great ally was becoming her soul mate. Or was she? The differences in how Americans answered that question would make the French Revolution an issue in American politics.

The first public fight over the issue broke out in 1791, and Madison helped provoke it. Thomas Paine, the journalist whose *American Crisis* ("These are the times that try men's souls") had earned him immortality and record-breaking sales, was in Europe promoting a suspension bridge he had designed when the Revolution broke out. He discussed the news with Lafayette, Jefferson, and Morris, and in February 1791 he published a blazing defense of the revolution, *Rights of Man*, in England, with a dedication to George Washington, president of the United States: "may [you] enjoy the happiness of seeing the New World regenerate the Old." A month later, Madison got one of the earliest copies to arrive in America, while it was en route to a printer. He let Jefferson see it first.

At the same time, John Adams, vice president of the United States, had been writing a work of his own, *Discourses on Davila*, a series of essays that first appeared in a Philadelphia newspaper in April 1790 and continued on into 1791 (his leisure for writing showed how little vice presidents had to do). Enrico Davila was a historian of an earlier period of French history; *Discourses* used him as a peg to discuss current events, and political science generally.

If Adams had had to make his living as a journalist, he would have starved; he hid diamonds of psychological insight in dunghills of pedantry. *Discourses* had a point, though: good government was always threatened by ambition and strife, and since elections encouraged both, hereditary succession might produce "fewer evils." Adams was indulging in gloomy thoughts, a favorite activity of his. But praising hereditary succession was a dangerous thought for an American to express; doubly dangerous coming from an elected officeholder; triply so from an officeholder who had lobbied for Washington to have a title.

In May the American edition of *Rights of Man* appeared, with a prefatory note from Jefferson, expressing the hope that it would refute "political heresies which have sprung up among us." Everyone, including Adams, concluded that Jefferson was using Paine as a stick to beat Adams.

Jefferson wrote Adams protesting that it was all a mistake. His words had been taken from a letter he had sent the printer, when he passed the book along; the printer had used them without his permission. "Nothing was further from my intention . . . than to have had either my own or your name brought before the public."

Adams believed him. Should he have? The truth is that Jefferson had mixed motives. The note at the head of *Rights of Man* helped him, showcasing him as a champion of republican values. It certainly hurt Adams, condemning him as a heretic. And yet Jefferson and Adams were old friends. They had served together in the Continental Congress, and in Europe as diplomats; Jefferson knew and liked Adams's family. Politics is a contact sport, and sometimes throwing punches hurts almost as much as taking them.

Madison, who was never friends with Adams, bucked Jefferson up. "Mr. Adams can least of all complain." If "one servant of the public [can] write attacks against its government" by defending hereditary succession, another could defend "the principles on which that government is founded." Adams had started the fight by writing *Discourses*, and he was wrong; Jefferson had answered him with his blurb for *Rights of Man*, and he was right. Jefferson struck the blow, but Madison primed him, then encouraged and congratulated him, like a trainer in a fighter's corner.

Just as Paine had told Washington that the New World would regenerate the Old, the Old World could also regenerate the New. If Madison and Jefferson had been losing their fights with Hamilton in New York and Philadelphia, they could draw sustenance from liberty's progress in Paris.

There is no record to tell us when exactly Madison and Jefferson decided to push back against the mistaken policies and opinions of their colleagues. Perhaps there was no single moment. One thing happens, then another; then one realizes war has been declared.

Madison and Jefferson certainly had no intention of founding a party, or "faction," as a political party was then often called. Although Madison thought factions were inevitable—"the latent causes of faction," he had written in *Federalist* #10, were "sown in the nature of man"—he also believed they were unjust. "By a faction I understand a number of citizens . . . united and actuated by some common impulse of passion, or of interest, adverse to the rights of other citizens, or to the permanent and aggregate interests of the community." Factions were like germs—ubiquitous and unhealthy.

Madison was not alone. His dislike of factions was a universal prejudice—parties/factions were corrupt and corrupting; they led to commotion and war. "[I would] quarrel with both parties, and with every individual of each" before joining either, Adams wrote of parties in Massachusetts when he was young. "Let me . . . warn you in the most solemn manner against the baneful effects of the spirit of party," said Washington at the end of his career. "I never submitted the whole system of my opinions to the creed of any party of men whatever," declared Jefferson. "Such an addiction is the last degradation of a free and moral agent."

And yet founding a party is exactly what Jefferson and Madison now began to do, while never admitting, even to themselves, quite what they were doing. Soon enough, Hamilton and his allies would found a party of their own, which even Washington ultimately joined, all of them showing the same un-self-awareness.

Madison and Jefferson embarked on their undeclared mission in the late spring of 1791. They took a trip through New York and New England—north from New York City to Lake Champlain, then back via Vermont, Massachusetts, Connecticut, and Long Island. They fished for trout and shot squirrels. Jefferson ordered trees from a nursery and Madison took the longest open-water voyage of his life—across Long Island Sound. They investigated the Hessian fly, a grain pest, at the behest of the American Philosophical Society (Jefferson was one of its vice presidents).

One of Hamilton's friends, Robert Troup, a New York lawyer, thought they were up to more than that. "There was every appearance of a passionate courtship between the Chancellor, Burr, Jefferson and Madison when the two latter were in town," Troup wrote Hamilton.

The chancellor of Troup's letter was Robert Livingston, who presided over New York's Court of Chancery. Livingston was a disappointed man. He had not gotten any post in the Washington administration. As partial compensation, he had expected one of New York's Senate seats to be awarded to a member of his large, powerful family. But Hamilton had arranged with the state legislature, which made the selections, for one seat to go to Hamilton's father-in-law, Philip Schuyler, and the other to go to one of Hamilton's friends from the Constitutional Convention, a transplant from Massachusetts no less, Rufus King. Livingston had been an ally of Hamilton's in the fight to ratify the Constitution in New York state, but once he felt disrespected, that was that. Livingston began to get his own back in January 1791, when Schuyler was up for a new term. (The first senators had drawn lots to pick short or long terms, so that their tenure would be staggered.) This time Livingston teamed with Governor George Clinton to throw Schuyler out of office.

The man who benefited from this maneuver was Aaron Burr, a thirty-five-year-old veteran and lawyer. He had attended Princeton with Madison, though they seem not to have known each other well there. Burr's father had been president of Princeton a decade before John Witherspoon, and his maternal grandfather was the great theologian Jonathan Edwards. Burr's own talents ran to wit, reading, litigation, and politics, and in recognition of the last, Livingston and Clinton tapped him to replace Schuyler in the Senate.

Biographers of Madison and Jefferson deny that the northern vacation was about anything except relaxing in the beauties of nature. But sometimes contemporaries see what is under their noses. If the two Virginians wanted to exert a new force in national politics, they could not do it alone. They needed allies—peers in other states who shared their views, or their enemies. Jefferson, Madison, Livingston, and Burr had all clashed with Hamilton or his father-in-law. "Delenda est Carthago," Troup told Hamilton, was "the maxim adopted with respect to you." Every educated person then knew at least some Latin; you didn't have to know much to understand the old slogan, *Carthage must be destroyed.*

A party is made of more than just leaders. Another way that Madison and Jefferson built their party was to find instruments—like-minded men, not peers, who could do the work, much of it tedious, some of it dirty.

John Beckley had come to Virginia in 1769, the same year that Madison went to Princeton, as an indentured servant, sent from England because his parents were too poor to support him at home. He rose in the world thanks to his clear hand and clear reading voice. He clerked for Edmund Randolph and the Virginia legislature, and wanted to clerk for the Constitutional Convention, though Madison told Randolph that the job would go to someone "more conspicuous." Beckley tried to make himself more conspicuous by getting elected to the Virginia ratifying convention, as the owner of some land in a remote western county, but he failed. He did serve as the convention's secretary, and in April 1789 (this time with Madison's help) he won the job of his life, clerk of the House of Representatives. "Beckley Clerk," Madison noted in a letter to Randolph.

Once he was at the center of things, Beckley made himself useful to his Virginia patrons. He dealt with House documents and printers, and he knew people's handwriting. "From hints dropped," he learned when Hamilton had been writing pseudonymous essays for the newspapers; another time he "happened to see" a manuscript in the handwriting of one of Hamilton's clerks—another clue. Gentlemen would not read other people's manuscripts, but they would read analyses of them by people who had.

Beckley knew people's business, and shared what he knew. "The following list of paper men is communicated to me by Mr. Beckley," wrote Jefferson, on a document in his own hoard of intelligence (paper men were congressmen who were invested in U.S. securities, and thus beholden to Hamilton's wiles). It was Beckley who gave Madison the fateful copy of *Rights of Man*, and he gave both his exalted colleagues advice (all the more welcome because it confirmed what they already believed). "It would be wise to be watchful . . . of this extraordinary man," he wrote Madison of Hamilton. "[He has] a comprehensive eye, a subtle and continuing mind and a soul devoted to his object." Madison and Jefferson, in turn, introduced Beckley to allies of theirs: a letter of introduction to Burr described Beckley as "possess[ing] the confidence of our two illustrious patriots, Mr. Jefferson and Mr. Madison."

No politician can do everything himself. He needs intermediaries, and eyes and ears. Beckley filled all three functions.

Another man the illustrious patriots turned to was a sometime peer, for he had known Madison at Princeton, though he had since come down in life: he was a journalist.

Philip Freneau, a descendant of Huguenot merchants, went to Princeton to study for the ministry. There he met, in addition to Madison, the muse.

> *A second Pope, like that Arabian bird*
> *Of which no age can boast but one, may yet*
> *Awake the muse by Schuylkill's silent stream.*

The enjambment of the first two lines makes us hope that Freneau might write well one day, though the clunk of "Schuylkill's silent stream" suggests that he will not.

After college he drifted from career to career—teacher, translator, privateer, ship's captain—interspersed with journalism and versifying. Early in 1791 Madison recommended him to Jefferson, who offered him work as the State Department's clerk for foreign languages. The job required only "a moderate knowledge of French," Jefferson explained, and would not "interfere with any other calling the person may choose." The other calling Jefferson and Madison had in mind was for Freneau to edit a Philadelphia newspaper, with national circulation, that would be an "antidote" to "monarchy and aristocracy."

The administration already had its own de facto mouthpiece, John Fenno's *Gazette of the United States*, which ran Adams's *Discourses* and made money from running Treasury Department notices. To take on the *Gazette*, Jefferson offered Freneau information and income: he could see "all my letters of foreign intelligence and foreign newspapers" and be paid to print all the State Department's proclamations and notices—a bonus to his clerk's salary, which was only $250 a year.

Madison hawked subscriptions for the new paper in Virginia. "With Mr. Freneau I have been long and intimately acquainted," went one of his letters. "He is a man of acknowledged genius" whose qualifications "promise a vehicle of intelligence and entertainment to the public." Jefferson, for his part, pushed Congress to cut the postal rate for newspapers. Freneau went to work as clerk for foreign languages in August 1791, and brought out the first issue of his paper, the *National Gazette*, on Halloween.

The third step in party building was taken by Madison alone, and it was a very Madisonian step. He read a number of books, and wrote a series of essays, which would become his party's platform for the next twenty years. They would define him and his allies as agrarian, expansionist, pacific, and populist.

Madison did most of the reading in the early spring of 1791. He had brought a load of books to Philadelphia with him when the government moved there, and he told Jefferson that he would perform "the little task" of studying them before they set off on their northern vacation. He marinated his thoughts until the fall, when he began publishing them in the *National Gazette* three weeks after its debut issue; by April 1792 he had written more than a dozen essays.

Madison made a few simple points, and made them repeatedly. Country life was good, cities and manufacturing were bad. "'Tis not the country that peoples either the Bridewells or the Bedlams"; such "mansions of wretchedness" belonged to "overgrown cities" (Bridewell was a London prison, Bedlam a London madhouse). Urban life was insecure as well as wretched, because the artisans and factory workers who populated cities depended on "the consumption and caprice" of the marketplace. "What a contrast . . . to the independent situation and manly sentiments" of those "who live on their own soil."

This was a slap at Britain, whose industries depended on American and other foreign buyers. Madison calculated that more than 200,000 British workers were employed making exports for America. He filed the thought for future reference: the great economic superpower might be vulnerable to American pressure.

He was also slapping Hamilton, who had presented the Report on Manufactures to Congress at the end of 1791, singing the praises of economic diversity: "The spirit of enterprise . . . must be less in a nation of mere cultivators, than in a nation of cultivators and merchants; less in a nation of cultivators and merchants, than in a nation of cultivators, artificers [manufacturers] and merchants." Madison believed this vision of prosperity was all a delusion; the enterprise of manufacturers was always vulnerable to uncontrollable market forces.

Madison admitted that human fertility caused overpopulation, which tended to flow into cities. His safety valve was emigration—from Europe to America, and from the eastern states to new states and territories farther west. This tracked his years-long interest in opening the Mississippi River valley. Population control provided a rationale for the second plank of Madison's platform: western expansion.

He also made a bold prediction: the American and French Revolutions might put an end to war. Kings fought wars to gratify their ambitions. Republics would not have that temptation, and, as their peoples became more rational, they would no longer fight to gratify popular animosities. The "progress of reason" was "the only hope of UNIVERSAL AND PERPETUAL PEACE" (caps in the original).

This was another hit at Hamilton, for surely Madison remembered that only four years earlier, his then-friend had written *Federalist #6*, a survey, as grim as it was brisk, of ancient and modern wars. Hamilton found republics as bellicose as monarchies. "Are not the former administered by men as well as the latter? . . . Is it not time to awake from the deceitful dream of a golden age" and admit "that we . . . are yet remote from the happy empire of perfect wisdom and perfect virtue?" Remote indeed. In April 1792, France, Austria, and Prussia went to war, inaugurating two decades of universal bloodshed.

The most interesting thoughts in Madison's *National Gazette* essays concerned public opinion (one of his essays was titled simply "Public Opinion"). Americans already had a rough-and-ready appreciation of public opinion: Why else did they write so much for the newspapers? Madison wanted to define its political and constitutional role.

He had touched on the importance of public opinion in *The Federalist*, when he remarked that better transportation would strengthen the "cords of affection" that bound Americans together. But the main guarantee of liberty he had put forward as Publius had been the very complexity of the government, and of the country itself. Now, four years later, he relied instead on public opinion. Americans could maintain their freedom by keeping in touch with one another, and with their own principles (via the *National Gazette* and like-minded newspapers). They should also keep watch over possible backsliders and seducers (Adams and Hamilton).

Madison called for "a general intercourse of sentiments . . . favorable to liberty." "Let it be the patriotic study of all . . . to erect over the whole [country] one paramount empire of reason, benevolence and brotherly affection." Then "every good citizen will be . . . a sentinel over the rights of the people." "Every citizen shall be an Argus to espy" threats to his rights. (Argus was a hundred-eyed giant of Greek mythology.)

Public opinion was so important that Madison felt entitled to correct Montesquieu, everyone's favorite political philosopher. Montesquieu had proposed a classification of all governments into three kinds, each infused with a different spirit. Despotisms ran on fear, monarchies depended on honor, republics relied on virtue. Madison respectfully proposed his own tripartite system. Despotisms were ruled by force. Sham republics were ruled by corruption, with bounties and bribes upholding "the real domination of the few" (Hamilton and his paper men). Finally, true republics were ruled by an interplay between government and society: the "will" of society gave government its "energy," while government's "reason" instructed society's "understanding." Public opinion was a loop, sustaining leaders even as they shaped it. "Such are the republican governments which it is the glory of America to have invented, and her unrivalled happiness to possess."

Madison denied that his party was partisan at all. He blamed partisanship on his rivals, chiefly Adams (without naming him, though the reference was clear). The vice president's fascination with titles and hereditary succession had introduced "new vices" into American political discourse. Madison admitted in passing that it might be necessary to create "one party [i.e., his own]" to be "a check on the other." But the blame would rest with Adams and his ilk, who had started the escalation in the first place.

Most of the planks of Madison's platform were old ideas put to new uses. Poets had sung the virtues of rural life since ancient Greece and Rome (since the emergence of cities, in fact). Americans had been champing to push westward since they were colonists clinging to the eastern seaboard. American history had been punctuated by conflict, and with the right leaders Americans could fight well. But Madison knew from his revolutionary experience that they tired of long wars. His thoughts on public opinion, however, were something new in political theory: an expression, and a defense of populism.

Madison scholars spend relatively little time on his *National Gazette* essays, and those who study them do not ask why they are so ignored. One reason surely is their quality. They are short, but not sweet. The writing is crude, and so are many of the thoughts. Madison relies on clanging verbal chimes (see Bridewells and Bedlams, above). One almost feels he is writing down, as if for readers who move their lips as they read.

Madison wrote better than Adams, but that was a low bar. For years his foil, politically and journalistically, would be Hamilton. Hamilton was not a great writer (the four great writers of the founding were Jefferson, Franklin, Paine, and Gouverneur Morris). But he was energetic, prolific, and versatile. Sometimes he wrote too much, and too vividly, for his own good. But he never sank to the childish level of the *National Gazette* pieces.

Yet Madison was not writing for the ages. He was not really writing to win specific arguments. He was getting his thoughts in order—laying out issues for the years and decades to come, identifying his enemies and ways to attack them. He did what every party platform does—he pointed with pride, and he viewed with alarm.

Most important, he was bringing his readers into the process. All Americans believed in government based on popular choice. Even Hamilton, arguing at the Constitutional Convention for an executive elected for life, pointed out that he would be elected. Even Adams, toying with hereditary succession, expected an elected bicameral legislature. Madison now believed in more than popular choice. He wanted the people to be consulted between elections, continually. They would be his partners in government. It was an insight appropriate to a family man, to the ideal partner of so many other founders. Madison put his faith in Argus.

He flattered his audience, playing to their pride. (When Argus was killed by Hermes, Hera put his hundred eyes in the peacock's tail.) But Madison knew from long experience that pride is a factor every good politician takes into account.

This is why Madison would win the battles of the next nine years, however often he lost. This is why Hamilton's arguments, however persuasive, never won the larger contest for popular favor. Hamilton focused on opinions—his own, and those of his enemies—and whether they were right or wrong. Madison understood public opinion.

CHAPTER FIVE

Leading an Opposition

In 1792, Madison's party named itself. Having used terms like "republicanism" and "the republican interest," he and Jefferson and their allies settled finally on "Republican party." "The Republican party, as it may be called," wrote Madison in yet another piece for the *National Gazette*.* Their enemies, meanwhile, took to calling themselves Federalists. Hamilton and his supporters appropriated the prestige and success of the Constitution; Jefferson and Madison claimed the spirit of the government itself.

Madison's most urgent task that year, however, went beyond politics—it was to persuade George Washington to stay in office. 1792 was the year of the second presidential election, and the president was beginning to feel his age—he turned sixty in February. In the spring he asked his longtime adviser how to let the country know that he would retire at the end of his term. Madison dutifully offered his opinions on the proper time for such an announcement (mid-September) and the proper manner (an article in the newspapers), and drafted an eight-paragraph Farewell Address. But he included an anxious plea. "Having thus, Sir, complied with your wishes . . . I must now gratify my own by hoping [that you

---

* The party still exists, though they call themselves Democrats. The modern Republican Party is a newer, different organization.

will make] one more sacrifice, severe as it may be, to the desires and interests of your country."

This was an effort to hold politics off, for Washington still seemed to be above it. Though he had backed Hamilton on important questions, he had not yet committed himself to one side or the other. More accurately, Madison, who cherished Washington and his own closeness to him, could not acknowledge how much closer Washington had become to his former staff officer. Washington's status as father of his country could be tough on his symbolic sons; family politics is even harder on losers than the ordinary kind.

Everyone else in Washington's official family also begged him to stay on—Hamilton, Jefferson, Secretary of War Henry Knox. After that unanimous chorus of advice, everyone promptly returned to the business at hand, which was abusing one another. Jefferson warned Washington, by letter and in person, that Hamilton wanted America to be a monarchy and that he had wanted it at the Constitutional Convention. This was clearly a reference to Hamilton's long speech in June 1787 when he had called for an executive elected for life. Washington knew about the speech; he had been there. How did Jefferson, who hadn't, know about it? His best friend had also been there, taking notes. Clearly Madison had shared his notes of the Constitutional Convention with Jefferson, now that he and Hamilton were friends no more.

Hamilton attacked in public. He wrote an operatic letter to Edward Carrington, an old army comrade from Virginia, outlining the plot against him. "Mr. Madison cooperating with Mr. Jefferson is at the head of a faction decidedly hostile to me." Though Hamilton flagged several of his points as confidential, such letters were manifestos, meant to be circulated among the recipient's important friends. He thought Jefferson was the worse of the two Republicans, "a man of profound ambition and violent passions." He found Madison's character "peculiarly artificial and complicated." Jefferson was dangerous, Madison simply devious. Both, though, held opinions that could harm "the union, peace and happiness of the country."

Hamilton next took his complaints to the press. Writing under a variety of pseudonyms, he told the story of the founding of the *National Gazette*, fingering Madison's role and laughing at the notion that Philip Freneau's only connection to Jefferson was as a translator. "Could no person have been found acquainted with more than one foreign language?" The *National Gazette*, for its part, called Hamilton "injurious to the liberty and enslaving to the happiness of the people."

Washington, growing alarmed at the journalistic fireworks, wrote his secretaries of state and the treasury asking for "mutual forbearances and temporizing yieldings on *all sides*" (Washington's italics). He could still float above politics, but he was trying to stop the scrum beneath him—a vain effort. His associates responded in character—Jefferson protesting that "not a syllable" in the newspaper wars had proceeded from him, which was true only literally; Hamilton admitting "some instrumentality"—and the fighting went on as before.

Voting for president and vice president took place in the fall. Washington decided to stay on—the feuding of his associates did not augur well for a world without him. He saved Madison's notice of retirement for later use and ran unopposed. But John Beckley, Madison, and James Monroe (now one of Virginia's senators) coordinated a Republican effort to replace John Adams. They wrote letters to Republican leaders in Pennsylvania and New York, with Beckley making a trip to New York City. The candidate they picked, after some discussion—freshman senator Aaron Burr put his name forward—was George Clinton, who had just won his sixth term as governor of New York; he received fifty electoral votes to Adams's seventy-seven, a respectable showing. Washington, of course, was reelected unanimously. National electioneering had been barely audible, like mice scurrying in a wall. The election of 1792 was the last in American history in which that would be so.

The little maneuvers of American politics soon paled before the spectacle of French politics. A cascade of events, beginning in August 1792 and filling American newspapers after the usual transatlantic delays, constituted a second French Revolution.

The king was arrested and deposed, and a republic set up in his place. Lafayette, failed champion of a liberal revolution, fled the country. France's new rulers repelled an invading Prussian army and massacred 1,400 prisoners in Paris jails. The ex-king himself was guillotined in January 1793; Britain declared war in February.

The last foreign ambassador left in Paris was Gouverneur Morris, tapped by Washington to be Jefferson's successor. Despite diplomatic immunity, he had to bluff revolutionary militiamen out of ransacking his house, and stopped keeping his diary for fear that it might be seized.

These events thrilled Madison, as a Francophile, and a republican. In April 1793 he learned that he had been made an honorary French citizen. His reply to Jean-Marie Roland, minister of the interior, shows the tone of his thought. The "artificial boundaries of nations," he wrote, could not divide the "great family" of mankind. America had a special "connection with France . . . endeared by the affinities of their mutual liberty." He wished "prosperity and glory to the French nation" and to its "dignified maxims" and "triumphs of liberty." (Roland had already resigned by the time Madison wrote him, and seven months later committed suicide after learning that his wife had been guillotined.)

The French also conferred citizenship on Hamilton, who found that they gave his first name in their announcement as "Jean." He filed the typo with a note: "Curious example of French finesse."

Madison was not the only American caught up in French radical chic. The death of Louis XVI, so recently the ally of America, was celebrated in banquets; people sang the Marseillaise, and in imitation of the revolutionary salutation "Citoyen" called one another "Citizen" and (more awkwardly) "Citess." French massacres were denied, or excused. "The French," wrote the *National Gazette*, "have made examples of two or three thousand scoundrels, to rescue the liberties of millions of honest men." Jefferson, better spoken but no less bloodthirsty, told an American diplomat that although he was "deeply wounded by some of the martyrs of this cause . . . rather than it should have failed I would have seen half the earth desolated."

The "cause" was not France's alone: Jefferson and Madison believed that the success of the French republic would boost the Republican Party's fortunes in the United States. Republicanism seemed to them an international cause; a stroke in one part of the world would rebound in another, like a bank shot in billiards.

They wrote of the common struggle in religious terms. Madison described the typical Federalist as a "blasphemer" of rights and an "idolater" of tyranny; critics of the French Revolution in America were "heretical," a French defector from it committed "apostasy." Such rhetoric choked the prose of Jefferson, from whom Madison may have picked it up. The Federalists committed their own verbal excesses: Hamilton, in his letter to Carrington, had accused Jefferson and Madison of "a womanish attachment to France." He unsexed them; they damned him—and felt entitled to do so because they served the cause of republicanism, which is divine. So it is—but if defined too literally, and too narrowly, it consigns a lot of people to hell.

In the same month that Madison accepted French citizenship, a bit of the French Revolution arrived in America, and seemed at first to confirm Republican hopes. France sent Edmond-Charles Genet, a young diplomat, as ambassador to her sister republic. (Morris met with him before he sailed, and thought he had the "look of an upstart.") His ship, blown off course, landed in Charleston, South Carolina, rather than Philadelphia; his monthlong trip to the capital was like the triumphal tour of a great actor, if America had had any then.

As Genet was making his way north, Republicans experienced a setback: at the end of April, President Washington proclaimed America's neutrality in the war raging in Europe. The United States still had a treaty of alliance with France dating from the Revolution, but it did not require America to go to war on France's behalf, and Washington decided to make it plain that America was not planning to do so. Any Americans who pitched in as volunteers would be breaking the law.

Such a blunt announcement struck Jefferson as too anti-French; as a sop to him, the proclamation did not use the word "neutrality," though everyone understood that neutrality was meant.

Genet arrived in the capital in mid-May. It was the apotheosis of his celebrity. "I live here in the midst of perpetual fetes," he wrote home excitedly. "I receive addresses from all parts of the continent." No one could be "more affectionate," Jefferson told Madison. "He offers everything and asks nothing." Genet in fact asked for a number of things—early payment of America's Revolutionary War debt and permission to launch privateers from American ports to attack enemy ships. Dealing with Genet as secretary of state, Jefferson simultaneously did his duty—telling him America lacked the money for an early payoff—and led him on—suggesting that, though there were Anglophiles close to the president (Hamilton), the people were "for us." Genet was so popular, it seemed that Jefferson might be right.

Hamilton went back to the press, with a series of essays signed "Pacificus," defending neutrality and the president's right to proclaim it. Legislative powers, he noted, were enumerated by the Constitution, but the president was vested with "the executive power," plain and simple. Jefferson begged Madison to respond. "For God's sake," he wrote in July, "take up your pen, select the most striking heresies, and cut him to pieces." Madison tried; his answers were signed "Helvidius," after a late supporter of the Roman republic, executed by the emperor Vespasian. The grim pseudonym showed Madison's discomfort with his task. He was good at laying out principles, not so good at rough-and-tumble. He snarled at "foreigners and degenerate citizens among us" and tried to make a clever point by quoting one of Hamilton's *Federalist* papers (#75), which had argued that treaty-making was not exclusively an executive power. But since the object of their present dispute was proclaiming neutrality, not making treaties, the point fell wide. Although Madison understood the importance of appealing to the public, Hamilton was actually better at it.

Freneau drew blood from Washington when he printed a satire, "A Funeral Dirge for George Washington," describing him being led to the guillotine. Henry Knox mentioned it at a cabinet meeting and Jefferson preserved what happened next in one of his little memos to himself. Washington became "much inflamed, got into one of those passions when he cannot command himself, ran on much on the personal abuse which had been bestowed on him . . . [said] that *rascal Freneau* sent him three of his papers every day, as if he thought he would become the distributor of his papers." Freneau did not need Washington to become a distributor of his papers; Jefferson and Madison were already doing that.

Freneau's attack exemplified the weak spot in the Republican strategy: however popular the French Revolution was in America, George Washington was more popular still. Genet, his head turned by perpetual fetes, also ignored this truth. After learning that under the terms of the neutrality proclamation, no privateers could sail from American ports, he threatened to appeal to the country over Washington's head: "It is not thus that the American people wish we should be treated," he blustered to Jefferson. Hamilton, told of this threat in a cabinet meeting, leaked it to the papers, and Genet's stock began to fall as Americans rallied around their insulted president.

Jefferson told Madison in September it was time for Republicans to abandon their obnoxious French friend: "quitting a wreck" that would "sink all who should cling to it." Madison and Monroe together prepared a tactical retreat, a series of resolutions that Republicans would offer at public meetings throughout Virginia. The resolutions were pro-Washington, but discreetly pro-French. Eight counties passed them, with minor variations "to avoid," as one of Madison's friends put it, "suspicion of their being coined in the same mint."

Back in France, the revolutionary faction to which Genet belonged had been replaced by a new one, which guillotined its predecessors and asked for Genet to be sent home, undoubtedly to be guillotined himself. After all the theatrics and threats, Washington let Genet stay in America as a private citizen; he married one of George Clinton's daughters.

Two other figures retired to private life at the end of 1793. A yellow fever epidemic in Philadelphia killed 5,000 people; the death and desolation killed off the *National Gazette*. Freneau survived but resigned his clerkship, complaining that he could not translate the Russian, Dutch, and German documents that crossed his desk. Republican journalism would not fall silent, however; the *National Gazette* would be replaced by other, even more strident voices.

More important, Jefferson himself left the State Department for what Madison called "his farm and his philosophy." Jefferson's retirement put James Madison in charge of the Republican Party's day-to-day workings.

P artisanship became violent in the woods of Pennsylvania, thanks to Hamilton's financial program.

The Constitution—Article I, Section 9—allowed Congress to levy direct taxes on property and income (so long as each state's share was apportioned according to the three-fifths rule), but no one liked them: Madison called direct taxes "obnoxious" and Hamilton thought them "impracticable."

That left tariffs and excise (or commodity) taxes. Hamilton had singled out "ardent spirits," which in America mostly meant whiskey, as a suitable item for excises in his Report on Public Credit in 1790. Two years later he told Washington that most distillers were in compliance with the whiskey tax; the only scofflaws "of any consequence" were frontiersmen in Kentucky, North Carolina, and western Pennsylvania.

It is a myth, still marching on in history books, that the only way farmers in the backcountry could ship their grain to market was by putting it into barrels as whiskey. Yet contemporary Philadelphia newspapers show no ads for western whiskey. Westerners sold whiskey to the army, which was fighting Indians on the frontier, and to one another. They liked to drink it, and they hated paying taxes on it, or anything else.

In July 1794, western Pennsylvania exploded. The federal tax collector outside Pittsburgh fought a gun battle with the local militia; two militiamen, including the commander, were killed. The countryside rose up, and Hugh Henry Brackenridge, a local lawyer, warned that angry westerners might march all the way to Philadelphia.

Brackenridge had been a friend of Madison's at Princeton (he, Madison, and Freneau had written abusive poems together). But Madison did not welcome insurrection as a political tool. Neither, really, did Brackenridge, who found himself in the tricky position of an ordinary politician who shared and expressed his neighbors' anger at the whiskey tax, while trying, without much success, to redirect it. The local congressman, Republican Albert Gallatin, a Swiss immigrant, was in the same spot.

Madison was a revolutionary. He had labored for the American Revolution and cheered France's. In *Federalist #46*, he had even warned that Americans could resist an oppressive government thanks to "the advantage of being armed, which [they] possess over the people of almost every other nation." The whiskey excise, however, did not rise to that level of oppression. It was a law, perhaps a bad one; there were many ways to repeal or modify it, and Madison, who had spent his career on the ins and outs of politics, knew them all. Violent resistance at this point was "resistance [to] the will of the majority."

Washington called up 15,000 militia, while sending a commission to western Pennsylvania to report on the situation. Only after the commissioners recommended a show of force did the army move, in late September. Washington reviewed the troops at their staging areas; Hamilton himself led them over the Alleghenies. Delay and numbers accomplished their purpose: tempers cooled, the ringleaders lost heart and fled, there were no battles. Two men were killed in altercations; two were convicted of treason and sentenced to death, but Washington pardoned them.

All this passed without protest from Madison. Aspects of the affair worried him nevertheless. Would it now be claimed that "a standing army was necessary for enforcing the laws"? Hamilton had had his first taste of military life since the Revolution; would the exercise whet his appetite for more? Madison even hinted, in a letter to Monroe, that the rebellion might have been a put-up job, a provocation, designed to justify a crackdown. "The real authors" of the rebellion, "if not in the service . . . of despotism," had served its ends. This was conspiracy theory politics, and there would be a lot more of it, on all sides, in the years to come.

Madison worried less about the attack on western Pennsylvania than an attack on public opinion by George Washington. Washington believed that the crisis had been stirred up by Democratic Societies. "Democratic" was a new and unsettled term of praise in American politics; to Federalists the word still smacked of anarchy. Democratic Societies had sprung up in 1793 in the flush of Genet's visit; he himself had named the Democratic Society of Philadelphia, one of the first and largest. In 1794, there were thirty-five throughout the country. They passed resolutions and lobbied for and against candidates for office. Madison thought they helped elect at least one congressman (Robert Livingston's younger brother Edward, in New York). They were pro-French, and pro–Republican Party.

Almost all of the Democratic Societies condemned the Whiskey Rebellion. But two in western Pennsylvania seemed to be implicated in it. Their leaders were also leaders of the rebellion, and Brackenridge called one of societies "the cradle of the insurrection."

When Washington addressed Congress in November after the rebellion was done, he singled out "certain self-created societies" that had propagated "suspicions, jealousies and accusations of the whole government." "Self-created" strikes us as a strange phrase, especially as a pejorative. American society and politics are full of "self-created societies"—pressure groups and lobbyists of all kinds. Yet this was a foreign notion to Washington in 1794. He and every congressman, governor, and state legislator had been elected by the people. They were the people's representatives, and they did the people's business until such time as the people voted them out; there should be no intermediary bodies between them and the Americans who had chosen them. The Senate agreed, echoing Washington's censure of the Democratic Societies in its reply to his message.

Madison had a different view, which he expressed in the House. Pennsylvanians who had committed crimes had already been arrested. Was the House now to take notice of opinions? "An action innocent in the eye of the law could not be the object of censure to a legislative body." He went further, reminding his colleagues that in republics "the censorial power is in the people over the government and not in the government over the people."

The ideas of the Democratic Societies, he concluded, "will stand or fall by the public opinion. . . . In a republic, light will prevail over darkness, truth over error."

The key phrase in Madison's rebuttal was "public opinion." The people did not express themselves only when they voted. Public opinion operated at all times; it was the sovereignty of the people in action, and it could endorse or rebuke elected representatives and self-created societies alike. Madison was putting his *National Gazette* essays into practice, though at the time his principles went unnoticed in the politics of the occasion.

Madison analyzed the politics in a letter to Monroe. "The game [of the Federalists] was to connect the Democratic Societies with the odium of the insurrection" and "to connect the Republicans in Congress with those Societies."

But what had been the game of Madison and the Republicans? To use the societies as noisemakers and ad hoc supporters, reserving the right to condemn those who ran into a ditch.

There was personal politics in the occasion, too. As the Whiskey Rebellion reached its climax, Edmund Randolph wrote Washington that a Democratic Society in South Carolina had named itself "Madisonian."

Washington, who was reviewing militia bound for western Pennsylvania at the time, had not liked that at all. There he was, trying to uphold the law, while Madison was—what? consorting with?—its enemies. "I should be extremely sorry," he wrote back, "if Mr. M———n *from any cause whatsoever* should get entangled with them, or their politics" (Washington's italics). Washington and Madison had disagreed on many things over the past four years, but now Washington began to suspect his old friend. His aside to Randolph was his version—short, acerbic—of Hamilton's aria to Edward Carrington.

Madison and his party had been put in some tight spots by real or reputed allies—Genet, the whiskey rebels. They had cut their losses, and Madison had advanced an important principle concerning public opinion and its role in politics. But they were still in search of political advantage.

I n 1794, Madison, for once, had a concern more important than politics. At age forty-three, he fell in love and married, though, Madison being Madison, this too would have political implications.

Dolley Payne, born in 1768, had grown up in Virginia. Her mother, Mary Coles, was a Quaker, and her father, John Payne, converted to his wife's faith; like many converts, he took his new beliefs seriously. In 1783, a year after the laws of Virginia allowed it, John Payne freed his slaves—Quakers were pioneer abolitionists—and moved to Philadelphia, where he tried to support his family by making starch. For his teenage daughter, the move was both a step up to a sophisticated capital and a step down in fortune. The religion that had inspired her father to make the sacrifice of manumission expelled him from its ranks when he went broke and failed to pay his debts. Strict Quakers told Dolley she was too fond of "the gayeties of this world"; her caps, gowns, and shoes gave "offense." Marriage to the young Quaker lawyer John Todd in 1790 gave her some security, which shattered when the yellow fever epidemic of 1793 killed her husband and her newborn baby, leaving her only a one-and-a-half-year-old boy, John Payne Todd.

Madison may already have known who she was—her uncle, Isaac Coles, was a Virginia congressman. The widow Todd was not destitute—her husband had left her some money. She was certainly attractive. As an old lady she lived long enough to have her daguerreotype taken, and as First Lady she would be painted numerous times, though these images caught her past her prime (one diplomat's wife would call her "*grosse*," stout, coarse). Other observers testified to her lovely throat and bosom—"the most beautiful . . . I ever saw." Young or old, she had a brightness that drew all eyes. "Thou must hide thy face," a Quaker friend reproved her, "there are so many men staring at thee."

In May 1794, the staring James Madison was formally introduced to Dolley Todd by Aaron Burr, who had been handling her legal affairs. "The great little Madison," she wrote her critical Quaker friend, "has asked . . . to see me this evening." George and Martha Washington also encouraged the courtship. The president was still personally fond of his former adviser—the Madisonian Democratic Society had not yet come to his attention—and he and his wife saw arranging the marriages of their protégés as a way of building an American leadership class. So the worst and the best of the founders lent a hand.

There is no paper trail for Madison's proposal and Dolley's acceptance until August, when Madison wrote, "I cannot express, but hope you will conceive the joy [your answer] gave me" (no wonder he had little to say about the Whiskey Rebellion). On September 15, the two were married at a small stone plantation house, still standing in Charles Town, West Virginia, belonging to one of Washington's nephews.

Madison added a wing to Montpelier for himself and his new family—Dolley, her son, and her younger sister, Anna—with a separate door and a separate kitchen; the custodians of Montpelier today describe the addition as a Philadelphia town house, spliced onto a Virginia plantation house. The only direct access from the new wing to the rest of Montpelier was on the second floor, where a passage led into Madison's library. Clearly he valued his new status as the head of his own household, but he needed unimpeded access to his books.

Madison gave his wife a life that combined the best features of her life so far. Marrying the son of a Virginia planter let Dolley reenter the world of her youth; marrying a politician guaranteed her a place in the high society of Philadelphia and the new Potomac capital, whenever that was built. Becoming Mrs. Madison also severed her connection with the Quakers, who in December 1794 disowned her for marrying outside the faith.

What Madison gained from his marriage was an expansion of his personality. He stayed the same—learned and thoughtful; at ease with friends, and devoted to them; silent, shy, and stiff in the outside world. Dolley completed him as a public figure. Her name, fortuitously, captured her character. "Dolley" was no nickname, but the name on her birth certificate, her marriage certificates, and her wills. Yet like "Doll" and "Dolly," it originated as a contraction, a short form of Dorothy. In the eighteenth century, "doll" was being used as the word for the child's toy. But an older use of both "doll" and "dolly" was as pet terms for a woman. The words were affectionate, sometimes with an erotic undertone (like "wench").

Dolley deployed her femininity all her life, enlisting the help of colors, fabrics, and accessories (such as turbans) as she aged. The malicious put an unfriendly spin on her sex appeal, contrasting it with Madison's lack thereof. Gouverneur Morris, wit and skirt chaser, told his diary that "Mrs. Madison . . . has good dispositions, which, from the shriveled condition of [her husband], are the less to be wondered at." Gouverneur thought Dolley was a flirt; was James taking care of business?

But most men and women met her on the open ground of friendliness. "Everybody loves Mrs. Madison," declared Henry Clay, with all the flattery of an air kiss, but meaning it, too. "That's because Mrs. Madison loves everybody," she replied. She didn't love everybody, of course. She knew who all her husband's enemies were and kept a running tally of their disasters and defeats, sometimes arranging a few. But she was expansive, gregarious, and outgoing. She would rather like people than dislike them. She would be an indispensable help to Madison when his career demanded that he navigate capital-city politics as both a right-hand man and an heir apparent. He had stopped being Washington's right-hand man (though it took awhile for him and Washington to acknowledge it). But his time would come again.

What came first was a new foreign policy crisis. Britain had gone to war with France in 1793, and at the end of that year it had begun seizing American ships that carried contraband (chiefly grain) to the enemy. The British paid for the cargo, but their actions were tedious and disruptive for American captains, besides insulting to American sovereignty.

In the spring of 1794, before the Whiskey Rebellion broke out, Washington decided to send John Jay as a special envoy to London. Jay was assigned to stop the seizures and to clear up unresolved issues from the treaty that had ended the Revolution: Americans had not paid all their prewar debts to British creditors, and Britain had not returned escaped American slaves; American ships had trouble trading with the British West Indies (formally, they were frozen out, though there were many local loopholes); British troops still occupied twenty forts on the American frontier, intriguing with Indians and menacing settlers. Though Jay was now serving as chief justice of the Supreme Court, most of his career had been spent in diplomacy. He was polite and patient, willing to take half a loaf if that was all he could get and to eat toads along the way. Madison, whose notions of diplomacy ran to stating unanswerable propositions, disliked him and expected little from his mission.

Jay signed a new treaty with Britain in November 1794; it arrived in Philadelphia in March 1795. The Senate debated and ratified it, and Washington signed it, all in secret, by the beginning of July. As soon as Jay's Treaty became public, "it flew," as Madison put it, "with an electric velocity to every part of the Union." "Electric" was a well-chosen word:

Franklin's grandson, Benjamin Franklin Bache (nicknamed "Lightning Rod Junior"), who had replaced Freneau's *National Gazette* with a new Republican newspaper, the *Aurora*, printed Jay's Treaty in pamphlet form and distributed it far and wide.

Washington and the Senate had kept Jay's Treaty secret because they had reservations about it and they knew many Americans would loathe it. On the plus side of the ledger, Britain agreed finally to evacuate its forts, and most Anglo-American disputes were referred to arbitration commissions. But slave owners would not be pleased that Jay, first president of the New-York Manumission Society, had not secured the return of escaped slaves. Merchants would be equally unhappy to find that American ships were admitted to the West Indies only under onerous restrictions. Even Federalists disliked the last provision, and the Senate excluded it from its ratification. To Republicans, Jay's collection of little provisions seemed like a sellout. Why should America settle commercial relations with an exemplar and defender of monarchy, rather than with embattled France? Madison knew why; as he told Monroe in cipher, the most fervent supporters of the treaty in America were "the *British party*" and "*British capitalists*."

Hamilton went to the press once again, with a series of thirty-eight essays titled *The Defence* (he had some help from Rufus King). He analyzed Jay's Treaty clause by clause, showing how it would stimulate the economy and avert strife with Britain. Jefferson wrote Madison in something like admiration, comparing their enemy to the medieval hero Roland. He "is really a colossus to the anti–Republican party. Without numbers he is an host within himself." Perhaps Madison could play the role of the Saracen army. "When [Hamilton] steps forward there is nobody but yourself who can meet him." But Madison, having already lost a skirmish over Genet, had no desire to fight Hamilton in the newspapers again.

Hamilton's arguments, renewed commerce with Britain, and peace on the frontier as the British evacuated their forts began to change public opinion about Jay's Treaty. There was another factor: when Spain got wind of the Anglo-American rapprochement, she suddenly decided to be friendly herself, granting Americans the right to navigate the Mississippi River, a benefit she had been withholding for years. Spain's new mood made Americans, especially in the west, happier yet. Maybe Jay had known what he was doing after all.

Republicans had one last option—attacking the treaty in the House, if only they could somehow bring it up for discussion there. The Constitutional Convention had considered giving the House a role in making treaties but rejected the idea; the Constitution (Article II, Section 2) assigned treaty-making power to the president, "by and with the advice and consent of the Senate."

"The situation," Madison wrote Jefferson in December, "is truly perplexing. . . . The treaty is not regularly before the House," and if the House were to ask Washington about it, it would bring him "personally into the question." If Hamilton was Roland, Washington was Charlemagne.

Impatient with Madison's perplexity, Edward Livingston moved a resolution in March 1796 calling on Washington to let the House examine documents and correspondence relating to Jay's Treaty.

Washington's response was brief and imposing. It began with a lecture. "The nature of foreign negotiations requires caution; and their success must often depend on secrecy." That was "one cogent reason" for restricting the treaty power, and all its associated paperwork, to the president and the Senate.

Next he made an ironic threat. The request for papers served no legitimate purpose of the House "except that of an impeachment, which the resolution has not expressed." If you really want a fight, let's really fight.

Then he played the trump card of personal testimony. "Having been a member of the [Constitutional] Convention," he knew what the Constitution said. "If other proofs . . . be necessary," he referred to the journals of the Convention—not Madison's notes, but Major William Jackson's record of motions and votes—which showed that the effort to involve the House in treaty-making had been "explicitly rejected." He also noted that "I have deposited" those journals with the State Department. He had done that because it had been one of the tasks assigned to him as president of the convention. He had been an eyewitness, the most important eyewitness, and he put that authority behind his rejection of the House's request.

Madison replied early in April. For years he had been grappling with Hamilton. Now he was taking on Washington directly, and his unhappiness showed. Despite their policy disputes, he and Washington had been friends and associates for more than a decade. He had supplied him with Madeira and helped him with canals and constitution-making; Washington had blessed his marriage. The man who never quarreled with his biological parents did not want to fight the father of his country.

Madison reminded the president that he was not a king—our government had no "hereditary prerogatives"—and reminded him of the power of public opinion—"the sense of the constituent body" would ultimately resolve all disputes. Yet Madison admitted Washington's "high authority" and insisted that he himself used only "decent terms" to refute it. Madison's divided mind weakened his argument, which was involved and arid, four times as long as Washington's message. He made one new point: the Constitutional Convention was not an "oracular guide." It was a "dead letter," brought to life only by "the voice of the people" as spoken in the state ratifying conventions. But if the convention was a "dead letter," why had Madison spent so much time recording its deliberations? He found it easier to devalue his own handiwork as a historian than to take on Washington directly.

Washington found it easy enough to react to Madison's opposition. He had never been a naturally even-tempered man; he was old (sixty-four in February) and tired. He ended the relationship. Though Madison would attend a few state dinners at the presidential mansion, he and Washington exchanged no more letters, paid no more visits. The collaboration had been effectively over for years; now so was the friendship.

Madison's own side was unhappy with him, too. They blamed him for not fighting Washington hard enough. The burden of the anti-treaty argument in the House shifted to Madison's younger colleague Albert Gallatin, who proved to be a powerful force, smart and tireless. Republicans were grateful for his leadership, and grumbled at Madison's. His "great fault[s] as a politician," thought Edward Livingston, were "want of decision" and "a disposition to magnify his adversary's strength."

As late as mid-April, Madison counted a twenty vote anti-treaty majority in the House. Yet one by one his supporters flipped. Samuel Smith, a Republican congressman from Baltimore, was one of many defectors, citing the pro-treaty views of "the people of Maryland, whom he had the honor to represent" (especially its shippers). Gallatin gave a great anti-treaty speech late in April, then Fisher Ames gave a greater one in favor. Ames's oration, ninety minutes long and delivered without notes, would become a staple of books of rhetoric: young Daniel Webster and Abraham Lincoln memorized swatches of it. Joseph Priestley, the English scientist and liberal who heard it from the House gallery, thought Ames had excelled the spellbinders of Parliament. On April 30, 1796, the House voted 51–48 to appropriate whatever money was necessary to put Jay's Treaty into effect.

"Mr. Madison," wrote Vice President Adams to his wife, "looks worried to death. Pale, withered, haggard." Seven years in Congress had taken Madison from being a child of fortune to being a goat. He needed a break.

CHAPTER SIX

Wilderness Years

M adison served in the lame-duck session of Congress, which then
ran from December 1796 to March of the following year; then
he would be out of office for the first time in twenty years. He gave no
elaborate explanation of his decision to retire; he simply wanted to be
home. He wrote his father that he was "inflexible" on the point, then
spent the rest of his letter discussing clover crops at Montpelier.

A more momentous announcement had already been made—George
Washington declined to serve a third term. The president followed the
advice Madison had given him four years earlier about how to stage-
manage his retirement. His Farewell Address appeared in mid-September
in a Philadelphia newspaper. The first paragraphs were the draft that
Madison had written for him, then begged him not to use—its appearance now an autumnal memorial of a lost friendship. The body of the
Farewell Address, written by Washington and Hamilton working closely
together, expatiated on the evils of partisanship and the danger of "passionate attachments" to foreign countries. Since these, in Washington's
mind, were traits of the Republican Party, the Farewell Address rebuked
Madison as much as it commemorated him.

Washington's retirement was the signal for a new thing in American
political history—a contested presidential election. Four years earlier,

when Madison had urged Washington not to step down, he suggested that his potential successors would be John Adams, John Jay, and Thomas Jefferson—two Federalists and a Republican. Jay's prospects had been consumed in the firestorm over his treaty. Adams, bruised but not broken by his talk of titles and hereditary succession, had age (he turned sixty-one in October 1796), seniority (he had been a prominent patriot since the Boston Massacre), and eight years of devoted if dull service as vice president to commend him. Jefferson had not been a day-to-day Republican leader (Madison and, more recently, Albert Gallatin had filled that slot). But he was eloquent, mature (fifty-three years old), and almost as eminent a revolutionary figure as Adams. He represented the south as Adams epitomized the north.

Tickets consisting of a presidential candidate and his running mate were flimsy things in those days, since the Constitution had not contemplated them. Article II, Section 1 said only that each presidential elector should cast two independent votes. Whoever got the most votes would become president; whoever came in second would be vice president. But now that political parties had emerged, so had de facto tickets. It was understood that Adams's running mate was Thomas Pinckney, a diplomat from a grand South Carolina family, while Jefferson's was New York senator Aaron Burr.

All the machinery of the Republican Party—quaint by later standards, but potent in its way, like some eighteenth-century contraption, a spinning jenny, or a steam engine—went to work. Burr spent six weeks in New England, homeland of his clergyman ancestors, rallying local political leaders. In Pennsylvania, John Beckley appealed to ordinary voters with a cross between a direct mailing and a media blitz, distributing 30,000 printed lists of the presidential electors Republicans should vote for (the names of presidential candidates did not appear on ballots). Since Pennsylvanians were forbidden by law from taking printed lists with them to the polls, Beckley also urged Republicans to copy the lists by hand as last-minute prompts.

Although Madison was looking forward to retirement, he had as always the key role of handling Thomas Jefferson. It was a particularly delicate task now because Jefferson was a reluctant presidential candidate. In 1789–1790, when Madison had helped Washington persuade his friend to be secretary of state, he had chased Jefferson around Virginia with the president's offer. This time he did the reverse, staying away from Monticello, so that Jefferson could not tell him face to face that he was not running. "*I* have not seen *Jefferson*," he wrote Monroe in cipher at the end of September, "and have *thought it best to* present *him no opportunity of protesting.*"

Jefferson really did want, as he wrote one correspondent, "to plant my corn, peas, etc. in hills or drills as I please." His touch-me-not reluctance was also calculated. The foreign policy issues raised by Genet and Jay were not going to get any calmer over the next four years, and Jefferson preferred to let Adams deal with them. If his talk about not wanting to run at all was largely pose, his not wanting to win was shrewd political and geopolitical instinct. Fortunately for him, presidential candidates in 1796 (and for many elections thereafter) were not expected to do anything as crass as campaign, so he could not run and run at the same time.

In 1796, neither popular voting nor statewide winner-take-all was the norm. In some states the legislature picked presidential electors; in some the people voted directly, but in electoral districts. Beckley's efforts in Pennsylvania were successful: Jefferson took fourteen of its fifteen electoral votes. Burr's in New England were not, as Adams won every vote there, and in New York, New Jersey, and Delaware as well. The two candidates split Maryland, and Jefferson swept the south—except for one electoral vote each from Virginia and North Carolina, which went to Adams.

In the end, Adams edged Jefferson, seventy-one votes to sixty-eight; Pinckney and Burr trailed (some electors in both parties cast their "second" votes for other men). So the United States would have a president and vice president who had run against each other. And yet they had been friends for years, years ago. As 1796 ended, Jefferson felt moved to write the president-elect a letter bathed in the warmth of reminiscence. "The public and the public papers," he began, "have been much occupied lately in placing us in a point of opposition to each other. I confidently trust we have felt less of it ourselves." He reviewed the contest, then concluded: "That your administration may be filled with glory and happiness . . . is the sincere prayer of one who . . . yet retains for you the solid esteem of the times when we were working for our independence."

On New Year's Day, Jefferson sent this letter—unsealed, to Madison, for his advice. Madison found himself in the same situation he had been in when he had to buck Jefferson up after the appearance of his blurb for *Rights of Man*. Then he had had to assure Jefferson that he had done the right thing. Now he had to prevent Jefferson from doing the wrong thing.

Madison's reply began in accents of modesty and deference. "I have felt no small anxiety" in answering, he wrote, given "the importance of [making] a wrong judgment." But this was also a cue to Jefferson: don't you make a wrong judgment, friend.

Then Madison got to work. What, he asked Jefferson, about "the zealous and active promoters of your election"? Should their efforts be "depreciated" by showing such fondness for the common foe? Everyone from Beckley to Burr had spent the fall working for you; don't sell them short by being nice to Adams. Madison pointed out that Adams as president was bound to say and do anti-Republican things. In that case, "there may be real embarrassments from giving [him] written possession" of so many compliments. Don't give hostages to fortune, and certainly don't do it in writing. Madison's advice as a party man was that Jefferson should behave like one, too, and his advice as a friend was that Jefferson should watch out for himself.

But if Jefferson still wanted the letter delivered, Madison, serviceable in all things, promised to do it, though he added that it would be wise to postdate it, to conceal the fact that Jefferson had hesitated in sending it.

Jefferson thanked Madison for his advice. A part of him truly cherished his friendship with Adams (better, the memory of his friendship). But another part of him knew how the game of politics was played, and knew that Madison knew it, too. Madison was like a box in which Jefferson could deposit his savvy, on occasions when it conflicted with his other impulses or emotions. But Jefferson always remembered how to find it again. The letter was never sent to Adams.

Jefferson was not the only man thinking of reaching across party lines. Adams wondered, on the eve of his inauguration in March 1797, whether he could make a diplomat out of Madison.

America needed an effective representative in France. The French were very angry over Jay's Treaty, construing peace with Britain as hostility toward them. America needed a representative, or maybe even a special commission of two or three. Who better to be that man, or one of them, than Madison?

So the incoming president thought. Adams asked Jefferson, the incoming vice president, if he would convey the offer.

Jefferson delivered the message, and the answer: no. Madison, with his history of ailments on the road, feared an ocean crossing. But a more important reason for his refusal was political. America's problems with France, in his view, had been provoked by the Federalists' tilt toward Britain. Repairing Franco-American relations now would be doing the Federalists' work for them, and binding oneself, however indirectly, to their agenda and their fortunes. Let Adams clean up his own (and Washington's, Hamilton's, and Jay's) mess. Party lines stretched beyond the three-mile limit.

B eyond all the considerations of politics, Madison needed time out. It was the only moment in his adult career that he would take it, but now was the time.

Family matters claimed him. His favorite brother, Ambrose, whose plantation abutted Montpelier and who had watched over Orange County politically for Madison (not that it needed much watching), had died four years earlier, at age thirty-eight. Madison's father, the old colonel, had meanwhile become truly old—he would turn seventy-four in 1797 (Madison's mother would be sixty-five). Montpelier and his parents needed attention just when Madison had lost his sibling surrogate. The plantation that had always supported him now needed his support.

While taking on new responsibilities, Madison also had to reconfigure Montpelier for his new family. Adding a new wing was only the first step; he then had to integrate it aesthetically with the older two-thirds of the building. Jefferson was adding a portico to Monticello, and Madison decided to add a portico, too. It would shift the axis of his house and tie it together visually.

The portico of Montpelier, the new front door it framed, and the new drawing room that would be built behind them became a long-running project, stretching into the next century. Madison borrowed workmen from Jefferson as well as inspiration, though he would not follow their advice in everything. James Dinsmore, a carpenter who had worked on both Monticello and Poplar Forest before coming over to Montpelier, suggested that Madison raise the second floor over the new drawing room "a foot or eighteen inches. . . . It is at present too low for the finish we wish to adopt over the doors and side lights." Madison's answer has not survived, but it was clearly no, for Dinsmore wrote a second letter promising to "accommodate our work to the present height of the ceiling." Today this story is told at Montpelier as a compliment to Madison's prudence and a joke at Jefferson's extravagance: if a carpenter had told the master of Monticello to raise one of the floors a foot, he would have answered: do it. But the story cuts both ways: if the beautiful is truly important to you, and an extra foot might make a difference, you will raise the floor, and pay for it (or not) later.

Madison used Dinsmore and John Neilson, another Jefferson carpenter on loan, to replace some of his father's handiwork. The old colonel's commercial blacksmith operation took the form of a row of sheds at the north corner of the house. But Madison and his family would look directly at them from their new wing. He had them replaced by a Greek temple—a small circle of ten columns supporting a graceful dome. The temple was practical in a way, for beneath it lay a belowground freezer: ice sawed from ponds in the winter was stored there, packed in straw, to cool drinks year-round and to make the ice cream for which Dolley would become famous. The temple and its icehouse provided a social and even a political benefit, though it was not as profitable as the smithies. (Madison downsized them, as well as moving them.)

The Republicans, meanwhile, could get along without Madison, for a time anyway, because he and Jefferson had built their party so well. Leadership in the House had passed to Gallatin, whom Madison called "a real treasure." Ten years younger than Madison and eighteen years younger than Jefferson, Gallatin was born and raised in Geneva, in a family of educated, industrious oligarchs. The Gallatins were rather broke by the time Albert came along, however, so in 1780 he came to America, age nineteen, to make some money. He sold tea, taught French, and speculated in land, none of which made him rich, although he did meet George Washington in a surveyor's office in western Pennsylvania. The great man was adding up the day's accounts, talking aloud to himself, when Gallatin offered the correct answer. Washington gave him a baleful look, finished his calculations, then looked up again and said, "You are right, young man."

Gallatin also had a talent for politics. The Pennsylvania legislature elected him to the Senate in the early 1790s, but the Federalist majority refused to seat him on a technicality. He came back to haunt them in the House, where they mocked his French accent: the stupidity of a party in power, attacking outsiders in ways that would turn all outsiders into opponents.

His position as a party man was fortified by his marriage to Hannah
Nicholson, daughter of a well-connected New York City Republican.

Buoyed by the election of 1796, Federalists had become strong enough
in the House to fire John Beckley as clerk, but he managed to get his own
back by using and abusing information. The Federalist he took down was
Alexander Hamilton, and he did it by raking up an old scandal.

Years earlier, a crook named James Reynolds had accused Hamilton of
insider trading (Reynolds said he made trades using tips from the Treasury Department, supplied by the secretary). Republicans in Congress—
including James Monroe, then still a senator—learned of Reynolds's
charges and threatened to expose Hamilton. But Hamilton was able to
convince them that his real connection with Reynolds was paying blackmail, because he had been sleeping with Mrs. Reynolds. The Republicans
backed off, but Monroe shared the story with Jefferson and Beckley. Five
years later, Beckley now offered it to a rising Republican journalist, James
Callender.

Callender had fled his native Scotland after writing a radical pamphlet.
He had an exalted notion of his calling: pamphleteers, he boasted, are in
the "van of every revolution" and "the first rank in storming the ramparts
of oppression." Arriving in Philadelphia in 1793, he got a job taking
notes of debates in the House for newspapers (today he would be called
a pool reporter). There he met Beckley. When that job ended, he felt he
knew Madison, or knew of him, well enough to write a letter asking if
he could find work as a schoolteacher in Virginia. Nothing came of it,
and Callender returned to pamphleteering.

He printed the scoop Beckley had fed him in a pamphlet published
in the summer of 1797. It instantly became the most lurid story in American politics.

Hamilton's reaction showed the weakness of his strength. He published
a ninety-five-page pamphlet of his own, denying that he was corrupt by
admitting that he was an adulterer; he printed both his mistress's love
letters and her husband's blackmail notes. The public was both titillated

and appalled. "A curious specimen," Madison wrote Jefferson, "of the in-genious folly of its author." Although Hamilton would continue to lead his party, he had been indelibly smirched.

The Federalist Colossus had defeated himself. His response to Callender was too detailed, too personal. He did not know when to let things alone, and he did not have auxiliaries to fight his battles for him. Madison could not beat him one-on-one, but he did not have to, for he had helped develop a cadre of auxiliaries for his party. In the Reynolds affair, they undertook the politics of personal destruction. This is not for gentlemen, but it is part of the political process nevertheless. Madison would not have touched the Reynolds affair with a barge pole, but there was no need; that was work for Beckley and Callender. A party, like a family, is larger than any individual. As in a family, its members do not have to like one another, or even know one another particularly well. As long as they share a common loyalty, each can work for all.

Jefferson was less cautious than Madison in his handling of Callender; he thought of him as "a man of genius" and sent him little payoffs. Callender had done good work for the Republican cause—for now.

The Madison-less mission that John Adams sent to France in the summer of 1797 consisted of Charles Coatesworth Pinckney, older brother of the diplomat Thomas; Elbridge Gerry, an old friend of Adams's from Massachusetts; and John Marshall, a smart and shrewd Virginia Federalist. What they found in France caused a storm that would knock Republicans flat, provoke Jefferson and Madison to desperate intellectual efforts, then sweep them to victory, all in under three years.

The current incarnation of the French Revolution, the Directory, was both milder and more aggressive than its predecessors. It relaxed the rule of the guillotine at home, while sweeping through Germany, Italy, and Austria (one of the new young generals it employed was a Corsican artillerist,

Napoleon Bonaparte). Everywhere the Directory was venal—squeezing tribute from foreign countries and bribes for its officers from all who dealt with them. The three Americans in Paris looked like new chickens to be plucked.

Pinckney, Gerry, and Marshall had been instructed to patch up relations with France as best they could, just as Jay had done with Britain. They met the foreign minister, Talleyrand, an excommunicated bishop, for fifteen minutes early in October 1797, but he then became inaccessible. Various intermediaries appeared instead, demanding a loan for France and "something for the pocket" for themselves. "No, no, not a sixpence!" Pinckney exclaimed in one meeting. The Americans had become characters in a very old drama: Innocents Abroad. Marshall sent home two letters describing their situation, identifying the grasping Frenchmen as X, Y, and Z.

The letters arrived in America in the spring of 1798 like a thunderstorm. The French stood revealed as bullies, shakedown artists, almost muggers. X, Y, and Z were even worse than Citizen Genet: then, one ambassador had made himself obnoxious; now, the French government had insulted America's honor.

Federalists were enraged—and energized. Congress created a new Navy Department, authorized hostilities against French ships in the West Indies, and voted to provide money for an army in case France tried to invade the United States (an unlikely fear—but rumor had it that the Directory might invade Britain itself). Washington would be called out of retirement to command; Hamilton would be his second-in-command. Pinckney's exclamation was transformed into a toast: "Millions for defense, but not one cent for tribute."

Madison watched it all from Montpelier with dread. Marshall's letters, he wrote Jefferson, had been used to "kindl[e] a flame among the people." It was a "solemn lesson" in the political effects of war fever. "Perhaps it is a universal truth that the loss of liberty at home" occurs under the threat of "danger, real or pretended, from abroad."

Madison wrote that letter in May, when no American liberties had been lost. As spring turned to summer, his fears were realized by the passage of two new laws. The Alien Act allowed the president to deport any noncitizen foreigner he thought "dangerous to the peace and safety" of the country, without hearing or trial. The Sedition Act made it a federal crime to say or publish anything "false, scandalous and malicious" about the federal government, or Congress.

These laws were as partisan as they were sweeping. Federalists were feeling oppressed by hostile newcomers. Irish immigrants had begun arriving, if not yet in the floods of fifty years later, still in a noticeable stream, driven by oppression and unrest in the old country; in their new country, Britain's Republican enemies would be their friends. And wasn't Gallatin a foreigner? (Wasn't Hamilton? The Federalists forgot that.)

Journalism was a free-for-all. Reading *The Federalist*, or Thomas Paine two hundred years later, we remember the heights. But turn-of-the-nineteenth-century American journalists gratified every taste, including bottom feeding. Newspapers—published daily in some cities, the most successful having weekly national editions as well—had created modern media culture: lively, au courant, hysterical, salacious. Philip Freneau's fantasia about Washington's execution by guillotine was only an early episode in a two-decade saturnalia of rumor and vituperation. Federalists had their own newspapers, which told their own lies, but as the party in power, with the most to lose, they also wanted to defend themselves legally. They designed the Sedition Act to expire on March 3, 1801—the day before the next presidential inauguration, in case the man being inaugurated were not John Adams.

Madison and Jefferson met twice, at Montpelier in July and at Monticello in October, to plan a counterattack. There is not much of a paper trail; they were evidently uncomfortable using the mail, even in cipher. The plan they devised was for each of them to write a set of resolutions to be adopted by a friendly state legislature—Madison's in Virginia, Jefferson's in Kentucky. The resolutions would function as Republican Party position papers—statements of grievances and rallying points for the party nationwide. Each set would be introduced by a surrogate (their true authorship would not be known for decades).

The Kentucky Resolutions were adopted in mid-November, the Virginia Resolutions the day before Christmas.

Madison's set is shorter and less urgent, but more compact and more forceful. He outlined his intellectual framework in one paragraph: the federal government is a compact between the states; its powers are limited to those enumerated in the Constitution; and "in case of a deliberate, palpable and dangerous" exercise of other powers, the states may "interpose for arresting the progress of the evil."

Next he discussed the present danger. He began with an overview that was, to speak plainly, nuts: "the obvious tendency" of Federalist measures was "absolute, or at best a mixed monarchy." Who was to be the monarch? King John Adams I? When he got down to specifics, however, he became clear and compelling. The Alien Act violated the Constitution in two ways: deporting aliens was a power nowhere delegated to the federal government, and by giving the president a free hand in exercising it, it mixed executive and judicial functions. The Sedition Act flew in the face of the First Amendment, which gave Madison one more opportunity to explain its importance: the "right of freely examining public characters and measures" was "the only effectual guardian of every other right."

His remedy was for Virginia to declare the Alien and Sedition Acts unconstitutional and for the states to take "necessary and proper" measures to defend their rights, and the rights of the people.

Madison began and ended his resolutions with praise of the Union and the Constitution, which he called "the pledge of mutual friendship and the instrument of mutual happiness." He was claiming the mantle of conservatism, of defending the established order, and he was reaching out for allies. He repeated the reaching gesture in his remedies: "the states," plural, should "interpose for arresting . . . evil," and together they should take "necessary and proper" measures of self-defense. ("Necessary and proper" were, of course, the very words of the Constitution that Hamilton and other Federalists had used to expand its powers. Was Madison winking at his enemies as he stole one of their weapons?)

Jefferson's Kentucky Resolutions had a different feel. They contained some blazing prose, Jefferson at his finest: "Confidence is everywhere the parent of despotism; free government is founded in jealousy and not in confidence. . . . In questions of power then let no more be heard of confidence in man, but bind him down from mischief by the chains of the Constitution." His references to the Constitution were not collegial, like Madison's. He parsed it like a divorce lawyer combing through a prenup. He reveled in an adversarial stance: he called unconstitutional acts "unauthoritative, void, and of no force"; he even said a state had the power to "nullify" them, until the Kentucky legislature cut that word out. Jefferson was revolutionary, not conservative; yearning to act, alone if necessary. He and Madison each fell back on the great episode of his life: Jefferson on the Declaration and the spirit of '76; Madison on the Constitution and the spirit of '87.

The 1790s were a frantic time, and Madison's paranoia on the looming threat of monarchy was not his alone. (When paranoia was in the air, Jefferson was never far away.) The Federalists were not in fact working toward monarchy, absolute or mixed. Adams, their outlier, wrote of monarchy's virtues, and even wrote in private that it would come to America after he was gone. But even he did not expect or want it in his lifetime. Yet Republicans looked for monarchists under every bed, because republicanism was so new and seemed so fragile. Who knew what relapses there might be?

Federalists, meanwhile, had their own paranoia: they conceived their enemies as atheists, Jacobins, guillotiners (didn't Republican cartoons and rhetoric, beginning with Freneau, employ guillotines?). Federalists brooded on all this because the French Revolution was indeed sweeping through Europe, overturning governments much older than ours, and America's Republicans admired it. Federalists had their own visions of fragility to frighten them.

F irst reactions to the Virginia and Kentucky Resolutions were over-whelmingly negative. There were at the time sixteen states—the orig-inal thirteen, plus Vermont, Kentucky, and Tennessee. The legislatures of ten explicitly rejected the resolutions (New York's called them "inflam-matory and pernicious"); the other four made no comment.

Madison and Jefferson were out on a lonely limb. But that was all right; the struggle had just begun. Not everything in politics is up to you. Sometimes the opposition is your best friend; it can break ranks, and overreach. Federalists did both.

In France the Directory began signaling that it wanted to negotiate with America in earnest; military reversals in Europe had made it more tractable. President Adams announced in February 1799 that he was sending a new mission, which had the effect of splitting his party between Adams loyalists and die-hards who wanted to keep the pressure on France and on Republicans at home.

Federalist pressure at home became overbearing, then odious. The mil-itary measures that had been voted to repel a possible French invasion were expensive, and the taxes that paid for them were heavy. In the spring of 1799, there was a second tax rebellion in Pennsylvania, as German farmers in the eastern part of the state chased off assessors of a property tax. Although there had been no violence, the army was sent to arrest the lawbreakers. It was a parody of the Whiskey Rebellion: the threat was slight, the response too harsh. "A sergeant and six men," wrote one officer, might have done the job.

President Adams never enforced the Alien Act, but there were fourteen prosecutions under the Sedition Act. Federalist judges threw the book at defendants. Matthew Lyon, a Republican congressman from Vermont, was convicted for writing in a newspaper he edited that John Adams "grasp[ed] for power" and "ridiculous pomp." He was fined $1,000 and spent four months in jail in a freezing cell with a stinking latrine. James Callender would be arrested for calling Adams a "hideous hermaphroditical character," fined $200, and sentenced to nine months in jail. Benjamin Franklin Bache, editor of the *Aurora*, escaped prison by dying of yellow fever while awaiting trial. William Duane, the Irish immigrant who succeeded him, avoided various prosecutions by threatening to expose administration secrets and by going underground. The government's tax and sedition policies were both niggling and fierce, and made the Federalists contemptible as well as hateful.

If Virginia and Kentucky were the bastions of Republican resistance, then it was time for their best Republican politicians to step forward. Madison ended his sabbatical from office by standing for a seat in the Virginia Assembly in April 1799; he won easily.

When the legislature met in December, they faced a sad duty. George Washington died on the 14th, at age sixty-seven, of an inflammation of the throat. Madison moved that the assembly wear mourning throughout their session. "Death," he said, "has robbed our country of its most distinguished ornament, and the world of one of its greatest benefactors." He had been fighting Washington politically for years, and Washington had cut him off for it. But Madison had never accepted their estrangement. He stayed loyal to his father figure to the end.

Madison used the assembly session to prepare for the elections of 1800. Despite a bout of dysentery, he wrote a 20,000-word Report on the Alien and Sedition Acts, published in January 1800, which defended and elaborated on the Virginia Resolutions. The silence or scorn of every other state except Kentucky did not faze him. He went ahead like a gambler doubling down on his initial bet.

The states, he argued, were the final arbiters of the constitutionality of laws. This role belonged to them because the Constitution had been ratified by their assent. Some of the states that criticized the Virginia

Resolutions assigned the arbiter's role instead to the courts. Madison would not hear of it. The courts themselves might act unconstitutionally: "the Judicial Department . . . may exercise or sanction dangerous power." The states had to sit in judgment over the judiciary. Madison was no doubt influenced by the fact that the courts just then were in Federalist hands, and Federalist judges were enforcing the Sedition Act zealously.

In his report, Madison let all the Republican Party's hobby horses out for a ride. Hamilton's Bank of the United States and his Report on Manufactures were as unconstitutional as the Alien and Sedition Acts. Federalism's slipshod lawmaking would "pave the way to monarchy." The president, he warned, might even "regulate" his successors in office "as he pleased." (This charge, raising the specter of an American dynasty, would prove to be prescient, if also ironic, for it would be Madison and his Virginia friends, not the Federalists, who would show how to maintain a presidential dynasty for a generation.)

Madison's Report was most eloquent defending freedom of the press. "To the press alone, checkered as it is with abuses, the world is indebted for all the triumphs which have been gained by reason and humanity over error and oppression." Defending the press's abuses was as important as defending its freedom; abuses were an inescapable consequence of press freedom. "It is better to leave a few of its noxious branches to their luxuriant growth than, by pruning them away, to injure the vigor of those yielding the proper fruits." Trying to control the press was trying to throttle history. If a sedition act had been in force for decades, Americans might never have replaced the Articles of Confederation or thrown off British rule.

Freedom of the press was not a privilege accorded journalists; it was another name for citizen responsibility. "It is the duty as well as right of intelligent and faithful citizens to discuss" the errors of their representatives, both "to control them by the censorship of the public opinion" and "to promote a remedy according to the rules of the constitution"—that is, to elect new representatives at the next election.

So Madison shifted, over the course of his Report, from the states to public opinion as the ultimate judge of constitutionality, fitness to rule—everything. The Virginia legislature was the forum he had been using for a year, so naturally he had emphasized the states in his polemical resolutions. But public opinion was his real home ground. Like Antaeus, he was strongest when he stood on it.

Madison's and Jefferson's resolutions had cast the Republicans as defenders of beleaguered liberty. Federalist excesses and divisions only reinforced their claim. If America was genuinely threatened by France, the taxes and the ham-handed prosecutions might have seemed worth it. But President Adams himself, by reopening negotiations with the Directory, had told the country that it was not threatened. Adams might win some credit as a peacemaker. Why then were he and his party supporting war policies?

The candidates in the election of 1800 were almost the same as in 1796. Despite intraparty division, Adams led the Federalist ticket. His Pinckney running mate this time was Charles Coatesworth, veteran of the XYZ mission. Republicans once again backed Jefferson and, after some hesitating over possible New Yorkers, Aaron Burr. Jefferson needed no coaxing to run this time—Federalist policies had truly alarmed him, and the geopolitical scene was propitious: Adams was preparing the way to peace with France, after taking on all the odium of war preparations.

Meanwhile, Madison tended to home-state political chores. He joined in an effort to change Virginia's election laws to winner-take-all (there would be no lone Adams vote from a rogue electoral district this time). He also helped assure Burr that southern electors would not waste their "second" votes on other candidates.

For all the Republicans' efforts and the Federalists' errors, the 1800 election was a close call. Since the states cast their electoral votes at different times—and since legislative elections, which would determine the electoral vote in many states, were even more spread out—results trickled in throughout the year. Adams and Pinckney swept New England, except for one wasted "second" vote. Burr justified his place on his party's ticket by masterminding a Republican sweep in the New York legislature, which would deliver the state's vote. Hamilton's home base was rudely snatched from his control. "We have beat you," Burr crowed to one Federalist, "by superior *management*." The Federalists won New Jersey and Delaware, the Republicans Virginia, Georgia, Kentucky, and Tennessee. Maryland and North Carolina, voting by electoral districts, split, as did Pennsylvania, whose electoral vote in this election was cast by a deadlocked legislature.

Everything came down to South Carolina, where yet another Charles Pinckney, this one a Republican despite being a second cousin of Charles Coatesworth Pinckney, held the state for Jefferson and Burr. When all was done, Jefferson and Burr had seventy-three votes each, Adams sixty-five, and the Federalist Pinckney sixty-four.

But, since the Constitution did not recognize tickets—even though the two parties had each run de facto tickets—Jefferson and Burr were tied. The tie would have to be broken by the House of Representatives, each state voting as a unit. Federalists were strong enough there to prevent Jefferson from winning outright. Out of spite they voted for Burr for thirty-five ballots. Finally, on February 17, 1801, enough Federalists gave in on the thirty-sixth ballot to make Jefferson president.

The endgame of this election was played out in the nation's new capital, named after Washington and located on the Potomac, as Hamilton, Madison, and Jefferson had arranged a decade earlier. Madison was not there. He had come down with rheumatism as the old year ticked over— and his father was dying. James Madison Sr. passed on February 27, 1801, a month shy of his seventy-eighth birthday. "Rather suddenly," the son wrote the president-elect, "though very gently, the flame of life went out." When Madison arrived in Washington in May, he would no longer be the young colonel, but secretary of state.

CHAPTER SEVEN

In Power

When James Madison first arrived in Washington in the spring of 1801, it was nowhere. The federal government had moved to its latest site in the summer and fall of 1800, but only small, stumbling steps had been taken to make the new capital a national city, or even a habitable place. The presidential mansion was a finished building, on the outside, at any rate, though the grounds were filled with the detritus of ongoing construction. The Capitol, a mile and a half away on a small hill, was just begun. There were a few boardinghouses, a handful of shops and taverns, and a scattering of private homes (many of them built on spec). The roads were unpaved paths. There was good partridge hunting on Capitol Hill, and locals grew vegetables in the Mall. Gouverneur Morris, who after a decade of high life in Europe was now a senator from New York, wrote a princess friend of his that "we want nothing here but houses, cellars, kitchens, well informed men, amiable women, and other little trifles of this kind, to make our city perfect."

If Washington had been even grimmer, the prospect facing Madison still would have been glorious. He and his allies and their leader, Thomas Jefferson, had accomplished something brand-new in the history of the United States, rare enough in the history of the world: the peaceful ascent to the highest offices of government by one set of men replacing their opponents. The Republican sweep had been striking. Not only was Jefferson president, but Republicans held a three-to-two majority in the House (almost reversing the Federalist majority in the last Congress), and they had pulled nearly even in the Senate. The change had not been accomplished by revolutionary means: the Federalists had not crowned their heads, and the Republicans had not had to remove crowns or heads, despite the fears of both parties. But the changeover was felt to be revolutionary in fact. Jefferson considered it a second American Revolution.

For his cabinet, Jefferson turned to two Massachusetts men, Henry Dearborn (secretary of war) and Levi Lincoln (attorney general). Samuel Smith, the Baltimore congressman and merchant, preferred staying in the House to becoming secretary of the navy, so Jefferson appointed his younger brother Robert. Since the office of attorney general was a minor one in those days, and Jefferson intended to pursue a peace policy (no more chest thumping against France), these were minor appointments. For Treasury secretary he turned to the obvious Republican, Albert Gallatin. To fill the office of secretary of state, the job that he himself had held in George Washington's cabinet, he turned to Madison.

The triumvirate of Jefferson, Madison, and Gallatin was almost as brilliant as the triumvirate of Washington, Jefferson, and Alexander Hamilton a decade earlier. The new trio, unlike that one, would hang together. The three great Republicans saw eye to eye. Not even ambition divided them. Gallatin could have dreamed of being president himself one day, for though he was foreign born, he had been a citizen when the Constitution was adopted, which made him eligible according to Article II, Section 1. Almost uniquely for a successful politician, though, he seemed entirely focused on doing his job, whatever that might be. Jefferson had already reached the top of the pole; his only ambition could be to stay there, with the nation's love. Madison was the heir apparent.

No member of a cabinet had been so close to a president; none perhaps ever would be again. Washington's cabinet had been separated from him by the barrier of his own uniqueness. Adams's cabinet had been alienated by its littleness and his willfulness. Jefferson had done Madison's job and therefore had opinions and hands-on experience, which is often a recipe for a president to overwhelm his secretary. But Madison's long record of advising his chief on every subject gave him a compensating intimacy.

For three weeks, Madison and his household—Dolley, her son, Payne, and her sister, Anna—lived with Jefferson in the White House. Then, after a two-month stay on Pennsylvania Avenue, over the temporary offices of the State Department, he rented a house on F Street.

Madison was uniquely favored—therefore conspicuous, therefore vulnerable. To the Federalists, who had been transformed overnight into an almost impotent minority, Madison was only a tool and a toady. They saved their carping for Jefferson, their displacer, archenemy, and hate figure. But if any Republicans were unhappy with anything the Jefferson administration did, whom would they carp at? The lightning rod and scapegoat for Republican unease thus became the right hand, James Madison.

He made enemies over patronage. Ideally, Republicans would not deal in patronage. One of their complaints against Federalism was that it fortified itself by creating needless government offices and doling them out. Yet Republicans had created a party, and while partisans work for common ideals, they also work for their own interest and advancement. After the election of 1800, many Republicans came begging.

Even though Madison was the man who had slipped Philip Freneau into Jefferson's State Department, he ran his own impartially, retaining a hard-line Federalist, Jacob Wagner, as chief clerk because he was capable. Madison's attitude perplexed William Duane, Benjamin Franklin Bache's successor at the *Aurora*, so much that he traveled from Philadelphia to Washington to urge Madison to do the right thing with his staff. Duane characterized the eight clerks he found at the State Department as four picaroons, or pirates, "a Hamiltonian, a nothingarian, a modest man and a nincompoop." Duane complained in vain and from then on marked Madison as a weak reed.

Another Republican journalist, James Callender, one of the Sedition Act martyrs, made a patronage claim for himself. Jefferson had issued him a retroactive pardon and ordered the repayment of his $200 fine. Callender, however, wanted more than vindication; a postmastership in Richmond, Virginia, would fit the bill. He wrote Madison an oily letter pressing his claim ("I was extremely happy to hear that you had accepted of an office under the new presidency because . . . I was interested in having one person among them whom I could without hypocrisy profess to feel an attachment for"). (Beware the man who says he addresses *you* without hypocrisy.) Callender followed his letter with a visit to Madison in Washington. Too late, Jefferson and Madison were beginning to suspect their erstwhile supporter. The secretary of state told Callender not to get his hopes up.

But the most consequential patronage decision of the Jefferson administration's first year concerned the new vice president. When the thirty-six-ballot drama of the tied presidential election had been performed in the House of Representatives, what role had Aaron Burr played? Innocent bystander, watching Federalists struggle to keep Jefferson out of the White House? Or backstairs intriguer, actively assisting their efforts? Contemporary gossips, Republican and Federalist alike, tagged Burr as an intriguer. Jefferson noted the talk—some of it conveyed to him by Madison—and kept his own counsel.

The first sign of his attitude toward his vice president came when Jefferson withheld a New York customs house appointment from Matthew Davis, a Burr ally who had been a poll watcher during the crucial legislative races a year earlier. (Davis was so zealous, he had gone fifteen hours without eating.) Burr wrote three letters on behalf of Davis, who even made a trip to Monticello to lobby for himself. At length Jefferson told his vice president that his policy on solicitations was to let his answer "be found in what is done or not done." Davis never got the job.

New York was a key part of the victorious Republican coalition. One of Jefferson's and Madison's tasks over the next sixteen years would be managing their northern junior partners—and making sure they remained junior. Who in New York would the Virginians be better off working with—Burr, ambitious, vigorous, and forty-five years old? Or George Clinton, beginning his valedictory seventh term as governor as he turned sixty-two?

Madison would make another enemy on a matter of principle. The chairman of the Ways and Means Committee of the new Republican House was a twenty-eight-year-old Virginian, and a second cousin of Jefferson's, John Randolph of Roanoke. All his life, his voice never broke and he never used a razor. He kept the world in awe with his quick tongue and quicker temper. In his twenties and thirties, he was not as crazy as he would later become, after alcohol, opium, and disappointment had done their work. But he was already willful and domineering.

His collision with Madison was set up by a crooked real estate deal hanging over from the last decade. The state of Georgia claimed a vast western hinterland called the Yazoo country, after a river in what is now the state of Mississippi. In 1795, Georgia sold twenty million Yazoo acres to four land companies for half a million dollars. But the next year, the state voided the sale, on the grounds that every legislator but one had been bribed. Georgia and the land companies were not the only claimants: the federal government said it owned the land, and several Indian nations—Creek, Cherokee, Choctaw, and Chickasaw—actually occupied it.

To settle the matter, Jefferson tapped Madison, Gallatin, and Attorney General Lincoln as a commission. In April 1802, without trying to resolve any of the underlying issues of possession, they brokered an agreement among the state, the Indians, and the investors. It was "expedient," the commissioners said, "to enter into a compromise on reasonable terms." But expediency was not acceptable to Randolph, who thought his party stood for states' rights and against corruption. He made Georgia's sovereign power to punish its lawmakers and the greed of the land companies who had bribed them touchstones for good and evil.

All these feuds came to a boil at different times, like pots on a stove. Burr made the least fuss, at least as far as Madison was concerned. Clintonian Republicans began to attack Burr in his home base, New York City, using the *American Citizen*, a newspaper edited by an English immigrant with the self-descriptive name of James Cheetham. Late in Jefferson's first term, Burr complained about the abuse to the president himself. Jefferson replied that he paid no more attention to it than to "the passing wind." Cheetham, he admitted, had a contract for printing federal laws in New York City, a valuable subsidy for any newspaper. But those arrangements were made "by the Secretary of the State, without any reference to me." In other words, all the dirt being done to Burr was done not with Jefferson's help, only with the help of Jefferson's best friend, who, additionally, had the most to gain by hobbling Aaron Burr. Burr decided he had better look outside the Republican Party for his future.

Randolph fell upon the Yazoo claims at the tail end of the term. He tried to read Madison and the other compromisers out of the party. The people of Georgia had a right to undo a corrupt contract, and anyone who disagreed must be corrupt himself. "What is the spirit against which we now struggle," he asked, " . . . a monster generated by fraud, nursed in corruption, that in grim silence awaits its prey! It is the spirit of Federalism—that spirit which considers the many as made only for the few, which sees in government nothing but a job, which is never so true to itself as when false to the nation!" Although his overheated rhetoric blocked Yazoo legislation for years, he would have less success blocking Madison. However wounding Randolph could be at any moment, he was not a bad enemy to have over the long haul; he palled through excess.

Duane remained a thorn in Madison's side for a decade, attacking him and Gallatin while maintaining ostentatious loyalty to Jefferson, supporting a populist faction in Pennsylvania politics, and denouncing Republicans he disliked as Quids, from "tertium quid"—third things, neither fish nor fowl.

Of all the Republican dissenters, Callender had the greatest impact on the American mind, for in September 1802 he told the nation about Sally

Hemings in an article for a Federalist newspaper, the *Richmond Recorder* (if he couldn't work for the post office, he would work for the other side). Two hundred years later, the sly scorn of his attack is still startling. "It is well known that the man, *whom it delighteth the people to honor*, keeps and for many years has kept, as his concubine, one of his slaves. Her name is SALLY. The name of her eldest son is Tom. His features are said to bear a striking though sable resemblance to those of the president himself." The italics allude to the sixth chapter of the Book of Esther, in which the villainous Haman thinks that Ahaseurus, king of Persia, delighteth to honor him, whereas the king actually delighteth to honor Haman's enemy, the Jew Mordecai; when Mordecai gets the upper hand, Haman and his sons are hanged. Callender hoped to turn Jefferson into an American Haman.

Ten months later, in July 1803, Callender was found floating in the James River, dead. A coroner's jury ruled that he had drowned accidentally, bathing while drunk. Callender did drink. But had someone helped him into the James and eternity?

When journalists went too far, it was not uncommon to beat them. A few months before he died, Callender had been attacked with a club by a Richmond lawyer who happened to be James Monroe's son-in-law. If gentlemen (a class to which journalists did not belong) gave offense, satisfaction was sought on the dueling ground. Madison never fought a duel himself, but he acknowledged the practice. Back in the Adams administration, two congressmen had rumbled on the floor of the House, armed with a cane and a set of fireplace tongs; Madison thought they should have dueled instead. A political revolution had occurred without revolutionary violence, but man-to-man, ad hoc violence flickered on the edges of American politics. History has accepted the verdict of the coroner's jury in Callender's case, but political violence would appear in shocking forms in Madison's later career.

The complaints against Madison by his fellow Republicans sound very modern; they are in fact eternal. Practical men (Duane) said he wouldn't get his hands dirty; purists (Randolph) called him corrupt and a sellout.

Neither Burr nor Callender attacked Madison directly; he could survive those who did, so long as he made no mistakes of his own and retained Jefferson's support. Eminence can be a lonely thing, but it is on the whole better than obscurity.

So much for politics. What of Madison's job?

Madison and Jefferson shared two goals, and two prejudices, which would guide their foreign policy for the next eight years and beyond. The goals were peace and expansion; the prejudices were a disposition to trust France and to distrust Britain.

They yearned for peace because war was expensive and vicious. War oppressed taxpayers, swelled the state, and caused panic and oppression (the Alien and Sedition Acts had just proven that). Their peace policy was not a passive one, however. American commerce, they believed, was so valuable to the world that it could be used as a weapon instead of armies and frigates.

They favored expansion because it was demographic destiny. American settlers were pouring into the Ohio Valley, Kentucky, and Tennessee. Neither Indians nor Europeans had any right to stand in their way.

As for their attitudes toward France and Britain, the passions awakened by the French Revolution had changed, both in them and in Europe. The French republic had been overthrown, in spirit if not yet in form, when Napoleon Bonaparte took the title First Consul in 1799. Guillotiners and extortionists gave way to a military man. When Napoleon first came to power, Jefferson wondered whether he would be more like George Washington or Oliver Cromwell—upholding the laws or twisting them to his own ends. Yet long after it became clear that Napoleon was a law unto himself, the two Virginians gave him the benefit of the doubt they were never willing to give Britain. Napoleonic France may have become an ex-friend, but they hoped it might be friendly once more; Britain was their lifelong enemy.

The secretary of state and the president could summon erudition, rhetoric, and (in Jefferson's case) poetry to support these beliefs. But the beliefs themselves were first principles, axioms from which all else flowed.
Jefferson's and Madison's agreement on their two goals and their two prejudices gave their actions consistency and, in many cases, force. But it
could also blind them to difficulties and failure. The Jefferson administration benefited from the unity of its leaders—and suffered from it.

Madison took over the State Department at what seemed to be a lucky
time. President Adams had resolved the ill feelings of the XYZ affair by
negotiating a treaty with France, the Convention of Mortefontaine,
which was signed in October 1800. Peace became general the following
year. The coalition of enemies that had tried to tame France broke up,
exhausted, and 1801 marked a pause in Europe's wars.

The first order of business for Madison was the question: Who will
get the Spanish empire? Spain's possessions covered a continent and a
half, from California to Cape Horn. They had even increased during the
eighteenth century, as Spain acquired the ancient French dominion of
Louisiana and lost, then regained Florida. (Both territories were larger
than the modern states of the same name, Louisiana vastly so: western
Florida ran all the way along the Gulf of Mexico to New Orleans, while
Louisiana stretched north and west to the sources of the Mississippi and
Missouri Rivers.) Madison believed that Florida and a small part of Louisiana ought to belong to America. Several of the Yazoo country rivers
flowed through the Florida Panhandle to the Gulf, and the Mississippi
was the watershed of a vast arc of the interior of the United States, from
Pittsburgh to Natchez. If American settlers, present and future, did not
have the freedom to trade through Pensacola, Mobile, and above all New
Orleans, they would be like people trying to live in a house with the
doors barricaded from the outside.

But dealing with Spain meant dealing with France. In 1795, Spain had
bowed out of the wars of the French Revolution, too weak to fight its
northern neighbor. In 1800, Napoleon had tightened France's embrace,

by forcing Spain to give him Louisiana. The Treaty of San Ildefonso, which confirmed the deal, was signed the day after the Convention of Mortefontaine.

France kept the Treaty of San Ildefonso secret, especially from the United States, because it was a threatening, almost hostile act. The United States now found itself sharing a border not with a fading colossus, but with a superpower looking to rebuild its overseas empire.

Although Europe buzzed with rumors of the treaty, Madison did not learn definitively that it existed until November 1801. A year later, he learned something worse: the Spanish official who still administered New Orleans had closed the port to American trade (worth $2 million a year), presumably with the approval of its new owners.

Madison reacted with three strategies. The first was to lecture Louis André Pichon, the French chargé d'affaires in Washington, about geopolitical destiny. Louisiana, he told Pichon, was a white elephant, remote and vulnerable; France could enjoy possession of it only if she had friendly relations with the United States, which she could secure by ceding New Orleans and Florida. (Florida was owned by Spain, not France, but Madison assumed that France could make the deal.) He also threatened Pichon—a threat Jefferson repeated through other channels—with a British alliance if France proved hostile. "We must marry ourselves to the British fleet," as Jefferson put it. Britain and the United States, the threat implied, would then divide the Spanish empire between them. Madison and Jefferson did not intend to marry themselves to the British fleet, but they were willing to use it as a bogeyman. Finally, Madison energized America's diplomatic presence in Paris. Robert Livingston was America's ambassador there—his consolation prize for never having been Jefferson's running mate. In the spring of 1803, he was joined by James Monroe as a minister extraordinary. They were instructed to regain the right to trade through New Orleans—or to buy the city, and western Florida, too, for as much as $10 million.

This was able and varied diplomacy, playing different tunes on different instruments. Napoleon heeded none of it. He sent an army commanded by his brother-in-law, Victor Emmanuel Leclerc, to St. Domingo, the present-day Haiti, formerly a French colony, then in the midst of a revolution by its black and mulatto populations. If France could pacify St. Domingo, then it would have a staging area for occupying and developing Louisiana.

Jefferson's and Madison's enemies, the Federalists, had helped St. Domingo's blacks win their freedom in the first place. At the end of the 1790s President Adams had given them naval aid and sent them an American diplomat, Edward Stevens, a childhood friend of Alexander Hamilton's from the islands. Hamilton himself sketched a constitution for the new black state. In his last appearance as Publius, Hamilton concluded that only a military government would do, though he suggested some internal division of powers (e.g., judges appointed by generals for life; an assembly of generals to reject or ratify taxes).

In the spring of 1802, France seemed to win a great victory when Toussaint-Louverture, Haiti's black leader, was tricked into surrendering (Leclerc and Napoleon sent him to a mountaintop fort in France, where he died of pneumonia). But the resistance of the liberated slaves, and the ravages of yellow fever, swept away Leclerc and his army before the year was out.

As soon as Napoleon saw that there was no quick route to empire in the New World, he decided to turn his attention back to the Old; he cut his losses by making a deal with the United States. In April 1803, an astonished Livingston wrote Madison that he had been offered all of Louisiana. Monroe arrived in Paris days later, and the two diplomats settled on a price of $15 million. With a few signatures, the United States nearly doubled in size. There had not been such a stupendous windfall since the treaty that ended the American Revolution, and this spurt of national growth had been accomplished without firing a shot.

Back home, Monroe got the credit for the Louisiana Purchase. His late arrival had coincided with the deal, and he was a Virginian in a Virginia administration. Hamilton and Gouverneur Morris noted that their fellow New Yorker Livingston was being given short shrift. "It is possible," Morris wrote Livingston, "that I am unjust to Mr. Monroe, but really I consider him as a person of mediocrity in every respect." So the bad blood between New York and Virginia continued to flow.

Actually, neither Monroe nor Livingston deserved as much credit as Napoleon, who had decided to make the United States the beneficiary of his own change of plan. Yet credit also belonged to Madison and Jefferson, who had pursued opportunities to expand with such single-mindedness that they were ready to grasp one when it came. Seek, and ye shall find.

There was only one problem: Jefferson and Madison thought the Louisiana Purchase included Florida. New Orleans and Florida had been their maximum goal; even though they had won so much more, they still wanted all of what they had originally desired. And, for little more reason than their wanting it, they believed they had actually gotten it. Napoleon would make use of their error.

Jefferson and Madison decided to teach Britain, the other great superpower, a lesson in American independence. A decade earlier, Alexander Hamilton had told Major Beckwith, the British agent, "We think in English." Jefferson and Madison wanted to think in American, and one instrument they used to show the difference was etiquette.

The etiquette of republican government was uncharted territory, since there were so few modern models. When President Washington lived in New York and Philadelphia, he held weekly receptions on Tuesday afternoons from three to four, which he described in a letter. "Gentlemen, often in great numbers, come and go, chat with each other, and act as they please. A porter shows them into the room, and they retire from it when they please, and without ceremony. At their *first* entrance they salute me, and I them, and as many as I can talk to I do. What pomp there is in all this I am unable to discover." The tone of Washington's last line was defensive, because others had discovered the pomp in his simple routine. At first the criticism was confined to a few anti-Federalists, who thought he was coming on too grand (he bowed to guests but would not shake hands). In time, it was taken up by the Republican Party. Presidents should not hold receptions; they seemed like royal levees. Perhaps they were even intended (if not by Washington, then by Hamilton, Adams, and others) to prepare the public for monarchy. Although Madison never criticized Washington personally, he, like all good Republicans, grumbled about "the pageantry of rank" in one of his *National Gazette* essays.

The Republican simplicity of the Jefferson administration was abetted by the plainness, even poverty of the new capital city. But Jefferson and Madison also made it a point of pride and a matter of principle.

President Jefferson held no receptions; he gave dinners in the White House to small groups of congressmen, plus diplomats. In doing so, he played to his strengths, for in small groups his conversation shone. So did his kitchen, and his wine cellar. "The wine," wrote one dazzled Federalist senator, "was the best I ever drank, particularly the champagne, which was indeed delicious. I wish his French politics were as good as his French wines."

As secretary of state, Madison too hosted dinners, playing to his own strengths. He lacked Jefferson's palate and his quirky brilliance, but in private Madison showed intelligence and humor. One evening he proposed an experiment to see how many bottles of champagne it would take to induce hangovers the next day. (No result was recorded.) Another of Madison's strengths was his wife. Since Jefferson was a widower, Dolley, with some help from Hannah Gallatin, became the administration's unofficial hostess.

In December 1803, Jefferson formalized the principles of Republican social life in a memorandum, Canons of Etiquette, written with the advice of his cabinet. In traditional diplomatic protocol, ministers (or ambassadors) outranked chargés d'affaires and secretaries of legations. Now all diplomats were considered equal—and all Americans were considered equal to them. At dinners or other public functions, gentlemen were to give precedence to ladies, but otherwise conduct was to be regulated by "the principle of equality, or *pêle-mêle*." "Pell-mell"—Jefferson's spelling reflected the French origin of the word—was not the most diplomatic word to use. It meant mingled or mixed-up, with a possible whiff of disorder, even violence. Shakespeare's unique use of it (*Henry IV, Part I*) describes a rebellion: "pell-mell havoc and confusion."

Republican *pêle-mêle* seemed disorderly enough to the British minister when he first encountered it. Anthony Merry had been sent to Washington in the fall of 1803. Merry was not some aristocrat marking time in the diplomatic service, but a wine merchant's son; one American described him as "plain, unassuming and amiable." But he was also a conventional Englishman, and a conventional career diplomat. He was thus surprised, when he paid his first call on the president in late November, that Jefferson received him in slippers. He was disconcerted by his first dinner at the White House early the next month, when Jefferson, instead of taking Mrs. Merry, the wife of the guest of honor, to the dinner table, took Dolley Madison instead. (Madison picked up Mrs. Merry.) He was angered a few nights later by a dinner at the secretary of state's house when Madison took Hannah Gallatin in to dinner. No one at all looked out for Mrs. Merry, leaving the job of escorting her to Merry himself.

These snubs were made worse by the administration's fondness for France. In December 1803, Jerome Bonaparte, Napoleon's youngest brother, married Elizabeth Patterson, the eighteen-year-old niece of the Baltimore Smiths (Robert, still secretary of the navy, and Samuel, now a senator). Napoleon, in fact, disliked the match: he wanted European royalty for his in-laws, not Yankees. But Republican Washington gloried in it. Jefferson gave the young couple dinner at the White House, and Robert Smith threw them a fancy ball.

Elizabeth caused a sensation. "Mobs of boys," wrote one of Dolley's women friends, "have crowded round . . . to see what I hope will not often be seen in this country, an almost naked woman. . . . Her dress was the thinnest sarcenet and white crepe." Sarcenet was a silk fabric, often used for undergarments—except when Elizabeth Bonaparte wore it as outer garments. "Her back, her bosom, part of her waist and her arms were uncovered and the rest of her form visible." Her face was riveting, too. Gilbert Stuart did a dreamy portrait of her with three faces—profile, half profile, and full forward—as if he could not get enough of her.

If the Bonaparte marriage did not improve relations with France, it helped worsen them with the British minister. Pichon, the French chargé, noted cattily that the Bonapartes' appearance in Washington "has furnished Mr. Merry with new griefs."

Jefferson, Madison, and their colleagues had a serious point to make, both social and ideological: a new form of government required new manners, and Britain, they believed, was still the greatest threat in the world to republicanism. But their fecklessness was striking: Britain and France had resumed fighting in May 1803; the contest would soon involve all of Europe. The world is not a debating society; it was not wise to be provocative, without a plan. The Louisiana Purchase had gone to their heads.

At this moment of confidence and success, Madison sat for the best portrait ever made of him. Gilbert Stuart had set up shop in Washington, where, besides the lovely Elizabeth Bonaparte, he painted diplomats, local bigwigs, and James and Dolley Madison. In their portraits, Dolley's eyes are bright and lips are slightly smiling; Madison wears the outfit that he settled on in early adulthood and favored till the end of his days—all black, with a white neckcloth. His hair is powdered, worn long at the sides and pulled back into a queue (a look that was already beginning to look old-fashioned). His hair comes to a peak over his forehead, receding on either side—a hairline that highlights his head, and the brains within. His expression is calm, perhaps determined. "Quite pretty he has made us," wrote Dolley of Stuart's handiwork.

Jefferson's first term saw the violent death of one of Madison's colleagues at the Constitutional Convention.

Richard Dobbs Spaight of North Carolina had been in Philadelphia the day the convention opened. He spoke up a dozen times, once joining Madison in an effort to give senators long terms (to give government "stability," as Madison put it). After the Constitution was ratified, Spaight served as governor of his state and as congressman. In September 1802, he was shot and killed by a political rival in a duel.

Almost two years later, the same fate befell another of Madison's former colleagues, Alexander Hamilton. In July 1804, the former Treasury secretary was shot and killed by Vice President Aaron Burr.

Hamilton and Burr had been rivals in New York politics since the early 1790s. During the endgame of the presidential election of 1800, when Federalists hoped to use the tie vote in the Electoral College to make Burr president, Hamilton had urged them to accept Jefferson. "If there be a man in the world I ought to hate," he wrote Gouverneur Morris, "it is Jefferson. With Burr I have always been personally well. But the public good must be paramount." Why was Hamilton so hostile toward Burr? For a reason that might have interested Madison, if he had known of it. Jefferson had bad principles, from Hamilton's point of view, but Burr had none. "Is it a recommendation to have *no theory*?" Hamilton asked another Federalist. Without theory, Burr, he believed, must be ruled entirely by ambition.

In the spring of 1804, Hamilton repeated these arguments. Burr, abandoned by Jefferson, hoped to arrange his post–vice presidential future by running for governor of New York. But since the state Republican Party was backing a candidate handpicked by George Clinton, Burr had to run as a Federalist. Once again, Hamilton begged his party not to support Burr. Unlike the presidential election of 1800, the 1804 New York governor's race was not even close. Burr was crushed and decided to challenge his nemesis. Each man shot once. Hamilton's shot went high and wide; Burr's pierced Hamilton's liver and lodged in his spine.

Neither Jefferson nor Madison said much at the time about their dead enemy. In a letter to Monroe, Madison referred in passing to "the adventure between Burr and Hamilton." Many years later, he took a longer view.

When James Paulding, a literary chum of Washington Irving, wrote the aged Madison asking for biographical details of long-dead fellow founders, Madison replied, "That [Mr. Hamilton] possessed intellectual powers of the first order, and the moral qualifications of integrity and honor in a captivating degree, has been decreed to him by a suffrage now universal." Madison's prose contains a lot of eighteenth-century filling. Usually it is just the way he writes, but sometimes it serves a purpose. Here the passive voice almost exempts Madison from the judgment. "If [Hamilton's] theory of government deviated from the republican standard," Madison went on, "he had the candor to avow it, and the greater merit of cooperating faithfully in maturing and supporting a system which was not his choice." This ironically echoes Hamilton's decision to back Jefferson over Burr: Hamilton had the wrong theory, but at least he had one, and he put his shoulder to the wheel nevertheless.

Toward the end of the letter, Madison warmed up a bit. Days before the duel, Hamilton had visited a friend's office, where he slipped into a book on a shelf a note assigning authorship of the *Federalist* papers. Hamilton claimed far too many for himself; after his account was published, Madison had, from time to time, diffidently set the record straight. Hamilton's "misstatement," he now told Paulding, "was involuntary. . . . He was incapable of any that was not so." His heart was pure, if his principles were not.

Two New Yorkers had been swept from the field, the brilliant intellect, the canny pol. No one, however brilliant or canny, could withstand Jefferson as the presidential election of 1804 came round. Gallatin had cut taxes; Jefferson and Madison had kept the peace, and acquired Louisiana. Callender's trash talk was ignored.

This election avoided the awkward tie of 1800, thanks to the Twelfth Amendment, ratified in June 1804, which brought presidential tickets into the Constitution. In 1804, and in every election since, each elector cast a vote for president and for vice president on "distinct ballots." This time Jefferson's running mate was a New Yorker whom Madison would have little reason to fear—sixty-five-year-old George Clinton, closing out twenty-one years as governor and looking forward to the vice presidency as a "respectable retirement." The Federalists put up Charles Coatesworth Pinckney, Adams's running mate four years earlier, and Rufus King, another veteran of the Constitutional Convention.

It was no contest. Out of seventeen states (Ohio had joined the Union in 1803), Jefferson and Clinton carried fourteen, plus nine of Maryland's electoral votes. Pinckney and King won two votes in Maryland and only two states, Connecticut and Delaware. The total electoral vote was 162 to 14. The Republicans swept four-fifths of the seats in the House and the Senate.

Victory could not be more complete.

CHAPTER EIGHT

Problems of Power

P resident Jefferson showed his contentment with the course of things by keeping his team virtually unchanged as his second term began. There was some shuffling of minor cabinet offices, but Madison and Gallatin stayed in the two most important, State and Treasury.

One of the administration's first tasks in foreign affairs was to round out the Louisiana Purchase by scooping up Florida. The peninsula—a wilderness of swamp, hostile Indians, and escaped slaves—did not greatly interest them; western Florida—the Panhandle and its Gulf Coast ports— did.

Madison began by assuming that western Florida was included in the Louisiana Purchase. On the eve of Jefferson's second inaugural, he had offered to show Louis Marie Turreau, a Napoleonic general who was the new French minister to Washington, a map proving that Louisiana ran almost all the way to Pensacola. Turreau dismissed him: "maps are not titles."

Madison also tried dealing directly with Spain. In 1805, he sent James Monroe, who had been posted to London as a reward for his success with the Louisiana Purchase, to Madrid to negotiate. But Spain was stubborn. She had surrendered Louisiana to France in 1800 because it was only a late addition to her empire; Florida was a centuries-old heirloom, going back to Ponce de Leon. Spain had no intention of surrendering it, or even adjusting its boundaries.

Or maybe the road to Florida ran through Paris after all. Napoleon, having abandoned his plans for American empire, planned instead to expand his European empire. ("Empire" was no longer a metaphorical term: he had crowned himself emperor at Notre Dame Cathedral in December 1804.) But expansion meant war, and war meant cash. Napoleon had earned $15 million from the sale of Louisiana; would the prospect of some millions more induce him to compel Spain to yield Florida? Could the United States buy Florida, not from its owner, but from a third party? In January 1806, the House, meeting in secret session, voted to appropriate $2 million for France to make the deal.

The appropriation enraged John Randolph, who saw Yazoo methods of bartering and buying infecting foreign policy. "I considered it a base prostration of the national character to excite one nation by money to bully another nation out of its property," he declared. He decided that the chief debaser was Madison, Yazoo negotiator and secretary of state: "from that moment . . . my confidence in the principles of the man entertaining those sentiments died, never to live again."

The deal did not go through, for Napoleon just then did not need the money. By December 1805, he had crushed the Austrian empire after a war of only three months and had other resources. Florida would glimmer as a possible prize before Jefferson's and Madison's eyes for years to come.

Even as these maneuvers played out, it became clear that they were a sideshow. The focus of American foreign policy would not be Florida, but Britain. The administration might be most interested in the Gulf Coast, but Britain was most interested in winning a world war against Napoleonic France.

The land phase of that war was being handled—mostly mishandled— by Britain's European allies (varying combinations of Austria, Prussia, and Russia). But the economic phase of the war was being waged at sea—which brought Britain into collision with the United States.

Britain had intermittently claimed a right, going back to the French and Indian War, to stop neutral nations from trading with its enemies in wartime. The so-called Rule of 1756 was not a measure of blockade, but an aspect of mercantilism; its main goal was not to throttle all commerce with the enemy, but to ensure that as much of that commerce as possible would be conducted by Britain. The rule sought to benefit British merchants and employ British seamen, the potential labor pool for the British navy.

In the 1790s, Britain had given the United States a loophole in the rule. American ships were allowed to make broken voyages—carrying cargo between enemy ports in the West Indies and Europe, so long as it was unloaded and reloaded in an American port along the way. Britain assumed that the cost and tedium of these artificial stopovers would cut into American profits, but Americans turned out to be good enough merchants to make a profit all the same, and American trade boomed. British sailors signed on with American vessels by the thousands to claim a share of it.*

In July 1805, Britain changed the rules. An American ship, the *Essex*, had been making a broken voyage between Barcelona and Havana via Salem, Massachusetts, when a British privateer seized it. (Spain's alliance with France made its cargo enemy goods.) A British admiralty judge ruled that the *Essex* was legitimately captured, and his decision closed the American loophole, restoring the Rule of 1756 in its full rigor.

There was no appeal from the *Essex* decision. In October, just as Napoleon was beginning his demolition of Austria, Britain destroyed a Franco-Spanish fleet at the Battle of Trafalgar. The British navy, and the policies it upheld, could not be disputed by any power on earth. Madison tried to challenge the Rule of 1756 nonetheless.

---

* Gallatin guessed 9,000, out of 24,000 sailors on American vessels overall, were British.

He did it first with arguments. In the summer of 1805, Dolley went to Philadelphia to be treated for a lingering knee ailment. (Her specialist had a name out of Smollett—Philip Physick.) Madison accompanied her, with a load of books about the law of nations, and produced a pamphlet, *An Examination of the British Doctrine, Which Subjects to Capture a Neutral Trade. . . .* When printed—the administration gave a copy to every congressman as a kind of briefing paper—it ran more than two hundred pages. Madison began with an ideal. "The progress of the law of nations, under the influence of science and humanity, is mitigating the evils of war, and diminishing the motives to it, by favoring the rights of those remaining at peace," that is, neutrals. He then paraded dozens of quotations, not only from the works of international law theorists—seventeenth- and eighteenth-century jurists and scholars such as Hugo Grotius, Samuel Pufendorf, and Emmerich de Vattel—but also from actual treaties and court decisions, in Britain and elsewhere, showing that the ideal of neutral free trade was being approximated in the world. The Rule of 1756, he concluded, defied this trend; its only possible justification was "*mere superiority of force.*" The *Examination* was an exhausting performance, but it has had its admirers, then and since: John Quincy Adams, John Adams's eldest son, a Federalist senator from Massachusetts, approved it; Henry Adams, the senator's historian grandson, would call it "clear, calm, convincing." But no book by itself could convince those who wielded superior force of the error of their ways. The *Examination* cleared the intellectual ground for an American strategy, but it would have to be supplemented by other measures.

Madison tried diplomacy. He instructed Monroe, back at his regular post in London, to demand a repeal of the Rule of 1756. Madison also told him to make an issue of an old practice: impressment. The British navy was manned by a crude form of conscription: it seized, or impressed, sailors from civilian vessels, and even debtors, paupers, and vagabonds on land. It did more, stopping foreign ships on the high seas, looking for British subjects in their crews. If a sailor could produce American papers, he might be spared—or he might not, depending on the attitude of the officer on the spot, or the navy's needs at the moment. (The practice, naturally, created a brisk business in bogus American papers.)

Impressment was backed by Britain's naval might, and it was accepted as one of the risks of life at sea, along with shipwreck, flogging, and weevils in the biscuits. But when American trade was being stifled, impressment suddenly looked like an additional affront. Madison decided it was unacceptable. In May 1806, he sent a second diplomat to London to reinforce Monroe—an ex-Federalist lawyer from Baltimore, William Pinkney (no relation to the South Carolina Pinckneys).

The British rebuffed them on every point. The most they would offer was an assurance to look into the cases of Americans who were wrongfully impressed, and an agreement to restore the broken-voyage loophole, if the United States would tax the cargoes that were offloaded during the breaks in American ports. Britain would guard the rights of American sailors, and America would enforce British commercial policy. These terms were as bad as anything in Jay's Treaty, but Monroe, like Jay before him, decided that something was better than nothing. Without consulting the president or the secretary of state, he and Pinkney signed at the end of the year.

As Britain and America negotiated, the world situation worsened, and kept worsening after they were done. In November 1806, Napoleon issued the Berlin Decree (he issued it in Berlin because he had just crushed Prussia in a three-week war). No ship that stopped in Britain or its colonies would be permitted to land in France or a French-controlled port. Early in the new year, Britain responded with an Order in Council—a royal proclamation—forbidding neutrals to sail from port to port of Napoleonic Europe. Over the months that followed, Napoleon and George III's ministers issued escalating restrictions until each superpower forbade the United States to trade with the other in any way whatever.

When Jefferson and Madison learned early in 1807 of the treaty that Monroe and Pinkney had signed, they refused even to send it to the Senate.

Its acknowledgment of British power was a betrayal of their view of the world. It made them sick, maybe literally: Jefferson developed a migraine; Madison caught a bad cold. Madison had written his *Examination* and had tried diplomacy. Yet the British would not do the right thing. What more could be done to prod them?

Monroe had asked himself this question as he struggled to produce a treaty in London and he had drawn a painful blank. Britain, he wrote a Virginia friend, would not yield "to a power which had no maritime force." Here, he believed, was where the policy of the administration ran aground. The Federalists had built a small navy during the Adams years and had fought a low-grade war with France after the XYZ affair. But Jefferson and Madison led the party of tax-cutting and peace. However much they might spend for Louisiana or Florida, they had no plans to build more ships, because they had no intention of fighting the great powers—and the great powers knew it.

That did not mean that the great powers would not fight America. In July 1807, an American frigate, the *Chesapeake*, cruising off the Virginia coast, was stopped by a British frigate, the *Leopard*, looking for deserters. (Even sailors of the Royal Navy sometimes jumped to American ships.) When the American commander would not let the British board, they opened fire. Three Americans were killed and eighteen wounded before the *Chesapeake* struck its colors; the British took off four sailors, one to be hanged.

When the United States blazed up at the outrage—John Randolph, for once no angrier than anyone else, proposed to attack Canada and Jamaica—what could it do? The U.S. military was tiny by design. A peace policy was appropriate to a world at peace, as it had been when Jefferson and Madison came into office. But now the world was at war. The submission of the *Chesapeake* seemed like the epitome of Jefferson and Madison's peace policy.

The administration did have one other option, however. At the end of December 1807, Jefferson decided that it was better for the United

States not to trade at all than to have its trade menaced and plundered by Britain and France, and asked Congress to impose an embargo. No American ships would be allowed to leave port for foreign countries. By large majorities and with little debate, Congress agreed.

There was a too-good-for-this-world streak in Jefferson's character that showed itself in many ways, from his mountaintop house, to his dislike of face-to-face argument, to his pride, which also found expression in the embargo. But as a policy, the embargo was Madison's child. He saw it as more than a way of avoiding pain; it was a way to inflict pain on others. All his adult life he had believed in the power of commercial warfare. In the 1780s, one of his arguments for a new constitution was that it would enable the United States to meet foreign slights with "retaliating regulations of trade." The only substantive discussion of embargoes at the Constitutional Convention came from him: they might be "of absolute necessity" in making other countries treat us "equitabl[y]." In the First Congress, he had argued for trade policies that would rebuke Britain and reward France; writing for the *National Gazette* in 1791, he had calculated how many Britons depended on American commerce (such knowledge would help him gauge the force of our rebukes). In 1805, when Spain was being difficult about Florida, his thoughts turned to an embargo: it could "force all the nations having colonies in this quarter of the globe to respect our rights."

As soon as the embargo became law, Madison defended it in a trio of anonymous newspaper essays, which were reprinted nationwide as statements of the administration's position. The embargo would "mak[e] it to the interest of all nations to change the system which has driven our commerce from the ocean." How would that work? "We shall be deprived of market for our superfluities," but "they will feel the want of necessaries." America's virtuous farmers and artisans would outlast Europe's idle rich and wretched poor. The embargo would make us even more virtuous by "forc[ing] frugality" on us. The world would be impressed by our "manly spirit"—"the cheapest of all defenses" against further aggressions. Madison was bringing the puerile rhetoric of his *National Gazette* days to bear on policy.

The only objection to the embargo in the cabinet had come from Gallatin, who recommended going to war instead. An odd recommendation coming from a Treasury secretary, but Gallatin understood the protean power of trade and the stubbornness of buyers and sellers. "Governmental prohibitions do always more mischief than had been calculated," he warned Jefferson, "and it is not without much hesitation that a statesman should try to regulate the concerns of individuals, as if he could do it better than themselves." Madison understood neither war nor trade. But he understood his own ideas of the way the world worked. When the argument for an embargo prevailed, Gallatin went along with his colleagues, despite his reservations.

Once in place, the embargo required ever more severe enforcement. Gallatin explained, "Congress must either vest the executive with the most arbitrary powers . . . or give it up altogether." American ships initially were forbidden from sailing to foreign ports. After ships sailing along the coast pretended to have been blown all the way to Europe, vessels were required to take out licenses and post bonds; if a revenue collector suspected ships of wanting to sneak off, he could seize them without warrants. When trade by water was hampered, goods were smuggled overland to Canada. The area around Lake Champlain was then declared to be in a state of insurrection. The embargo made great strides in strangling American trade: in 1808, exports declined by nearly 80 percent, imports by almost 60 percent. One visitor to New York reported that "grass had begun to grow upon the wharfs." But Britain and France slugged it out as before, and neither offered to treat us better.

Jefferson supported the embargo throughout the grim year of 1808, his last in office. He was making a stand for America's purity, and for peace. But the effort tore him up. Was he appalled by the means he had been driven to use? The party of liberty and light government was behaving more odiously than the Federalists had a decade earlier, although this probably did not bother Jefferson, even unconsciously. The Federalists had restricted free speech, something Jefferson himself engaged in, while the embargo restricted trade, something Jefferson had never done (except to maintain Monticello).

Certainly Jefferson was dismayed by the erosion of his popularity. His enemies said so; even his friends said so (Madison, of all people, told a foreign diplomat that Jefferson's popularity was "dear" to him). He converted his distress into illness, suffering punishing migraines. Madison and Gallatin tried to pull Jefferson out of his tailspin, in vain; he told his allies in November that he would do nothing for the remainder of his term. Since he would soon be only "a spectator," he determined to behave like one.

Madison was made of tougher stuff. Myopia helped. In March 1808, he wrote that the embargo "continues to take deeper root." In May, he saw "the public mind . . . everywhere rallying." In July, he still saw "solid support." In August, Virginia at least seemed "unshaken." Gallatin judged his colleague, the secretary of state, objectively, and not without admiration: "Mr. Madison is, as I always knew him, slow in taking his ground, but firm when the storm arises."

Madison forged on because the embargo was his policy. At the same time, he could ignore criticisms because he was not the national symbol of the policy; Jefferson was. Jefferson was the president. He was only the third president, but already the office had become the crown jewel and the crown of thorns of American politics. As secretary of state, Madison was at the president's right hand, but in his shadow. It may also be that Madison suffered less because he loved popularity (or needed it) less than Jefferson did.

Neither man, in truth, was prepared for the ebb and flow of politics as it had been remade and nationalized by the Constitution. In the 1790s, Jefferson and Madison had been down. But then they had shot up to the heights. Who would have thought they would sink down again?

M adison's job as secretary of state was to handle America's dealings with the world. His job as a politician was to win his next job, the presidency.

The Constitution prescribed no term limits for the president, but Washington had retired voluntarily after two terms and Jefferson had already decided, on the eve of his second inauguration, to follow Washington's example. Madison's chance, therefore, would be in 1808.

In two elections, Jefferson had made good use of a partnership between Virginia and New York Republicans. George Clinton, his second New York running mate, had served as vice president without flamboyance, as intended. Clinton could have the Republican Party's nod for the number-two spot again in 1808, when he would be sixty-nine years old. Madison had to watch the vice president's nephew, DeWitt Clinton, however. The younger man had resigned a seat in the Senate to take the locally more powerful job of mayor of New York. He might push his uncle to run for higher office if he thought there was anything to be gained by it.

The most serious challenge to Madison in his own party, however, came from Monroe. Monroe was the obvious choice for any Republican who was unhappy with the Jefferson administration but did not want to repudiate Jefferson directly. Monroe, like Madison, was a Virginian, a friend and protégé of the party's leader. He too could plausibly claim to be Jefferson's heir, and since he had had fewer responsibilities than Madison, he could claim to be a worthier one. The less tried always carry less baggage.

Unfortunately for Monroe, his greatest champion was John Randolph, who not only damned Madison and all his works but now also attacked Jefferson himself. "I came here," he told the House in April 1806, "prepared to cooperate with the government in all its measures. . . . I found I might cooperate, or be an honest man." So every Republican who would not turn on Jefferson—which is to say, every other Republican—was dishonest.

But Monroe had other admirers besides Randolph. John Beckley, the old fixer, who had gotten a job as congressional librarian, corresponded with him (unsigned, and in the third person, to avoid what Beckley called "accidental miscarriage"). Perhaps he could work his wiles for Monroe's benefit.

Monroe, finally, had the friendship of Thomas Jefferson. Madison had a greater share of it, but Jefferson never liked to cut anyone off. Madison would be wise not to cut Monroe off himself; long-running home-state feuds are always unpleasant. Madison's task was to kill Monroe, but gently, and only for the present election cycle.

Madison also had to give some thought to the Federalists. Not much— Federalism was a sickly plant. Some of its fronds had also become poisonous. In the run-up to the election of 1804, a handful of New England Federalist congressmen, despairing at the Republican electoral lock, had actually discussed taking their states out of the Union. Their leader in rebellion and treason was Massachusetts Senator Timothy Pickering, a veteran of the Revolutionary War and the Federalist cabinets of the 1790s. Pickering was a man of ramrod self-righteousness. He thought that the Republicans threatened America with ruin and the French Revolution threatened the world; to him, the only logical next step was to break up the United States and ally the north with Britain. He was a Federalist John Randolph in arrogance and bad judgment, minus the charm. One potential plotter Pickering reached out to was Aaron Burr, who might be willing to aid any anti-Jefferson effort. The Hamilton/Burr duel ended the outreach, and the effort, but the Federalist die-hards might stir again.

Madison spent the most energy on his Monroe problem. The fact that Monroe was a diplomat, answering to Madison as secretary of state, helped Madison greatly. Sending William Pinkney to London in the spring of 1806 to negotiate with the British alongside Monroe was a shrewd move. Monroe would have recognized it, since he had been in the role of auxiliary helper in 1803, having been sent to Paris to join Robert Livingston. If such a double-headed negotiation succeeded (as

Livingston's and Monroe's had), the new diplomat got the credit. If it failed, both would share the blame. As soon as Pinkney joined him, Monroe was in a lose-lose situation politically. When Jefferson and Madison repudiated the treaty, refusing even to show it to the Senate, Monroe's loss was complete.

In May 1807, Madison wrote Monroe, breaking the news of the treaty's fate. The tone of Madison's letter is hard to judge. "It has been a painful task with the president to withhold from the joint work of yourself and Mr. Pinkney the sanction which was expected, as it has been to me to communicate the event." Read one way, it exemplifies the courtesy of a Virginia gentleman, giving bad news with a bow. Read another way, it is the victory dance of a favored son: *Jefferson shares my pain, but he also shares my decision.* Only the future could show which of the two possible meanings Madison and Monroe would draw from this episode.

Madison benefited from the help of his many allies. (The builder of the Republican Party well knew that one must never be in the position of having to do everything oneself.) Two Virginia congressmen with family ties to the administration—John G. Jackson, a brother-in-law of Dolley Madison's, and Thomas Mann Randolph, a son-in-law of Jefferson's—fought John Randolph on the House floor with his own weapons, giving him insult for insult.

Dolley herself spoke slightingly of Monroe in private. Randolph returned that blow by making insinuations about Dolley. She was no Elizabeth Bonaparte, but her charms and her fashion sense were always grist for those whose minds were in the gutter. Madison's marriage, Randolph wrote Monroe, was "unfortunate," then added, "I can pursue this subject no farther. It is at once too delicate and too mortifying."

But it was Dolley's skill as a hostess that helped her husband most. Besides the administration and the diplomatic corps, Washington's tiny social scene consisted mostly of congressmen. And congressmen were the constituency that Madison needed most to cultivate, for they were the gatekeepers of the process. Party candidates for the two previous presidential elections had been picked by each party's congressional delegation, meeting in a caucus. Dolley's dinner guests were thus the electorate that would decide on Madison's nomination. All the dinner parties in the world could not have boosted a nobody, but Dolley's did their bit to lift her already-prominent husband. Samuel Mitchill, Republican senator from New York, noted that the Madisons' entertaining made an effective contrast with George Clinton's loneliness and isolation. Madison "gives dinners and makes generous display to the members" of Congress, while Clinton, who was a widower, "lives snug at his lodgings and keeps aloof." Madison had "a wife to aid in his pretensions"; Clinton had no "female succor." And so "Mr. M is going greatly ahead of him."

Madison's most important ally, apart from Jefferson, was Gallatin. Despite his specialized expertise and his foreign birth, Gallatin had his own network of friends in the Republican Party, not all of them in Madison's camp: he had even been close, eight years earlier, with Aaron Burr. He had reservations about Madison's love child, the embargo. Yet Gallatin admired Madison's intelligence, earnestness, and public spirit. He had, as he later wrote, a "personal attachment to Mr. Madison . . . of old standing, I am sure reciprocal, and strengthened from greater intimacy." He could have made trouble for his colleague; instead he stood silently in his corner. Cultivating Gallatin's loyalty had been one of Madison's wisest tactics.

Republicans held several caucuses in January 1808. More than a hundred members of the Virginia legislature met in Richmond to nominate a slate of presidential electors pledged to Madison. Monroe's supporters, meeting separately to pick their own slate, were only half as numerous. In Washington, three-fifths of the Republican congressional delegation—almost ninety senators and congressmen—met and endorsed a ticket of Madison and George Clinton (they were joined by Sen. John Quincy Adams, increasingly unhappy with Federalist extremism). The sixty no-shows did nothing, except for a dozen irreconcilables led by John Randolph, who issued an angry blast: "We ask for energy, and we are told of [Madison's] moderation. We ask for talents, and the reply is his unassuming merit. We ask what were his services in the cause of public liberty, and we are directed to the pages of the *Federalist*." In Randolph's mental universe, the *Federalist* papers were a devil's dictionary. If Beckley had not died in 1807, perhaps Monroe might have made a stronger showing.

Madison's caucus victories were substantial, though not overwhelming. The pockets of Republican resistance to him were symptoms of unease with Jefferson, after seven years—and unease with Madison, for not being the Jefferson of everyone's dreams. Madison was lucky that the caucuses came when they did—so early in 1808, the embargo had not begun to bite. Once it did, it would be a problem for him, but not a fatal one unless some rival took advantage of it. Madison was even luckier in his opposition. Monroe, who had returned to the United States, his diplomacy done, was being touted as the icon of lost Republican purity. The Clintons were opportunistic New Yorkers. The Federalists had a closet full of maniacs. It would have taken genius and selflessness to meld these disparate factions into a united anti-Madison campaign, and these qualities were lacking.

In the summer, the Federalists renominated their slate from four years earlier, Charles Coatesworth Pinckney and Rufus King. They were not wild men, but they were also not exciting. When the states chose their electors, Pinckney and King carried Connecticut, Delaware, and two of Maryland's electoral votes, as they had in 1804. But this time, with the embargo at their backs, they added Massachusetts, New Hampshire, Rhode Island, and three electoral votes from North Carolina. Still, their total was only forty-seven; outside commercial New England, Federalism did not seem to be a serious option.

Madison meanwhile beat down his Republican opposition. Monroe's slate of electors in Virginia lost to Madison's, four to one, leaving Monroe empty-handed. George Clinton was in the odd position of running both for vice president and, in his home state, as favorite-son candidate for president. Clinton's halfheartedness crippled him; if he was not going all out, why should New Yorkers go all out for him? He won only six of New York's nineteen presidential electoral votes. Madison was the heir apparent, a known quantity, and one man, not three. He won 122 electoral votes, and the White House.

Before Madison took the oath of office, the fate of the embargo had to be decided, and the decision was not in his hands. The embargo's enemies did not need to unite behind a common candidate to oppose it; all they needed were their own votes in Congress. In February 1809, Republicans weary of the embargo joined Federalists in voting that it should end on March 4—Jefferson's last day in office. In their home states, New England Federalists were even more decisive; the governor of Connecticut, borrowing a word from Madison's Virginia Resolutions, declared that states must "interpose" between the people and a usurping national government. Jefferson signed the bill repealing the embargo, attended the inauguration of his protégé, then retired "to my family, my friends, my farms, and books."

Madison had won the highest office in the system he had helped create, following in the footsteps of Washington, the man he most admired, and Jefferson, the man he most loved. He faced a small but angry opposition, a divided party, and a world war.

CHAPTER NINE

President

Washington was a little more built up for James Madison's first inauguration than it had been for Thomas Jefferson's. In March 1801, only the north or Senate wing of the Capitol had been completed, and that was where Jefferson had taken the oath and made his maiden address. Madison spoke in the new House chamber in the south wing.

His short speech, seven paragraphs long, began by admitting that the country faced "difficulties" but denied that the last administration had done anything to bring them on. The United States, he said, had "cultivate[d] peace by observing justice. . . . If there be candor in the world," the world would recognize it. Some doubt about the world's candor made him add that "posterity at least" would recognize it.

He put his trust in his "purposes" and "principles," the main ones being neutrality, support of the Constitution, economy, and a limited military. He looked for additional help from his fellow Americans, his fellow politicians, and the Almighty. Madison's mild speech was a holding operation, promising more of the same from him and hoping for better from the world. He evidently spoke better than he often did, for a spectator in the gallery wrote that he was audible there.

The day ended with an inaugural ball at a hotel off Pennsylvania Avenue on Capitol Hill, where the Library of Congress now stands. Dolley Madison shone, but by then the president looked "woebegone."

It was all right if Madison looked woebegone; it was his wife's job to shine, and early in the term she set about constructing a proper stage. As her set designer, she enlisted Benjamin Henry Latrobe, an English-born architect who had moved to the United States in the 1790s. Latrobe knew Jefferson and had helped him finish the White House. But Mrs. Madison wanted to use it for more than intimate dinners. She and Latrobe planned a parlor and a drawing room for large functions.

Client and designer soon quarreled: Latrobe fretted about Mrs. Madison's taste in curtains (crimson velvet). Descriptions of her color schemes and her props—a piano, a parrot, a guitar—suggest early signs of nineteenth-century clutter and surfeit; Empire, Biedermeier, and Victorian were looming over the horizon, ready to sweep in and stifle. But Dolley Madison knew her own tastes, and those of her audience. White House guests responded to her extroversion and her glamour. Washington Irving, an observant, young out-of-towner, described a visit to her White House. "I emerged from dirt and darkness into the blazing splendor of Mrs. Madison's drawing room. Here I was most graciously received— found a crowded collection of great and little men, of ugly old women, and beautiful young ones. . . . Mrs. Madison is a fine, portly, buxom dame—who has a smile and pleasant word for everybody." The president, however, made a bad impression. "Ah! poor Jemmy! He is but a withered little apple-John" (an apple-john was an apple left in storage too long). Should Dolley have toned it down to make Jemmy look better? No; you have to play the cards you hold, and bluff the rest.

Madison had more trouble furnishing his administration. He wanted to move Albert Gallatin from the Treasury to fill his own shoes as secretary of state. Managing America's foreign policy problems would be the focus of his efforts, and he wanted the help of the Republican Party's best mind, besides his own and Jefferson's.

The Senate, however, balked—not just its Federalists, who were too few to block anything all by themselves, but members of Madison's own party. Now that Madison was president, the role of lightning rod passed to Gallatin. Intelligent and honest, and a sharp-eyed deficit hawk, the Treasury secretary had made enemies in Congress.

Making Gallatin secretary of state also raised a serious question of patronage. Most Republicans had rallied to Madison to elect him over Monroe, Clinton, and Pinckney. Now wasn't each member of the winning team as entitled as any other to the fruits of success?

Virginia's senior senator, William Branch Giles, wanted to be secretary of state himself. He had been a member of the House or Senate almost continuously since 1790. He had the opinions of his great Virginia colleagues, without any of their abilities. Another senator, Samuel Smith of Maryland, wanted the State Department for his brother Robert, Jefferson's secretary of the navy. John Randolph, reduced by his rebelliousness to the role of angry scold, wrote that Robert Smith would be a better choice than Giles, since "he can spell."

Giles and Samuel Smith were the core of a Senate faction, all Republicans, but more devoted to their own power and perks than to party loyalty. A third member was Michael Leib of Pennsylvania, an early urban machine politician who represented Philadelphia's German and Irish immigrants, and who was backed by *Aurora* editor William Duane. Today such congressmen are called Old Bulls; Giles, Smith, and Leib were known as "the Invisibles." The Invisibles were visible enough to Madison, who saw their potential for intraparty strife if he challenged them openly.

Madison tried to co-opt Senator Smith by offering to make brother Robert Treasury secretary, as a trade-off for letting Gallatin go to State. But this move was nixed by Gallatin. If Robert Smith went to Treasury, Gallatin knew he would have to do Smith's work as well as his own. Gallatin was a good soldier, who would do whatever job he was assigned. But he wanted to do only one. Madison finally let Robert Smith have the State Department, knowing that the man who would then have to do Smith's work would be himself.

Moving Smith left a vacancy in the Navy Department; there was another in the War Department, which Jefferson's secretary, Henry Dearborn, was leaving. For Navy, Madison tapped Paul Hamilton, a South Carolina planter and politician; War went to William Eustis, a Massachusetts doctor who had been an army surgeon during the Revolution and had served two terms in Congress. The military departments had not seemed serious in peacetime, eight years ago, but that time was long gone. Hamilton and Eustis provided sectional balance, south and north, and were good Republicans. Otherwise, they seemed like nonentities. They would actually be much worse.

As president, Madison was able to resolve one problem that had frustrated him as secretary of state. After years of vainly arguing that the Florida Panhandle had already been sold to the United States along with Louisiana, or vainly urging France to make Spain surrender it, in 1810 he simply took half of it. In the summer, American settlers had stormed a Spanish fort in Baton Rouge on the east bank of the Mississippi, eighty miles upriver from New Orleans. In October, Madison told the governor of the Louisiana Territory to send in the army, which he did, as far east as Mobile. The deed was done by presidential proclamation, without troubling Congress, and it showed, as the Louisiana Purchase had shown on a grander scale, that Republican presidents could act swiftly, decisively, and even extralegally when their foreign policy interests were clear.

Britain and its war with France were Madison's most obdurate problems. The war between the superpowers, which had lasted more than fifteen years with only a brief break, was truly a battle to the death. Britain ruled the waves; France dominated the continent. But Britain believed it had found a vein: Spain had revolted in 1808 against French overlordship, and Britain had put an army on the peninsula to exploit the opportunity. Neither belligerent was likely to have much concern left over for the United States.

And yet Madison was greeted by a windfall just weeks into his presidency. Congress, in ending the embargo, had replaced it with a Non-Intercourse Act, which banned trade with Britain, France, and their colonies but allowed it with neutral nations. Everyone understood that trans-shipment and subterfuge would allow covert trade with belligerents; Congress had exchanged masochistic pride for profitable dishonesty.

Now, in the spring of 1809, David Erskine, the British minister in Washington,* offered to reopen trade with Britain freely and publicly. Britain, he told Robert Smith, would repeal its Orders in Council and restore the seamen taken off the *Chesapeake* (minus the one who had been hanged). Britain would even wink at American broken voyages, so long as direct trade with France and its empire were forbidden. In return, Smith (coached all the while by Madison) assured him verbally that the Non-Intercourse Act would remain in force against France. Both sides were satisfied, and in June the Atlantic was flooded with American ships bound for British ports.

In July, Madison went to Montpelier for the summer—where he learned it was all a mistake. Erskine, wanting an agreement as a trophy for himself, had exceeded his instructions. His superiors in London required the ban on French trade to be an explicit part of an Anglo-American rapprochement, not a gentleman's agreement, and they insisted on a strict interpretation of the Rule of 1756. Since the United States had not accepted these conditions, Britain's trade restrictions remained in force. The situation returned to the status quo ante—except that relations between the two countries were chillier for the false thaw. Madison cut short his vacation and returned to Washington, complaining to Jefferson of Britain's "fraud and folly."

Late in the summer of 1809, London sent a new minister, Francis James Jackson, who was not calculated to patch things up. Jackson had shown how he treated neutral nations two years earlier when he served

---

* He had replaced Anthony Merry in 1806.

as the diplomat accompanying a British expeditionary force assigned to capture Denmark's navy, lest it fall into Napoleon's hands. After the Danes rejected Jackson's demands for their fleet, the British bombarded Copenhagen, killing several hundred civilians, until the ships were handed over. Jackson brought no fleet with him to Washington, but he did bring his own temperament and his wife. Jackson found Madison to be "a plain and rather mean-looking little man" and his government "a mob" with "mob leaders." His wife, a German baroness, called Dolley "*une bonne, grosse femme, de la classe bourgeoise*" (a pretty, fat woman of the bourgeoisie). After some unprofitable diplomatic skirmishes, the Jacksons decamped to Baltimore, then New York and Boston. Even away from Washington, Mrs. Jackson still suffered "detestable" food and "indifferent" Madeira.

London's repudiation of Erskine and the Jacksons' arrogance in America helped Madison politically: a swell of Anglophobia boosted Republican fortunes in states where they had suffered from the embargo.

But reacting to British feints and moods was one thing. Madison and Congress had to create an American policy of their own. In the spring of 1810, Congress produced a bill named after Nathaniel Macon, a North Carolina Republican, which opened trade to both Britain and France. If either country should then repeal its restrictive decrees, then the United States would ban trade with the other in three months, unless it too abandoned its restrictions. With Macon's bill the Republican doctrine of strength through trade sunk to the depths of feebleness. The United States would submit to the blows of both bullies and stand up to the one who stopped hitting us last.

Madison still yearned for an embargo. "Too late," he wrote Jefferson, Americans would see its "expediency and efficacy." But surprisingly, in August Napoleon appeared to accept America's offer. His foreign minister, the Duke of Cadore, sent a letter to John Armstrong, the American minister in Paris, announcing that the Berlin Decree and other French restrictions were revoked. Napoleon, Cadore added, "loves the Americans." Madison accepted France's revocations in November.

For all Napoleon's love, Cadore's letter contained an escape clause: it was "understood," he wrote, that Britain would also drop its Orders in Council. Since that had not yet happened, France could continue to seize as many American ships as it liked ("we commit ourselves to nothing," Napoleon said privately). Erskine had offered friendship, then Britain had taken it back. France had nothing to take back since Cadore's offer of friendship was false in the first place. Some Americans saw the flaw. John Randolph, like a stopped clock, was occasionally right, and he blasted the Franco-American truce. "It is a bargain which credulity and imbecility enter into with cunning and power."

It was all these things, but it also served, like the invasion of western Florida, at long last to fulfill one of Madison's goals. It untangled (nominally, if not actually) our relations with France, and it put on Britain the onus of untangling ours with her. Unless Britain acted, we would impose non-intercourse in March 1811. Slowly, almost unconsciously, and by sideways motions, Madison was leading America to a break with Britain. When in doubt, he could always fall back on Anglophobia. It was Madison's natural equilibrium point.

March 1811 would be the midpoint of Madison's term, and he marked it with a cabinet reshuffle that displayed his abilities both as a politician and as an executive.

He brought James Monroe back into the fold, the culmination of a long wooing. For a year, the defeated presidential candidate had kept to his tent. Jefferson, offstage, labored to bring his two protégés together. In the spring of 1810, Monroe visited Washington, where Madison received him "with great kindness. . . . Indeed," Monroe wrote, "I had proofs of kindness from everyone." The Madisons returned the visit to Highland, Monroe's new home in Albemarle County, near Monticello.

Once kindness had resumed, face had to be saved. By the spring of 1811, Madison assured Monroe that their differences were such as political gentlemen could negotiate. "Differences of opinion must always be looked for even among those most agreed on the same general views," the president wrote him. "These differences, however, lie fairly within the compass of free consultation and mutual concession." So the man whose treaty had been rejected and the man who had rejected it could work together.

The most important offer Madison could make did not have to be stated. If Monroe became his ally again, Monroe could also be his heir— the next Virginian in line for the White House. (Jefferson was eight years older than Madison, and Madison was seven years older than Monroe; their spacing was perfect.) So the Virginia Dynasty was born. One Virginia Republican in the White House was an event; two made a partnership. The prospect of three was like a royal act of succession. Virginia Republicans, with the persistence of cicadas, accused Federalists of yearning for monarchy, but they had established the elective equivalent. As soon as John Randolph saw what was happening, he dropped Monroe forever, consigning him along with Jefferson and Madison to the ranks of the damned. But he was a crank and an outlier. The Virginia Dynasty arranged the future and solidified Madison's home-state base.

Monroe's presidency was still two or six years away. In the meantime, he needed some tangible mark of his status as heir apparent—and Madison needed his help. As Madison closed the deal with Monroe, he made a vacancy for him in his cabinet by dismissing Robert Smith.

After two years of working with Smith, Madison's proximate complaints against his secretary of state were disunity and indiscretion. Smith disagreed with administration policy, and told people about it. He had passed diplomatic news to Federalists in Congress (Smith's brother, Samuel the senator, represented Baltimore's merchants, and they, like the Federalists, had cause to complain about the administration's fluctuating trade policies). He had even criticized America's reaction to the Cadore letter to a British diplomat (the Smith brothers could marry a niece to a Bonaparte and sympathize with Britain at the same time). Madison confronted Robert Smith with these betrayals during a meeting in March, telling him that "a remedy had become essential." To soften the blow of dismissal from the State Department, Madison offered to make Smith minister to Russia. Smith asked whether he could be sent to Britain or the Supreme Court instead, but when Madison held firm, he seemed willing to go to St. Petersburg.

Madison's meeting with Smith revealed as much about the president, however, as it did about his soon-to-be former secretary. In a memo to himself, Madison wrote a detailed account, in which he comes off as both timid and snide. He pulled the bandage off so slowly, it caused maximum irritation. He hid his criticisms behind passive constructions—"it had long been felt and had at length become notorious," "it was well understood," "it was no secret"—then suddenly raked Smith, telling him his diplomatic letters were "so crude and inadequate that I was . . . generally obliged to write them anew myself." Madison indulged in self-pity: he had given "constant aids . . . in discharging [Smith's] duties," he had "labor[ed]" for Smith's "credit," Smith's business had been "thrown . . . into my hands." Madison's real reason for firing Smith seemed to be his accumulated anger at covering for a man unsuited to the job in which he had put and kept him. And now he was going to foist that man on the czar.

Before Madison, two presidents had lost their secretaries of state. It was never pretty. During the debate over Jay's Treaty, George Washington suspected that Edmund Randolph had been dealing secretly with the French; when he demanded an explanation, Randolph quit. After John Adams decided to repair relations with France, he fired Timothy Pickering, and Secretary of War James McHenry for good measure (he had been unhappy with both men for years). Washington handled his problem clumsily, but he handled it quickly and, except for one private exclamation of ill temper, made no comment on it. Adams fired McHenry face-to-face in a tantrum that was like a fireworks display (Pickering got a letter). Madison expressed his temper differently than Adams did— steaming and sulking rather than fulminating. But he behaved more like Adams than like Washington—more like the man he disdained than the man he worshipped.

Why had he carried Smith on his back for two years? So as not to provoke a fight in his own party in the Senate. (Robert Smith was never an
individual, but a political Siamese twin, linked to Samuel.) But why had
party peace been Madison's top priority? Madison was a keen politician,
but the politics he knew best was that of legislatures, committees, and
party councils. Madison the legislator and party leader was a coalition
builder, and every coalition that is big enough to rule includes its share
of fools, incompetents, and troublemakers. They each have a vote, and
you need every vote to win. Executives, by contrast, are focused on the
tasks at hand. Dead Hamilton had explained it in *The Federalist*: "Energy
in the executive is the leading character in the definition of good government." To executives the weight of unsatisfactory associates is not a
trade-off but a dead loss, to be jettisoned as soon as possible. The very
qualities that enabled Madison to bring Monroe back—pliancy, a little
saving hypocrisy—allowed him to haul Smith along for two weary years.

After a week of thinking about St. Petersburg, Smith told Madison
that he would not go there after all. The Russian mission, he said, was "a
mere expedient to get rid of him." He threatened Madison with the wrath
of his friends and left the White House and the administration. Monroe
immediately took his place. In June, Smith published an attack on Madison and a defense of himself. It made a scandal, then a fizzle, as such
things usually do; we can be titillated by losers and what they reveal, but
no one really likes them. Madison did not reply but fed dirt to allies who
cut Smith up for him. So Madison won even that round, though the bad
habits—passivity, too much focus on intraparty dynamics—that had produced the situation in the first place remained.

While Monroe was coming and Smith was going, Congress
wrapped up a session. (Lame-duck Congresses then sat until
March of odd-numbered years; barring special sessions, their successors
did not meet until after the spring/summer recess.) Having accepted the
Cadore letter in the fall of 1810, Congress had given Britain three months

to repeal its Orders in Council. When this was not done, it voted, in February 1811, to impose non-intercourse. This was a step toward war.

At the same time, Congress took a step that would make war difficult to fight, by allowing the Bank of the United States to lapse. Its twenty-year charter would expire at the start of March 1811. Two decades earlier, Madison had fought the Bank in the House and in an appeal to Washington, challenging its constitutionality.

But Gallatin, however much he disagreed with Federalist economic policies, found the Bank a useful and efficient instrument. When he first took over the Treasury Department, he had been asked by Jefferson to look for evidence of Hamilton's financial shenanigans (Jefferson was certain that Hamilton was a crook as well as a monarchist). Instead Gallatin reported, "I have found the most perfect system ever formed." Gallatin now lobbied Congress hard to charter the Bank for another twenty years. He needed to lobby: Giles, Smith, and Leib were against re-charter, partly to boost smaller banks in their home states and partly to spite Gallatin, and other Republicans would be reluctant to overturn a historic position of their party.

Where was Madison? He had come around to Gallatin's position. When Madison was an old man, he wrote that the constitutionality of the Bank had been settled by its long existence: two decades of operation, "under the varied ascendancy of parties"—both Federalists and Republicans—"amount[ed] to the requisite evidence of the national judgment and intention." He had thought the Bank was unconstitutional in 1791 and throughout the decade, up to the Virginia Resolutions. But Congress and the country had accepted it all that time, and then the triumphant Jeffersonians had continued to accept it after 1801. This was enough to "overrule individual opinions." Madison's opinion in 1791 had been plausible, maybe even correct, but (like several of his arguments at the Constitutional Convention) it had lost out.

Madison was not willing to defend the Bank in 1811 when it counted, however, so Gallatin had to lead the fight himself. Years later, Gallatin wrote that Madison "made his opinion known" that the Bank was constitutional.

But he did not make it known forcefully, and even though presidents did not then lead as conspicuously as they do now, they could give clear indications of what they thought, when necessary. Madison's reticence left a confusing void. His 1791 arguments against the Bank were reprinted in newspapers; a rumor even started that, having changed his mind once, he had changed back and opposed the Bank again. Madison never explained why he remained aloof in 1811, so one must guess his reasons. The best guess is that he did not wish to seem inconsistent. But politicians change their minds. Not, one hopes, constantly, nor for light or corrupt reasons, nor (except in remarkable circumstances) on bedrock issues. But politicians do change their minds, and when they do they have to say why, or at least say so. If they do not, they cannot expect others to follow them.

The vote on the Bank was as close as it could be. The House voted to postpone action, waiting on the Senate. The Senate split, 17–17 (7 Republicans and 10 Federalists for re-charter, 17 Republicans against). Vice President George Clinton, acting as presiding officer, broke the tie with a nay, on constitutional grounds: "the power to create corporations is not expressly granted." Madison's old arguments defeated the Madison administration. He had failed as an executor of policy, as well as an executive leader of men.

The new Congress that met in the fall of 1811 was the Twelfth, and it was the first in American history that was not dominated by founders, or by junior partners still in their thrall. Its leaders were a cadre of new members, Republicans all, who were both young and self-assertive. The two destined to be most famous were Rep. Henry Clay of Kentucky and Rep. John C. Calhoun of South Carolina. At age thirty-four, Clay had already served the stubs of two Senate terms left incomplete by resignations. On his first day in the House, which was the first day the new House met, he was elected Speaker. Clay put twenty-nine-year-old Calhoun on the Foreign Relations Committee.

In a Senate speech the year before, Clay had announced the arrival of a new cohort. The key sentences were a painfully honest mix of inter-generational admiration, dismissal, and yearning. "The withered arm and wrinkled brow of the illustrious founders of our freedom are melancholy indications that they will shortly be removed from us. . . . We shall want the presence and living example of a new race of heroes to supply their places, and to animate us to preserve inviolate what they achieved."

In 1811, President Madison, illustrious founder, turned sixty. Clay and his peers were not scrambling for office like the Smiths, or squabbling over who was more Jeffersonian than Jefferson like Randolph; while pro-fessing all honor to their predecessors, they claimed the right to rule be-cause they were more alive. Madison and the Twelfth Congress might want the same things, but they would want them in a different tone of voice. Clay asserted his rule over the House by packing its committees with like-minded junior members, such as Calhoun, and by enforcing discipline: when Randolph brought his dogs with him to the House chamber, one of his little quirks, Clay had the doorkeeper remove them.

Just because the Twelfth Congress was more spirited did not mean it yet knew how to conduct the nation's business. Congress voted to in-crease the army and outfit the navy. They deferred tax increases, however, until war was actually declared. The government's three sources of rev-enue were loans, tariffs, and taxes. Loans would become more difficult in the absence of a Bank of the United States; non-intercourse and war would slash tariff receipts; and the Republicans were historically the party of low taxes. Congress was stripping for a fight, while tying an arm be-hind its back.

Meanwhile, Madison and Secretary of State Monroe did their best to rouse the country's fighting spirit. At the beginning of 1812, they got an unusual opportunity. Elbridge Gerry, another illustrious founder who was now Republican governor of Massachusetts, had met an Irishman, John Henry, and a Frenchman, Count Edward de Crillon. Henry said that he had been traveling for some years in New England, sending ac-counts of Federalist disaffection to the governor general of Canada. He was now unhappy with his British paymasters, and he and his friend Crillon were willing to sell the correspondence to America. Gerry wrote a letter of introduction to Madison, and the two went to Washington, where Monroe bought the letters for $50,000. In early March, Madison sent them to Congress.

He hoped to show the British and Federalists scheming together, but the Henry letters backfired. It turned out, on closer examination, that none of Henry's New England informants had known that he was a British agent or had entered into actual treasonous plots. Meanwhile, the American minister to France informed Madison that no such person as Edward de Crillon existed. "Crillon" was in fact a con man. By the time his identity was exposed, he had already left America to serve, he said, in the French invasion of Russia.

And yet the Henry letters referred to a truth: Federalists, in New England particularly, were disaffected. Timothy Pickering, leader of the abortive 1804 secession plot, had lost his Senate seat in 1811 when Republicans captured the Massachusetts legislature, but New England Federalists still held him in honor. They hated France under Napoleon as much as they had hated her under the guillotine; in their eyes Britain was the only bulwark against her, while Madison was France's dupe. One day he believed the Cadore letter, the next he believed the Count de Crillon. If he led America into war, he might reawaken Federalist patriotism, but he might equally drive Federalists to madness.

Madison's foreign policy toward Britain came to the crisis point as spring turned to summer. For decades, he had tried to discipline Britain with commercial restrictions, including the embargo. As president he had threatened to impose commercial restrictions again. Napoleon professed to yield to his threats; Britain held firm. Non-intercourse had come a year ago, but Britain still would not rescind its Orders in Council.

So on June 1, 1812, Madison sent a war message to Congress, listing American grievances against Britain. He led with impressment—"violating the American flag on the great highway of nations." The body of his message concerned "the complicated and transcendent injustice" of the Orders in Council. He would not let go of John Henry—"a secret agent . . . employed in intrigues" (people become attached to their inside information, even if it is worthless). He ended with a grievance, sometimes lost in the political maneuverings on the East Coast and the diplomatic maneuverings between Washington, London, and Paris, but vivid to Americans on the frontier—"warfare just renewed by the savages."

For the last seven years, two Shawnees, Tenskatawa and Tecumseh, had led an Indian revival in what is now the Midwest. Tenskatawa was a self-proclaimed prophet who preached temperance and offered immunity to white men's bullets. His twin brother, Tecumseh, was a statesman who sought alliances with the Indians of the Yazoo country, and the British in Canada. Jefferson had pushed America's borders to the Rockies; a hostile Indian alliance backed by Britain might shove them back to Ohio and Georgia. In November 1811, the governor of the Indiana Territory, William Henry Harrison, had captured the brothers' headquarters, a settlement on Tippecanoe Creek, and burned it down, though the brothers remained at large. Attacking Canada could cut the Anglo-Indian connection; conquering Canada might be a bargaining chip in resolving maritime issues.

Behind Madison's stated reasons for war loomed a larger one: national self-respect. Britain's provocations could be explained away, sometimes plausibly; America had committed follies of its own, showing meekness when it should have been firm, or firmness (like the embargo) that did no good. Yet the sum of it all was that Britain, fighting for its own survival, ignored and bullied America, and enough Americans could no longer tolerate it.

Barely enough. After two and a half weeks of debate, mostly in the Senate, Congress voted, 74–49 in the House and 19–13 in the Senate,

for war. The split was partisan—every Federalist in both houses, 39 men
in all, voted nay. It was also regional—Federalists were concentrated in
the commercial and maritime northeast, and were joined in their nays
by a number of their Republican neighbors. In the Senate, where the
vote was closest, war squeaked through with the support of the Invisibles,
who chose to back Madison on this issue. It stands as the narrowest vote
to declare war in American history.

Madison signed Congress's bill and visited the Departments of War
and of the Navy the same day. Richard Rush, comptroller of the Treasury,
described him as "stimulating everything in a manner worthy of a little
commander-in-chief, with his little round hat and huge cockade!"

Europe had been soaked in blood for twenty years, but there had been
no major battles in America since Yorktown. The army had fought Indians,
and the militia had rounded up whiskey rebels. When it came to the arts
of war, America was out of practice. Winfield Scott, a young lieutenant
colonel in 1812, would remember the army thus: "The old officers"—
Revolutionary War veterans—"had, very generally, sunk into either sloth,
ignorance, or habits of intemperate drinking." Newer officers were "coarse
and ignorant men . . . swaggerers, dependants, decayed gentlemen, and
others 'fit for nothing else.' . . . How infinitely unwise, then, in a republic
to trust its safety and honor in battles . . . to imbeciles and ignoramuses!"

There was no chance of improvement under the secretaries Madison
had appointed in 1809. William Eustis had eleven clerks to help him at
the War Department, a large staff for those days, but all of them were
inexperienced; Congress had blocked a proposal to give him two assistant
secretaries of war. The former army doctor was overwhelmed by his duties. He "consumed his time," one senator complained to Monroe, "in
reading advertisements . . . to find where he may purchase one hundred
shoes or two hundred hats." The Navy Department was in better shape—
luckily, for Paul Hamilton was a drunk who stopped working at noon.
Madison liked Eustis and Hamilton personally and they were loyal foot
soldiers of the administration: both secretaries had turned on Robert

Smith after he had turned on Madison. The only problem with them was that they could not do their jobs.

It is possible that Madison believed the war would be short, even negligible. Britain was deeply committed in Europe; its army had been fighting the French in Portugal and Spain for four years. Napoleon crossed the Neman River into Russia a week after America declared war. In the midst of these cataclysms, could Britain afford to fight a new war across the Atlantic? "It was a fair calculation," wrote Madison years later, with the cold-bloodedness of age, that she could not.

Certainly Madison put out peace feelers almost immediately, outlining America's terms to the British minister in Washington himself, and writing the American chargé d'affaires in London authorizing negotiations for an armistice.

In fact, Britain had already made a significant concession. In May, Spencer Perceval, the prime minister, had been assassinated by a madman; a new government had been formed; and on June 16 the Orders in Council were repealed. In Washington, Congress was still debating whether to go to war, but in the days of transatlantic communication by sailing ship, the news from London would not arrive until after the debate was done. Would the news have made any difference? The countries were at loggerheads; Madison had put impressment at the top of America's list of grievances, and Britain would not abandon that, too.

The first casualties of the war were Americans. Maryland was a politically divided state, splitting its electoral votes in every contested presidential election between Republicans and Federalists. Baltimore, its largest city, was a boom town with a rough immigrant underclass. In late June, a mob demolished the office of the *Federal Republican*, an antiwar Federalist newspaper in Baltimore (one of the publishers was James Wagner, Madison's old clerk from the State Department). A month later, the newspaper's supporters armed themselves and gathered in another building, brought out another issue, and battled a second mob. This time the local authorities called out the cavalry, which took the Federalists to jail for their own protection, but the mob broke in, hauled them outside, and tortured them for hours, beating them, stabbing them, and scorching them with hot wax, to test whether they were still alive. The Federalists had killed one rioter. The mob tortured one Federalist to death; another— Henry Lee, one of George Washington's cavalry officers—was crippled for life.

It is a credit to Madison's consistency that he would refuse Republican calls for a sedition law throughout the war. They came not just from party hacks, but from top legal minds as well: William Pinkney the diplomat, whom Madison had made attorney general, and Joseph Story, a congressman he had put on the Supreme Court. His reaction to mob law was less creditable. When the Federalist editors tried to mail copies of their newspaper into Baltimore, Madison refused to protect the post office. The Baltimore City Council published a report whitewashing the violence; Madison welcomed the report as a "seasonable antidote" to attacks on "the friends of true liberty."

Madison defended rights that he practiced (freedom of speech) when they were attacked by means he understood (laws). His attitude toward private-sector political violence was more laissez-faire, perhaps because it was so foreign to his nature; perhaps because in a wild town like Baltimore it was inevitable that a party would have its own outlaws. Republicanism ran in a great chain from philosophers on down. The Baltimore mob was the lowest link.

At the beginning of the war, America's military strategy was to attack the British in Canada. Jefferson, playing mountaintop strategist, wrote that conquering Canada all the way to Quebec would be "a mere matter of marching"; the British naval base in Halifax, Nova Scotia, could be scooped up the next year.

But American arms failed at all points. William Hull, a fifty-nine-year-old Revolutionary War veteran, was put in command at Detroit. His fault from Winfield Scott's list was sloth, with a dash of fear. In the summer he ventured into Upper Canada (now Ontario), pulled back, then surrendered to an inferior British force. Jefferson wrote Madison suggesting that he be shot as a traitor. (A court-martial sentenced Hull to death but spared his life in view of his age.) In October, an American attack across the Niagara frontier failed when the New York militia refused to cross the border.

The only good news came from the ocean: an American frigate, the *Constitution*, captured and sank a British frigate, the *Guerriere*; the American captain was Isaac Hull, nephew of the man who had lost Detroit.

I n the midst of war, Madison stood for reelection. A caucus of Republican congressmen and senators had renominated him in May. Vice President Clinton had died in April, at the age of seventy-two; the caucus tapped the almost equally elderly Elbridge Gerry to run in his place.

George Clinton's passing made his forty-three-year-old nephew, DeWitt, the leader of the family faction, and unlike his uncle the mayor of New York made an all-out run for the White House. Paintings of DeWitt Clinton capture his bifurcated political personality: his high brow suggested his intelligence (suited, unlike Madison's, to executive achievements: in later years he would plan and complete the Erie Canal); his mouth, shut like a leg trap, reflected his monumental arrogance. Clinton's campaign, like the anti-Madison efforts of 1808, was a rallying of malcontents, and the homecoming of James Monroe meant that there were none to be found in Virginia. But Clinton could appeal to Republicans in his own state, now the largest in the Union, and across party lines to Federalists nationally.

Gouverneur Morris, Madison's old colleague at the Constitutional Convention, expressed the mentality of Federalism in his diary; though he found Clinton "an unprincipled fellow who cares for nothing and for nobody but himself," he was "weary of Virginia domination." A secret Federalist convention in New York in September agreed to endorse Clinton without naming him, lest it jinx him. Clinton tapped as his running mate Jared Ingersoll, a Federalist lawyer who had signed the Constitution for Pennsylvania.

Clinton's program was "vigor in war, and a determined character in the relations of peace." Historians scoff at this all-things-to-all-men platform, though it was no more contradictory than Madison's declaring war and sending out peace feelers the same week. Yet Madison could say in his own defense that he was showing the responsible flexibility of an executive; challengers are in no position to make that argument.

Eighteen states voted in the election of 1812 (Louisiana, the southernmost portion of the Louisiana Territory, had gained statehood in April). Madison won one state in New England—Vermont. Every other state there, plus New York, New Jersey, Delaware, and five of Maryland's electors, voted for Clinton. Madison took six votes in Maryland, and all eight states in the west and south. The election was decided by Pennsylvania, which held firm for Madison; even William Duane, his scourge at the *Aurora*, backed him (Duane would be rewarded with a military appointment). Madison won 128 electoral votes to Clinton's 89. If Pennsylvania had gone the other away, Clinton would have won, 114–103. Madison's presidency, and his war, would continue.

CHAPTER TEN

War Leader

J ames Madison had failed his first test as a war leader. He had not put the right people in the right places, and therefore everything had come to grief. So in the gap between his reelection and his reinauguration, he addressed himself to the second test of a war leader: when you fail, try again.

In December 1813, Paul Hamilton and William Eustis quit, and Madison replaced them both with better men. His choice for secretary of the navy was a pure improvement. William Jones, like his predecessor Hamilton, was a Republican politician, having won a congressional seat in Philadelphia by fourteen votes. Unlike Hamilton, Jones had experience of ships and shipping—he had served on a privateer in the Revolution, and he was now a merchant—and he proved to be a capable administrator.

Madison's first idea for replacing Eustis was to make James Monroe, the secretary of state, secretary of war pro tem. In two years Monroe had gone from outsider to indispensable; a Virginian who could take direction and do his job was a godsend. But the concentration of power in one man was unseemly, and sectional balance required Madison to find a northerner to fill the War Department slot permanently. The man he picked was John Armstrong. A Pennsylvanian by birth, Armstrong had married a sister of Robert Livingston's and plunged into the intricacies of New York Republican politics, threading an upward path between Burr and the Clintons. He had spent a few years in the Senate, then served both Jefferson and Madison as minister to France.

Armstrong was an energetic man with military experience. In the Revolution he had fought bravely at the Battle of Princeton and served as an aide to Gen. Horatio Gates. It was while he was at Gates's side that he earned a dark place in history, for he wrote the inflammatory Newburgh appeal to the officer corps, urging them to mutiny if they were not paid. The antimilitarism of the Republican Party left it in the paradoxical position of relying on dubious military characters. They had disdained Washington, Knox, and Hamilton, the founders and champions of the army, for their Federalism. Who did they have instead? Burr and Armstrong. Monroe at least was trustworthy.

Monroe disliked Armstrong as a schemer. The great Virginians thought of anyone whose ambition differed from their own as a schemer—especially if he was a New Yorker. Yet Armstrong, with all his abilities, was indeed prickly, willful, and out for John Armstrong. Madison hoped, as he put it years later, that "a proper mixture of conciliating confidence and interposing control" would keep his new secretary of war in line.

While Madison was regrouping, the larger war of which his was only a sideshow took a bad turn. Napoleon had entered Moscow in September 1812 and evacuated the city a month later; his army was destroyed by desertion and death during the retreat from Russia, and by December he was back in Paris, raising new levies. The only enemy of America's enemy would be fighting for his life in central Europe. America had been unable to invade Canada while the British were preoccupied. What would happen if the time came when they could concentrate on this side of the Atlantic?

Madison's second inaugural address in March 1813 reprised the justifications of his war message: America was fighting for "national sovereignty on the high seas," and against "savages" on the frontier and British scheming with traitors at home ("attempts to disorganize our political

society"). He asked Americans to show "cheerfulness" and said that all
they needed to win was "the discipline and habits" of warfare, which they
were making "daily progress" toward acquiring. Nine months into a war
was a little late for the people or the president to be acquiring good
habits, but better late than never.

T he main political crisis of 1813 was the collapse of Madison's health.
In June, he was prostrated by a bilious fever. Doctors gave him qui-
nine to bring his temperature down, but he was bedridden for weeks.
Rep. Daniel Webster, a young Federalist, wrote that he "did not like
[Madison's] looks any better than his Administration." With Vice President Gerry turning sixty-nine in July, the political class began speculating
who should be president pro tem of the Senate—next in line of succession. Madison rallied and by August was able to travel to Montpelier,
which helped him recover more rapidly, but a major war and the presidency were a double burden on him—and he was the first man in American history to shoulder both simultaneously.

Madison and Armstrong promoted younger officers to higher ranks
in 1813 and focused America's efforts on Lake Erie and Lake Ontario.
Since the Midwest and Upper Canada were mostly wilderness, ships were
the quickest means of moving troops and supplies over long distances. If
America controlled the lakes, it could undo Britain's victory at Detroit
and disrupt its ties with its Indian allies.

Results were mixed on Lake Ontario, where the Americans gained no
decisive advantage but did burn a British base in the town of York, now
Toronto. They also burned the town's public buildings, after discovering
a scalp—presumably American—in one of them, and stole books from
the lending library. York was the capital of Upper Canada; the British
noted its destruction for future reference.

Lake Erie was a different story. In September, a twenty-eight-year-old
naval officer, Oliver Hazard Perry, destroyed a British fleet in an engagement

at the western end of the lake. Perry's report on the battle, "We have met the enemy and they are ours," became a watchword. The victory secured the army's communications and flanks, and the next month William Henry Harrison, marching into Upper Canada, caught the only British force in the region on the Thames River fifty miles east of Detroit and defeated it. Tecumseh was killed, reputedly by Richard Johnson, a Kentucky congressman who led a regiment of mounted riflemen. Johnson's achievement became the chorus of a square dance: *Ripsi, Rantsi, Humpsy, Dumpsy, I Dick Johnson, Killed Tecumseh*. Tecumseh's southern allies were beaten five months later when another frontier fighter, Andrew Jackson of Tennessee, exterminated a band of Creeks in what is now eastern Alabama.

These victories secured the safety of the frontier, but Madison's other war aims were as remote as ever. Operations sputtered along the Niagara and St. Lawrence Rivers; America could raid Canada, not conquer it. American ships won more duels against enemy ships, and even a defeat produced a slogan when James Lawrence, the dying American captain of the *Chesapeake*, said, "Don't give up the ship." But these triumphs, brilliant and small as flares, did not alter the overall maritime balance of power.

Even as he fought, Madison kept trying to end the war he had declared. In this he had the help of a better foreign friend than Napoleon—Czar Alexander I. Americans did a substantial Baltic trade; the czar's unwillingness to give it up was one of the reasons Napoleon had attacked him in 1812. Alexander was a strange amalgam of reaction, romance, and liberalism who was fond of the American minister to St. Petersburg, John Quincy Adams. In the spring of 1813, he offered to mediate the Anglo-American conflict.

It took months to get negotiations going. The czar's mediation was rejected, but the idea of two-party talks flickered on. The possible venue flitted from Russia to Sweden to London. The British were distracted; the Senate was difficult.

So Madison turned to his staunchest political supporter, Albert Gallatin, who after a dozen years was finally sick of the Treasury Department and the enemies it had made him. Madison had let Gallatin down twice: by not making him secretary of state and by not fighting hard enough for the Bank of the United States. Now, in his hour of need, Madison insisted on making him a peace negotiator. Gallatin's departure from the Treasury would leave it to the dogs but without credit, tariffs, or taxes, it was headed there anyway. Peace was the essential thing, and Gallatin was the best man Madison knew; every other consideration had to give way.

In the Senate, Federalists and Gallatin's Republican enemies resisted the appointment, the former out of mischief, the latter out of spite. When a committee of senators came to the White House to speak with Madison about the deadlock in July, Madison said he was sorry they did not share his views, and said no more. "The committee . . . remained a reasonable time for the President to make any other observations" was how the scene was recorded in the Senate's journal. "Observing no disposition manifested by him to enter into further remarks, the committee retired." Madison had the strengths of his weaknesses; he could be unforthcoming and rigid, but in this contest he made those qualities work for him. The Senate did not back down, but neither did Madison.

In the fall came word that Napoleon's last army had been shattered at Leipzig and that a British army had pushed into France from Spain. Britain would soon be able to give its full attention to the United States, on the battlefield or at the negotiating table. The Senate relented, and a team of American diplomats was finally approved in February 1814—Gallatin, John Quincy Adams, Henry Clay, and two others.

Meanwhile, Britain pursued the military option in tandem. Napoleon abdicated in the spring of 1814; over the summer and fall, Britain doubled its forces in North America.

The British often found a tougher enemy, better manned and better led. In one of many battles on the Niagara Frontier, near the Chippewa River on the Canadian side, the British engaged troops commanded by Winfield Scott, now a brigadier general. "Those are regulars, by God," said the British commander, marveling at the Americans' discipline under fire. Despite sharp fighting, neither side could break the stalemate around Lake Ontario. When the British tried to move down Lake Champlain, between New York and Vermont, the old invasion route from the French and Indian and Revolutionary Wars, they were routed.

They had better initial success with their operations in Chesapeake Bay. A British fleet under the command of Admiral Sir George Cockburn had been plundering the Maryland countryside for a year, burning supplies and towns and liberating slaves. The American navy, for all its one-shot triumphs, had been powerless to stop it. By August, Britain had put a new force of twenty ships and 4,500 veterans of combat in Spain in the Chesapeake, commanded by Gen. Robert Ross and Admiral Sir Alexander Cochrane, with Cockburn's assistance.

Madison and his administration had foreseen the possibility of such a stroke and assigned a brigadier general to prepare the region's defenses. Every effort was vitiated by two personnel problems. The brigadier general Madison picked (over the advice of Armstrong) was William Winder, a Baltimore lawyer who had been in the army for two years. His only combat experience had been in a battle along the St. Lawrence in which he had been captured. His uncle Levin Winder was the governor of Maryland, a Federalist. Involving nephew William in the defense of the area made political sense (so the Baltimore riot came back to bite Madison: if Maryland politics had not been so poisonous, it would not have been necessary to go to such lengths to navigate it). But the new commander proved to be a bad choice in every other way—both nervous and incompetent, frittering away his time in scouting and minutiae.

At this important moment, Madison's relations with Armstrong collapsed. Working together, the two men had done much to restore the army's performance and confidence. But Madison had come to resent Armstrong's independent ways, which amounted to insubordination. The secretary had taken serious decisions—consolidating regiments, arranging the careers of general officers—without consulting the president; Madison first learned of some of these decisions in the newspapers. Early in August, he sent Armstrong a letter spelling out what he wanted to be told. It was a bad sign to be having such a discussion a year and a half into their partnership. In reaction Armstrong resolved to do nothing unless he was explicitly told to do it. The president was still looking for ways to work with his secretary, but his secretary had decided not to work with the president.

On August 19, the British armada landed its troops at Benedict, Maryland, on the Patuxent River. Benedict was thirty-five miles southeast of Washington, fifty miles south of Baltimore. Armstrong was certain the British would head for the latter, the country's third-largest city and a center of shipping. As the British force strolled up the Maryland countryside, harassed only by the humidity, Madison's inner circle was seized by a rage for motion. Monroe scouted, as well as Winder. (Why was the secretary of state acting as scout? He seemed to distrust both Winder and Armstrong, and was vain of his own military service forty years earlier. Whatever his reasons, scouting is a job for the cavalry.) On August 22, Madison himself, Secretary Jones, and Attorney General Richard Rush* rode out to the main American camp in Old Fields, Maryland, now Forestville, eight miles southeast of the capital. Madison reviewed the troops—who were in "good spirits," he wrote in a note to Dolley—then returned to the White House the following afternoon.

Whatever the spirits of the troops, no one had yet decided what to do with them or where to deploy them. Winder believed that if Washington were threatened, it would be from the south, where a long bridge crossed the East Branch of the Potomac near the Navy Yard. The more obvious

---

* He had taken this post in February.

point of attack to everyone else (except Armstrong, who thought Washington was in no danger) was Bladensburg, northeast of the capital, where there was both a short bridge over the East Branch and a road through the hills. The troops Madison had visited at Old Fields were equidistant from both points, and good for nothing, especially if they were not seeking the enemy.

At midnight August 23, Madison got word from the peripatetic Monroe that the British were coming. The consultations and cross-purposes of the morning of the 24th, which ended with Madison and his cabinet on a hill outside Bladensburg, have been told. When Secretary Armstrong offered his verdict that "arrangements . . . appeared to be as good as circumstances admitted," the battle had already begun in earnest. The British deployed across the bridge, despite American fire, and went to work. Among their weapons were Congreve rockets, a newish invention, halfway between artillery and fireworks, which had been used to good effect in Europe. The Americans, badly disposed and led, broke and ran. (Self-hating wits called the battle the Bladensburg Races.) Only the five hundred sailors who had marched in from the Navy Yard held their ground, raking the British with grapeshot until their gunners were bayoneted at their cannons.

Madison had left Bladensburg once the action commenced, telling Armstrong and Monroe "it would be proper" to leave military matters to the military. Coming to the battlefield had been a show of seriousness far more meaningful than touring the War and Navy Departments in a cockade, as he had done in 1812. That had been theater, verging on farce; this was putting himself literally on the line. But staying would only distract his commanders and men.

The sixty-three-year-old president, who had already ridden from the White House to the Navy Yard to Bladensburg, rode back to the White House, accompanied by Rush. It had already been evacuated. Madison had sent a messenger, a free black man, on ahead of him who warned

Dolley to "clear out!" She and a few servants, including Paul Jennings, a fifteen-year-old slave, had packed up some valuables, including a Gilbert Stuart portrait of George Washington. Dolley's macaw went for safekeeping to the Octagon House, at Eighteenth Street and New York Avenue, the town house of a Virginia planter. Madison paused at the empty White House only briefly, then rode off with Rush to take a ferry to Virginia.

The British arrived in the capital in the evening. The Navy Yard was already burning, torched by the Americans to keep it from enemy hands. Mindful of the fate of York, the British proceeded to burn the Capitol (their Congreve rockets helped), then moved to the White House. A party of officers sat at the dinner table, including Admiral Cockburn, who toasted "Jemmy's health" and made lewd jokes about being in Dolley's "seat." Then the British burned that building, too.

The destruction was Miltonic. The midnight darkness of an abandoned town was set off by columns of fire and smoke. "I never saw a scene at once more terrible and more magnificent," wrote Jean Serurier, the French minister. A gale of rain and wind the next day quenched the flames but only added to the desolation.

M adison and his wife spent the night of their evacuation at different plantations on the Virginia side, neither knowing where the other was. But by the evening of the 25th, they had reunited at a tavern overlooking a stream appropriately named Difficult Run. The next morning, accompanied by the faithful Rush, Madison went in search of Winder, whom he believed was on the Maryland side. After a long day of bad weather and swollen streams, he had not found Winder, but on the morning of the 27th he learned that the British had left Washington for their ships. He sent word to his cabinet (Armstrong was in Frederick, Maryland, Monroe was with the army near Baltimore) to return to the capital.

The British had respected private property by and large, but public Washington was in ashes. The White House was walls, the Capitol a shell. The Madisons stayed with Rush, in a row house on Pennsylvania Avenue.

Madison had his last discussion with Armstrong, which he transcribed in a memo to himself. The story that he had played out with Robert Smith as farce now repeated itself as tragedy. Madison began by describing to his secretary of war the anger that swirled around him: Armstrong even more than Winder was blamed for the burning of Washington; one militia officer had threatened that every other officer would "tear off his epaulettes" rather than serve under him any longer. Armstrong defended himself, blaming his unpopularity on "intrigues" against him and saying that he "knew the sources" (meaning Monroe).

Madison went back on the attack. "It would not be easy to satisfy the nation that the event was without blame somewhere, and I could not in candor say that all that ought to have been done had been done." Madison's second point was obvious; his first, translated, meant *We need a scapegoat, and you are it.* Armstrong, he continued, had never taken the danger to Washington seriously. "Everything" that had been suggested for its defense had been "brought forward by myself," Madison insisted, though he had held back, "in order to obtrude the less on a reluctant executive." In other words, *I would have done everything, but I didn't because of you.*

Armstrong suggested that he take a leave of absence to visit his family in New York; Monroe would then act as secretary of war pro tem. Madison agreed and concluded by saying that he had always treated Armstrong with "friendliness." Armstrong set off for home, and by the time he reached Baltimore, he wrote to say that he was resigning. Monroe replaced him as secretary of war, while continuing to serve as secretary of state.

This wretched interview, yet another example of Madison's management style, simultaneously hands-off and carping, changes its character, for better and for worse, when seen in context. Armstrong's exit had two fortunate consequences, one administrative, one political. It removed a man with whom Madison finally could not work. Both men were responsible for that, but now at last the problem was solved. It also cleared the road for Monroe. He was thane of Glamis and of Cawdor, and would be king hereafter if the Republican Party kept its feet. Making way for the right Virginian was always a prime political task for Madison and Jefferson. Using and then discarding New Yorkers was a necessary means. Armstrong was the latest in a string of former allies going back almost twenty-five years: Livingston, Burr, the Clintons (thirty years, if one counted Hamilton). The capital might be in cinders, but the future of the Republican Party, and Virginia's role within it, had been defined.

Although Armstrong took the fall for the destruction of Washington, he was not the only man at fault, nor even the main one. Madison had put him, Winder, and Monroe in their jobs. It was his responsibility to spot incompetence and be rid of it, or misdirection and correct it, and he had done neither. He preferred to try to work with people, and he took a long time to make decisions, especially negative ones. Washington had paid the price.

Yet, how serious was that? The burning of Washington was a psychic scar, one of those wounds to national pride that marked the Anglo-American relationship in peace and war, and that had been inflicted by both sides, from needling Anthony Merry to impressment. Yet Washington was a town of 8,000; so little had been built, it could be rebuilt.

Armstrong had said all along that the British must really be after Baltimore: "No, no! Baltimore is the place, sir." In this he was right. The British made their move early in September. Sen. Samuel Smith, Madison's old enemy, was also a major general of the militia and had taken charge of Baltimore's defenses, drilling troops and building earthworks—doing all the things that no one around Madison had done for Washington.

Ross's army landed on North Point to the east of the city on September 12, while Cochrane on succeeding days tried to silence Fort McHenry at the mouth of the harbor so he could bring his ships in to bombard the city directly. Ross was killed by a sharpshooter as his troops approached, and Cochrane, for all his gunnery and Congreve rockets, could make no impression on the fort. So the British withdrew.

Francis Scott Key, a Georgetown lawyer who had come to Baltimore to negotiate a prisoner release, watched the bombardment from a ship along with Cochrane and Cockburn. The next day, when he saw the American colors flying, he wrote a poem, which he set to a fifty-year-old English drinking song. The jauntiness of the tune enlivens the gravity of its new subject.

> *On the shore dimly seen through the mists of the deep,*
> *Where the foe's haughty host in dread silence reposes,*
> *What is that which the breeze, o'er the towering steep,*
> *As it fitfully blows, half conceals, half discloses?*
> *Now it catches the gleam of the morning's first beam,*
> *In full glory reflected, now shines on the stream:*
> *'Tis the star-spangled banner: O, long may it wave*
> *O'er the land of the free and the home of the brave!*

When Congress returned to Washington in the fall, they met in a hotel. Madison, after bunking first with Rush, then with Dolley's sister Anna and her husband, moved into the Octagon House, where he and Dolley would live while the war lasted.

The administration faced great, gaping problems, which it proposed to solve with neo-Federalist measures. The government was broke. Gallatin's successor at Treasury, George Washington Campbell, a Tennessee senator, had been unable to handle the job and had retired due to poor health. Campbell's successor as of October 1814 was Alexander Dallas. A Philadelphia lawyer, born in Jamaica and raised in Scotland, who powdered his hair and wore it in a queue, he looked like Hamilton reborn. Like Hamilton, he now proposed a whiskey tax and a new Bank of the United States.

The army needed men. In his new role as secretary of war, Monroe called for conscription. He told Congress it had "a right by the Constitution to raise regular armies, and no restraint is imposed on the exercise of it." John Randolph asked scornfully what Monroe would have said to a similar argument from John Adams, and answered his own question: Monroe would have urged armed defiance.

Congress muddled along, trying to cope with the nation's disasters and the administration's new mood. It passed the whiskey tax but rejected the bank and the draft.

The main political issues, concerning presidential succession and the capital, were resolved decisively. Vice President Gerry died in November at age seventy, at a time when Madison was sick once more, and Federalists made a bid for power in the guise of bipartisanship. Rufus King, running mate on two losing Federalist tickets and senator for New York since 1813, might become president pro tem of the Senate, and thus first in line behind Madison. Or perhaps he or some other capable Federalist could strengthen Madison's cabinet.

At the same time, the city of Washington became the focus of a sectional controversy. Instead of rebuilding the ungainly southern town, why not move the seat of government to real cities, perhaps New York or Philadelphia, which had already hosted it? Jonathan Fisk, a Long Island Republican, called for a House committee to study the matter.

The administration fought both ideas. Republicans did not want a Federalist presiding over the Senate or sitting in their cabinet. "Such a bargain," wrote Monroe, "would ruin the administration, the [Republican] party, and perhaps the cause of free government." He wrote with the self-interest of an officeholder and a partisan, but he also offered a précis of the role of parties in a republican system. "There can be no change of administration but by the people. That must be by change of party." Parties came to power by popular will expressed at the polls, and the Republicans were going to hang on until the people voted them out.

Virginians could not accept moving the capital northward. Madison had a personal interest in the question, since he had made the original

deal with Hamilton for the Potomac site. When the House considered a
bill to move the government to Philadelphia for the duration of the war,
Madison lobbied against it and it narrowly failed. The deal Madison had
made twenty-five years ago was sweetened by a new transaction: to replace
its incinerated library, Congress voted to buy Jefferson's 10,000 volumes.

But at year's end, neither Madison nor anyone else in Washington was
a major actor. The war and their fates were being decided in Belgium,
Connecticut, and Louisiana. Distance and slowness of travel gave all these
scenes, simultaneous but incommunicado, a dreamlike dissonance.

American and British diplomats had been meeting since summer in
Ghent, the rendezvous they had picked at last. The five-man American
team was strong (also quarrelsome: Gallatin rode herd on them all).
Britain sent three second-raters, including the admiral who had bombarded Copenhagen—a sign of overconfidence and inattention. Gallatin
had warned Madison in June that Britain was vindictive and that the best
America could hope for was status ante bellum—turning the clock back
to prewar 1812. Another option, to use the Latin phraseology of international jurists, was *uti possidetis*—as you possess. Wherever the contending armies stood would mark the new boundaries of the United States
and British North America. Since the British occupied eastern Maine,
this would leave the United States at a loss. Britain's opening offer was
even harsher than *uti possidetis*—the United States should agree to an independent Indian homeland in the Midwest. Henry Clay, a devoted
poker player—when John Quincy Adams rose before dawn, he would
hear all-night card parties breaking up in Clay's room—thought the
British were bluffing. "Mr. Clay," wrote Adams in his diary, "has an in-
conceivable idea that they will recede from the ground they have taken."

The diplomats kept working throughout the fall, but the most important contribution to the process was made by an offstage Englishman—
the Duke of Wellington, hero of Britain and Europe for liberating Spain.

One thought in London was to send the duke to America, along with new troops. In November, Wellington wrote Lord Liverpool, the prime minister, a lecture, as blunt as it was genial, on military strategy. "I feel no objection to going to America, though I don't promise to myself much success there. . . . That which appears to me to be wanting in America is not a General, or general officers and troops, but a naval superiority on the lakes [e.g., the Great Lakes and Lake Champlain]." If Britain could not achieve that, "I shall do you but little good in America; and I shall go there only . . . to sign a peace which might as well be signed now." A week later, he sent the prime minister a second lecture, on international politics. "Does it not occur to your Lordship that, by appointing me to go to America at this moment, you give ground for belief all over Europe that your affairs . . . are in a much worse situation than they really are?" Wellington was saying, this war is a bother and a distraction; settle it.

The bargain the diplomats finally struck was status ante bellum. Britain would evacuate Maine, and Indians would have no home. Nothing was said of three of Madison's war goals, ending impressment, Orders in Council, and British scheming with Federalists, though in the event of world peace, these issues would become moot. The treaty was signed the day before Christmas, but it would have to be ratified in London and Washington, which would take weeks.

On December 15, the flower of New England Federalism—twenty-six delegates from Massachusetts, Connecticut, Rhode Island, and three counties in New Hampshire and Vermont—met in Hartford to consider what their states should do about the Madison administration and the War of 1812. Two and a half years of war and several years more of political defeats—close enough to be encouraging, never great enough to teach them a lesson—had driven Federalists beyond reason. They had not schemed as treacherously as Madison thought they had with John Henry and the governor general of Canada, but they had grumbled and fantasized among themselves. The letters of Gouverneur Morris, who was nursing a case of gout in New York, were a barometer of their temper.

He hated Madison: "[I have] been told that he never goes sober to bed. Whether intoxicated by opium or wine was not said." He hated the south. "[Shall] the slave holding states . . . exercise the privilege of strangling commerce, whipping Negroes, and bawling about the in-born inalienable rights of man"? He wanted the northern, virtuous half of the Union to secede, and to let the south and west carry on the war alone. "I hear some of the brethren exclaim, 'O Lord! O Lord! Why, this is civil war!' Unquestionably it is civil war. And what of it?" The draftsman of the Constitution had rejected his own handiwork.

Such opinions raged like a virus in Federalist ranks. Timothy Pickering of Massachusetts, who had plotted secession ten years earlier, now sat in the House representing Essex County, north of Boston. Federalist governors in New England had refused throughout the war to call up their militias for national use. Britain had encouraged them by not blockading New England ports, and the people of northern New England had returned the favor by smuggling supplies to the British army in Canada (after all, the enemy paid good money for them).

Madison and Monroe sent Colonel Thomas Jesup, a veteran of the Battle of Chippewa, to Connecticut, ostensibly to recruit, in fact to report on the doings of the Hartford Convention. What the Hartford Convention did, when they finished deliberating on January 5, 1815, was to issue a report that threw Madison's own words back at him. No one (outside of Jefferson and a handful of others) yet knew that he had written the Virginia Resolutions of 1798, but everyone knew that he and the Republican Party had approved them. In 1798, Madison the opposition politician had written this about an overweening federal government: "in case of a deliberate, palpable and dangerous exercise of other powers not granted by [the Constitution], the states who are parties thereto have the right, and are in duty bound, to interpose for arresting the progress of the evil." In 1815, the opposition politicians at Hartford now wrote of Madison's government: "in cases of deliberate, dangerous and palpable infractions of the constitution . . . it is not only the right but the duty of . . . a state to interpose its authority." In 1798, Madison had stressed that interposing states should act together. The Hartford men wrote "state" (singular) at first, but in the next few sentences, spoke of "states" and "the several states," so their meaning was identical to Madison's.

The only difference was that Madison in 1798 was protesting Federalist almost-war measures, while the Federalists in 1815 were protesting Madison's war measures.

Who had changed more? Federalists now accepted a principle—interposition—which they had rejected in 1798 (when they had said that constitutional disputes should be resolved by the courts). Madison still approved the principle, but that did not mean he had to approve every invocation of it (certainly not when it was invoked against himself). At such a moment, however, no one was awarding points for consistency.

The Hartford Convention suggested a list of constitutional amendments—among them, requiring a two-thirds vote of both houses of Congress to declare war or restrict trade, and a sixty-day limit on embargoes—and warned that if they were not adopted, New England would call another convention in June to decide what "a crisis so momentous may require." The threat was obvious: give us what we want or we will secede. At the end of January, Massachusetts and Connecticut chose delegates to deliver the suggestions and the threat to Washington.

Two days before the Hartford Convention met, a British expeditionary force, assembled in Jamaica, reached the offshore islands in the Gulf of Mexico east of New Orleans. The fleet was commanded by Admiral Cochrane of the Chesapeake campaign, the army by Gen. Sir Edward Pakenham, the Duke of Wellington's thirty-six-year-old brother-in-law. Methodically they moved, by lake and bayou, to the Mississippi downriver from the city. Gen. Andrew Jackson, scourge of the Creeks, commanded the defense.

Even as Britain's diplomats patched up their treaty in Ghent, the military was mounting a major operation in the Gulf. Wellington had mentioned the expedition in his November letters of advice but did not think it affected the strategic picture. In this he was wrong. The Mississippi River valley had been Madison's desire for thirty years—to say nothing of Napoleon's and Spain's. Britain would like to have it, too, or at least New Orleans. After years of plots and peaceful transfers, ownership now would be decided in battle.

New Orleans was the sixth-largest city in the United States, more than twice as big as Washington. Its population was a grab bag of Spaniards, Frenchmen, free mulattoes, slaves, and recent American arrivals; Barataria Bay to the south was infested with pirates. Jackson knocked heads, enlisted recruits, signed up the pirates, and fought delaying actions. The main British attack came at dawn January 8 on a field between the river and a swamp five miles below the city. Jackson was dug in with well-placed artillery. Pakenham's flanking attack miscarried, and his main force was shattered. The casualty lists told the story: the British lost 2,000 men, dead, wounded, or captured, one-third of their total force (Pakenham was among the dead). The Americans lost seventy. After ten more days, Cochrane withdrew.

News of all these events trickled into Washington slowly. The first to arrive was of the Battle of New Orleans, on February 4. Rumors of the city's fall had been swirling through the capital, which made Jackson's remarkable victory all the more remarkable.

America's copy of the Treaty of Ghent arrived in New York a week later. Word reached Madison at the Octagon House on the 13th. "Mr. Madison," wrote one congressman, "was much more excited than usual with his calm temper." The Senate ratified it unanimously on the 16th, and Madison addressed both houses two days later, to hail peace and sum up the war.

Neo-Federalism reigned. The man who had called the Report on Manufactures unconstitutional now asked Congress to "preserve and promote" manufactures. The man who had yearned for "universal peace" now called for a standing army and service academies. "Experience has taught us," he explained, "that . . . the pacific dispositions of the American people" cannot "exempt them from that strife which appears . . . to be incident to the actual period of the world." He could have read all about it in *Federalist #6*, but even for great minds experience can be a better, if slower, teacher than reading and reasoning.

In his message to Congress, Madison praised "the wisdom of the legislative councils . . . the patriotism of the people . . . the public spirit of the militia," and "the valor of the military and naval forces of the country." The patriotism of some of the people, and the valor of the military, deserved it. His war goals from June 1812 had shrunk to one: the war had been "necessary . . . to assert the rights and independence of the nation." As a justification of the war, this was only half true—America's rights were exactly where they had been two and half years earlier, that is, up in the air—but the half that was true was the half that counted. The War of 1812 was a war of national self-assertion—a second war of independence. In such contests, the underdog has bragging rights. By not losing, America had won. Tacitus had one of his barbarians say of the conquering Romans: "they made a desert and called it peace." Madison made a peace and called it victory, and the nation was so giddy from a combination of relief and pride that no one disputed him.

In the midst of these celebrations, the delegation of New England Federalists arrived in Washington from Hartford. Madison—one of the Massachusetts men called him a "contemptible little blackguard"—would not speak with them. Why should he? In the new state of things, the Federalist threat, and Federalist wrath, faded like ghosts.

Four days after Madison's address to Congress, Dolley gave her weekly reception, on Washington's birthday. Rep. Charles Ingersoll, a Philadelphia Republican, described the scene. For once the president, not his wife, was the center of attention. "Madison's wrinkled and withered face wore a placid smile, as he received the compliments of political opponents and the homage of adherents. None but the bitterest antagonists stayed away from such a jubilee. . . . All gay, some merry, more than one excited, even to convivial vivacity, pressed round the chief magistrate."

Then Ingersoll struck off a once-in-a-lifetime sentence, packed with wisdom. "It was one of those moments when joy or grief, and even bodily illness, hush the bad passions of human nature."

Madison's term had two more years to run, but his great effort had been made. The remainder was tying up loose ends. Treasury secretary Dallas proposed another plan for a Bank of the United States at the end of 1815, which Congress approved the following March. The second Bank, like the first, had a charter of twenty years and began operations in January 1817. The bad passions of human nature, or at least the venal ones, revived when Congress voted itself a pay raise in the spring of 1816. That fall, angry voters hammered them at the polls.

The presidential election was decided, as it had been in 1804 and 1808, by the Republican congressional caucus. One of the contenders to succeed Madison was forty-four-year-old William Crawford of Georgia. Smart and ambitious, Crawford had been tapped by Madison to follow Armstrong as minister to France and (once the war ended) Monroe as secretary of war. But Virginia managed one more victory for one of its own, with Monroe edging him out for the Republican nomination. In the presidential election, Monroe faced the Federalist stalwart Rufus King, who carried three ghettos of Federalism, Massachusetts, Connecticut, and Delaware, for 34 electoral votes. Monroe won 16 states (including Tecumseh's former home of Indiana, which had been admitted to statehood that year) for 183 votes.

It may seem strange that a major party, after years of frantic activity, should simply collapse. But so it happened. The wrath of the Federalists left them exhausted, while the Republican Party's appropriation of so many of their policies left them without purpose. Gouverneur Morris spoke for the new mood, as he had for the old. "Let us forget party, and think of our country." The Federalists never contested another national election.

Monroe's election marked the final triumph of the Virginia Dynasty. He, Jefferson, and Madison had built a party that obeyed, and shaped, public opinion, and they had carried all before them. A new party system would arise, but for now the only party that counted was the Republicans, who soon came to use their modern name of Democrats.

M adison ended his presidency with a surprise. In his seventh annual message to Congress, in December 1815, he had called for roads and canals. The states, he said, were already building them, "with a laudable enterprise." (His old rivals DeWitt Clinton and Gouverneur Morris were pushing for a canal across New York.) But the federal government should do likewise, to complete the nation's transportation network "systematically. . . . Any defect of constitutional authority," he went on, "can be supplied in a mode which the Constitution itself has providentially pointed out."

Congress heeded his exhortation but ignored his caveat. A bill for constructing roads and canals was introduced at the end of 1816 by Rep. John Calhoun of South Carolina, who praised transportation as an antidote to "a low, sordid, selfish and sectional spirit." The bill landed on Madison's desk in the new year, and on his last day in office, March 3, 1817, he vetoed it.

Building roads and canals, he explained, was not an enumerated power of Congress, under Article I, Section 8, nor did it fall "by any just interpretation" under the necessary and proper clause, the commerce clause, or the preamble when it spoke of providing for the common defense and promoting the general welfare. Such loose constructions of the Constitution "would have the effect of giving to Congress a general power of legislation." If Congress wanted to build roads and dig canals—and Madison agreed that it should—it could propose and send on to the states an amendment giving itself that power—"a safe and practicable" solution. The veto message was a testament, to himself even more than to the country: the retiring politician wanted to show that his reasoning and his distinctions were as firm as ever.

How firm was that? After more than forty years in public life, Madison had shown steady allegiance to certain things: religious liberty; freedom of the press; Anglophobia and Francophilia; trade war as an instrument of policy; expansion, especially to the west and south. On some things he had changed his positions: he supported a stronger national government when he expected to be influential in it and stronger state governments when his power base shifted to that level. His intelligence and his knowledge of history showed him how this tension between different political spheres could be built into the Constitution as a bulwark of liberty, though he came to believe that appealing to popular opinion through the arts of argument and politics was a bulwark at least as strong.

Madison biographers who want their hero to be consistent in all things will not be pleased with this analysis; political philosophers who value intellectual elegance and constitutional lawyers, who seek guidance from the Father of the Constitution, will be even less so. But we have to remember Madison's job: politics. We will not find complete consistency in his career; we should not look for it. Politics always creates new situations, springs surprises, and throws unexpected problems, friends, and enemies at those who practice it. It should be enough for us that a great mind gave it his best thoughts for as long as Madison did.

Although the Madisons hoped to leave Washington immediately after Monroe's inauguration, a round of parties held them for a month. When Madison, now sixty-six years old, was finally homeward bound, one friend said he looked like "a school boy on a long vacation."

CHAPTER ELEVEN

Retirement, Death

As the fourth former president in American history, Madison did what his predecessors had done—he lived at home and received visitors. Like Washington and Jefferson, he was well suited, by his upbringing and his class, for the role. A Virginia gentleman's home was a hearth and a stage, open to family, neighbors, friends—and, in the case of presidents' homes, also the patriotic and the curious. Dolley ran the show at Montpelier with her accustomed panache, and her macaw provided color and excitement (it tended to bite people). But the main attraction was Madison. He was a sight, like the Natural Bridge. One young male visitor to Montpelier expressed the universal view, despite the distractions of the young women who were visiting along with him. "The truth is pretty girls I can find plenty of, I could see but one Mr. Madison."

Age enhanced his stature. After all the years of bad health, and of worrying about his bad health, Madison nevertheless kept marching on. He outlived Washington, Adams, and Jefferson, his predecessors in office—not surprisingly, since they were older men—but he also outlived his immediate successor, James Monroe, who was younger. As the years passed, the thirty-eight other signers of the Constitution, and the sixteen who had attended the Constitutional Convention without signing, fell away, some from unnatural causes—besides Richard Spaight and Alexander

Hamilton, killed in duels, George Wythe of Virginia was poisoned by an impatient heir, and John Lansing of New York disappeared one night after walking out to mail a letter. Madison was the last framer standing. Loneliness increased his eminence, like a hill on a plain.

His retirement years were not cloudless. Like every other Virginia gentleman, he spent a lot of time considering how to get a better return from his land. He was elected president of a local agricultural society, which he lectured about contour plowing and manure. None of it helped, much. Montpelier had done well during his years as secretary of state and president, despite the care of overseers, because American wheat fetched good prices in war-torn Europe. But the return of peace and competition drove prices down; new American farmland wrested from the Indians was more productive. In 1825, Madison's prospects were so poor he could not get a loan from the second Bank of the United States.

Another drag on him was his stepson, John Payne Todd. Portraits show attractive eyes and hair, set off by a thick nose and an even thicker air of self-satisfaction. The tragedy of Payne's childhood—father and infant brother killed by yellow fever—and some flaw in his mother's character meant that Dolley never disciplined him; like many stepfathers, Madison was unwilling to do the job in her place. So young Payne ran wild. In 1813, Madison had made him Albert Gallatin's secretary when Gallatin went to Europe as a peace negotiator; Payne abandoned his boss in Paris to frolic. In later years he ran up immense gambling debts. Madison bailed him out, sometimes telling his wife, sometimes keeping the bad news from her, to the tune of $40,000.

To make ends meet, Madison sold land and other assets, and took out mortgages on what remained. He managed to hold off bankruptcy, which had swallowed Jefferson and Monroe, but he knew his patrimony was dwindling.

In his old age, Madison pioneered yet another political role—the former president as sage and counselor. Washington, in his brief retirement, had accepted command of the army, in case the French invaded. Jefferson wrote letters of advice to his protégés, Madison and Monroe, and John Adams wrote to whoever would correspond with him. All three were opinionated men, who continued to follow politics. But the aloof and tender part of Jefferson's nature made him embrace the role of Cincinnatus, forsaking the arena for his plow; Adams was so peculiar and unpopular—and so proud of his peculiarity and unpopularity—that the only politician who would actually listen to him was his own son, John Quincy Adams. Madison kept his hand in. His collegial habits served him in good stead. Early in his career he had been the ideal junior partner; now, in the evening of his life, he was the ideal senior, often silent partner.

One of Madison's most important tasks in his new role was to watch over his own legacy as a constitution maker. His triple role as a planner, framer, and advocate gave him special standing to speak, and his career told him that persistence often won the day. So he made his opinions known.

Several of his opinions brought him into conflict with Chief Justice John Marshall. Federalists had disappeared as a national political party, but a Federalist still presided over the Supreme Court. Madison had never liked Marshall (in the early 1790s, he told Jefferson that he was corrupt: "It is said that Marshall . . . has lately obtained pecuniary aids from the Bank or people connected with it . . . which will explain him to every one that reflects"). Washington had persuaded Marshall to run for Congress in 1798; Adams tapped him as secretary of state, after firing Timothy Pickering, then nominated him for the Supreme Court. Jefferson in his first term tried, and failed, to purge the courts of Federalist holdovers. But Marshall stayed on and on, issuing his rulings, and administering the presidential oath of office to Jefferson, Madison, and Monroe in turn.

In 1819 Marshall heard a case involving the second Bank of the United States. Maryland had passed a tax on the transactions of out-of-state banks. James McCulloch, clerk of the Bank of the United States' branch in Baltimore, had conducted business without paying the tax, whereupon Maryland sued him. The appeal rose to the Supreme Court. Marshall

ruled for the Bank and its clerk, revisiting the argument over ends and
means which had pitted Madison and Hamilton against each other in
1791 when the first Bank of the United States was proposed and taking
Hamilton's side. "If the end be legitimate, and within the scope of the
Constitution," wrote Marshall, "all the means . . . which are plainly
adapted to that end, and which are not prohibited, may constitutionally
be employed to carry it into effect." Establishing a Bank of the United
States was a legitimate end, branch banks were a means, and neither
Maryland nor any other state could hobble them with taxation.

Madison took up the argument in a letter to Spencer Roane, a Virginia
judge. He found himself standing on different ground than he had in
1791, because he supported the second Bank, and he seemed to support
McCulloch in the present case. Nevertheless, he criticized "the general
and abstract doctrine" that Marshall had "interwoven" with his decision.
Madison thought the chief justice's pronouncements about ends and
means gave Congress too much leeway. "Everything is related immediately or remotely to every other thing; and consequently a power over
any one thing, if not limited by some obvious and precise affinity, may
amount to a power over every other. Ends and means may shift their
character . . . according to the ingenuity of the Legislative Body." Gallatin
had persuaded him that a Bank of the United States was useful, and the
chaos of wartime finance had shown him that its absence could be disastrous, but he resented Marshall's invitation to Congress to propose
other innovations and curtail other states' rights.

Four years later, Madison engaged the Marshall court in a letter to Jefferson. Madison merely disliked the chief justice; Jefferson, who was his
cousin, loathed him. Jefferson had sent Madison an anti-Marshall blast,
of which he was justifiably proud, for it showed many of his characteristic
touches. Marshall's decisions, wrote Jefferson, "hang . . . inference on inference, from heaven to earth, like Jacob's ladder. . . . The Chief Justice
says, 'there must be an ultimate arbiter somewhere'" when state and federal governments collide. "True, there must; but does that prove it is

either party? The ultimate arbiter is the people of the union, assembled by their deputies in convention. . . . Let them decide to which they mean to give an authority." Don't take constitutional issues to court, Jefferson was saying; call conventions, like those to ratify the Constitution.

In reply, Madison slipped on the armor of tact he always wore when correcting his friend. Calling conventions to settle every disagreement would be "troublesome." On the other hand, letting state and federal governments simply fight it out would produce "a trial of strength between the posse headed by the marshal"—did Madison intend the pun?—"and the posse headed by the sheriff." The judiciary, Madison concluded, was a legitimate constitutional venue for deciding such disputes. Like Jefferson, he deplored Marshall's "extrajudicial reasonings and dicta. . . . But the abuse of a trust does not disprove its existence."

Madison could be pro- or anti-court, depending on the circumstances. In 1800, in his Report on the Alien and Sedition Acts, when Federalist judges were zealously upholding the latter, he had said that the states might sit in judgment on the courts, and in his retirement he thought Marshall went too far. But he acknowledged that the courts had a place in the federal machine.

Madison never arranged his opinions on the courts into a summa. He had a philosophical turn of mind, but comprehensive philosophical statements were not his style. His last large work would be not philosophy, but reporting-as-history—a finished version of the notes he had taken at the Constitutional Convention in 1787.

Madison was surprised by the publication, in 1821, of a competing set, by Robert Yates, the New York anti-Federalist who had walked out of the convention after a month and attacked the Constitution under the name of Brutus. Yates had died in 1801; his notes were brought out by the other New York anti-Federalist, John Lansing (whose disappearance was still some years off). Madison probably wished that Yates's notes had disappeared; in letters he called them "egregious," "erroneous," and "mutilated." They showed that Madison had been much less friendly to state power and popular opinion than anyone would have suspected of a founder of the Republican Party and the author of the Virginia Resolutions. They also quoted him speaking bluntly, without the mollifying phrases so characteristic of his rhetoric, and dear to his temperament. For example, Yates had Madison say, during a discussion of the length of a senator's term of office, that the Senate would be a check "on the democracy." In Madison's own notes, he spoke of the Senate checking "the popular branch" and "the instabilities of the other branches." Madison did not suspect Yates of lying, but he knew from painful experience how hard it was to take notes, and he wanted the notes of such an important event to be his.

Yet Madison refused to publish his own notes in rebuttal to Yates's— or to publish them at all while he lived. He sensed that the longer he held them back, the greater impact they would have: "the older such things grow, they more they are relished . . . the distance of time like that of space . . . . giving them that attractive character." He also did not want to be embroiled in quibbles, to be questioned or contradicted; if the notes came out after he was gone, he would truly have the last word. Madison was not by nature a dramatic person; he did not have the fire of Patrick Henry or even of Hamilton, or the masterly economy of Washington. But where his notes were concerned, he showed excellent timing.

His notes also showed, yet again, the importance of collaboration in his life—and how he used it for his own fulfillment. In them he would appear alongside fifty-four other delegates, several of them as intelligent and as voluble, a few of them more eloquent than he was. He would be seen losing arguments, and coming as close as he ever came to losing his cool (as when he lectured Oliver Ellsworth about proportional representation in the Lycian confederacy). What kind of a Father of the Constitution did that make him? His notes would show him to be one of a cohort, of a band of contentious brothers. Yet they would be his notes. His were the ears that heard it all and his the hand that wrote it all up. His role as on-the-spot historian would restore his constitutional paternity. What he lost as an actor in the drama of the convention he would recover as its dramatist.

A last aspect of Madison's concern for his legacy was tending to the most important collaboration of his life—his partnership with Jefferson.

Jefferson enlisted him in a new project—the University of Virginia. Jefferson dreamed of establishing an institution of national repute on his doorstep. In 1818, the state of Virginia agreed to support a university and to put it in Charlottesville, down the mountain from Monticello. Madison served as one of the visitors, or trustees; Jefferson oversaw everything from laying out the foundations of the buildings to hunting for faculty. Among the few places Madison ever traveled, after he retired to Montpelier, were Monticello and Charlottesville, almost always on university business.

Madison conceived of his role as helping the great man, just as he had once helped Washington plan canals. "As the scheme was originally Mr. Jefferson's," he told his fellow visitors, "it was but fair to let him execute it in his own way." He and Jefferson picked books for the library and the curriculum. Making book lists was an old pastime of theirs; it was a form of vicarious shopping, vicarious reading, almost vicarious thinking.

In their selecting of books, one discipline required their special attention. "There is one branch" of learning, Jefferson wrote, "in which I think we are the best judges . . . it is that of government." He suggested as required texts for the law school the Declaration of Independence, the *Federalist* papers, and the Virginia Resolutions (one by Jefferson, one and a third by Madison). Madison added Washington's first inaugural and his Farewell Address (two more contributions, in whole or in part, by Madison—though in fairness to both Virginians, they admitted Hamilton, via the *Federalist* papers and the Farewell Address, as a coauthor).

The list suggested a larger problem, which would not become evident in Jefferson's lifetime: the University of Virginia could not be a great school in the nineteenth century because Virginia was no longer a nursery of intellectual greatness. At its best, certain achievements of the Virginia mind had matched or surpassed those of Athens, Rome, and Elizabethan England. But Virginia's greatest thinkers were taking that mind with them to the grave, and they were not being replaced. They left texts, which their heirs cherished, like creeds. The Virginia gentleman's code of behavior lasted longer, but unguided by intelligence, it lost half its goodness.

Planning the University of Virginia was Jefferson's last job, and both he and Madison knew it. In February 1826, Jefferson sent a valedictory letter to his friend. After a page of university business (trying, but not hopeless) and another of personal business (quite hopeless: the master of Monticello was broke and grasping at financial straws), Jefferson opened his heart. "But why afflict you with these details? Indeed I cannot tell, unless pains are lessened by communication with a friend. The friendship which has subsisted between us, now half a century, and that harmony of our political principles and pursuits, have been sources for constant happiness to me through that long period. . . . You have been a pillar of support through life. Take care of me when dead, and be assured that I shall leave you my last affections."

Madison wrote back the following week. "You cannot look back to the long period of our private friendship and political harmony with more affecting recollections than I do. If they are a source of pleasure to you, what ought they not to be to me?" Deferential to the last: my pleasure in knowing you was greater than yours in knowing me, because you were the greater man. "Wishing and hoping that you may yet live to increase the debt which our country owes you, and to witness the increasing gratitude which alone can pay it, I offer you the fullest return of affectionate assurances."

This was their personal farewell, the acknowledgment, decorous yet loving, of all they had had and were about to lose: no more books, no more trips; no more letters about weasels, rights, or sad, starving women. It was also their pact with politics and with history. Jefferson asked Madison to take care of his reputation; Madison would do his best to see that the country showed him its gratitude.

As former president, Madison found himself paying more attention to slavery than he had in the prime of his life.

Madison the working politician had tried to keep slavery off the table in part because discussing it would distract from his goals. In the home stretch of the Virginia ratifying convention in 1788, Patrick Henry tried to derail the Constitution by warning that the preamble would allow Congress to free slaves in wartime to fight as soldiers. "Have they not power to provide for the general defense and welfare? May they not think that these call for the abolition of slavery?" Madison scoffed at this red herring. "Such an idea never entered into any American breast, nor do I believe it ever will."

Two years later, in the thick of the debate on Hamilton's financial plan, Congress received a petition signed by Benjamin Franklin criticizing the slave trade. When southerners blazed up in wrath, Franklin, in his last journalistic hoax, published a speech by "Sidi Mehemet Ibrahim of the Divan of Algiers" in which their arguments reappeared as justifications of Moslems enslaving Christians. Madison wanted everybody to shut up. Southerners should let Franklin and the other petitioners "proceed with as little noise as possible." Thus Madison the legislative tactician: don't get bogged down in slavery when we have a constitution to pass, or a Hamilton to fight over.

But Madison the Virginian had particular reasons to keep slavery off the table: it put slave owners like himself in a paradoxical position. How could they be in the vanguard of liberty when they held men and women in bondage? European liberals, otherwise sympathetic to the American cause, taxed Madison with the paradox. In the 1820s, Lafayette, America's favorite Frenchman, visited Montpelier. The old hero was making his final triumphal tour of the United States, but amid the nostalgia and the plaudits he pressed his host about "the rights *that all men without exception have to liberty.*"

Northern Federalists made the point more rudely, as in Gouverneur Morris's crack about Virginia Republicans "whipping negroes" while "bawling about the in-born inalienable rights of man." Morris had little

right to joke, because many Federalists, from both north and south—
Jay, Marshall, Pinckney—were also slave owners. But the potential for
embarrassing Madison and his peers was there.

Three ways out of the paradox presented themselves to Madison in
his retirement years. One was to weaken slavery by spreading it more
widely, and more thinly—a strategy known as diffusion. In the new
American west, the Louisiana Territory, slavery could be diffused as far
as the Rockies. Madison described how diffusion was supposed to work,
in an 1819 letter to Robert Walsh, a Philadelphia journalist. It would
"better the condition of the slaves, by lessening the number belonging
to individual masters, and intermixing both with greater masses of free
people." In a freer environment, owners would find encouragement to
manumit, and to lighten the lives of their slaves in the meantime.

Diffusion reflected a reality of slavery: wherever it was denser—tidewater
versus the mountains, South Carolina versus Virginia, the West Indies versus the United States—it was harsher. But it ignored another reality—that
slavery was a tenacious institution even where it was not dense. The New-
York Manumission Society had been founded in 1785, yet there were
still slaves in New York (the last would not be freed until 1827).

Madison was more taken with a second plan, colonization, which he
outlined in another 1819 letter to Robert Evans, another Philadelphian.
This plan also required movement—sending blacks back to Africa. Blacks
had to be "permanently removed" from white society, Madison wrote
Evans, since the "prejudices" of both races were "probably unalterable."
Whites felt "contempt" for the "peculiar features" of blacks, while blacks
had "vindictive recollections" of their slave status. Madison envisioned
an immense program to buy and resettle slaves. Assuming 1.5 million
slaves, he calculated that $600 million would do the job. That money
could be raised by selling several hundred million acres of western land.
The whole operation should be a federal project: "It is the nation which
is to reap the benefit. The nation therefore ought to bear the burden."
Amendments could supply whatever constitutional power was lacking.

Madison was not alone in such thoughts. An American Colonization Society, whose goal was to resettle ex-slaves in Africa, had been founded in 1816; the destination they picked on the west African coast is now Liberia. British abolitionists had begun a similar settlement in Sierra Leone in the 1780s. What made Madison's scheme utterly unreal was its scope: he proposed to spend more than five times the cost of the War of 1812 ($109 million, not counting veterans' benefits). Was a country that had not passed a constitutional amendment to build roads and canals going to take on a project of that magnitude?

Both diffusion and colonization shared an eerie psychological similarity: they solved Madison's slavery problem by putting blacks elsewhere, either beyond the Mississippi or across the Atlantic. Madison would not have to move; blacks would move away from him.

A third option involved change closer to home.

Edward Coles was a young cousin of Dolley's, on her mother's side. The Coleses were well-connected Albemarle County planters. Edward's older brother Isaac had been Jefferson's private secretary during his second term, and Edward filled the same role for Madison during his presidency. Young Coles had become convinced that slavery was wrong, and he was comfortable enough with Madison, whom he revered, to jibe him about it. When the two, in Washington, would see "gangs of negroes, some in irons, on their way to a southern market," Coles would congratulate "the chief of our great republic, that he was not then accompanied by a foreign minister" who might witness the "revolting sight."

In 1819, Coles took his slaves to Pittsburgh, put them on rafts in the Ohio River, then told them that when they reached their destination, the new state of Illinois, he would free them. He gave each head of a household 160 acres, and each slave a certificate: "Not believing that man can have of right a property in his fellow man, but on the contrary, that all mankind were endowed by nature with equal rights, I do therefore, by these presents restore to (naming the party) that inalienable liberty of which he has been deprived." Coles was diffusing freedom, not slavery.

Coles's solution was not for Madison: Coles was thirty-two years old with two dozen slaves, Madison was sixty-eight with a hundred. Nevertheless, Madison wrote his former secretary a congratulatory letter. Coles was not just flinging his slaves off but helping to set them up. "You are pursuing, I observe, the true course with your negroes, in order to make their freedom a fair experiment for their happiness." Madison added, however, a sober thought: "I wish your philanthropy could complete its object, by changing their color as well as their legal condition."

Madison's worries were justified. Life was tough for free blacks in Illinois. The certificates that Coles gave his former slaves were not just testimonials to his principles: Illinois arrested blacks who could not show proof of their freedom. In 1822, Coles, who had moved to Illinois himself, ran for governor, to thwart an effort to make the new state a slave state; he won narrowly and Illinois remained free, but harsh laws and prejudice remained. He joined the American Colonization Society and encouraged his ex-slaves to move to Liberia, but they refused to go. After all, they were Americans.

The option that is always open to men and society in the face of any problem is to do nothing. This is where Madison and Virginia ended up. The last constitution-making experience of Madison's life stands as a model of inactivity, as far as slavery was concerned. In 1829, Virginia held a convention to rewrite its Revolutionary War–era constitution, and in October, Madison and Dolley left their Montpelier/Charlottesville neighborhood for the only time in their retirement to go to Richmond. All Virginia's eminences were there—Monroe, Marshall, John Randolph—but Madison was the most eminent. The years had taken a toll on his frame, but not his mind or his spirits: one dinner-table observer noted his "abundant stock of racy anecdotes."

He gave one speech, early in December, on the issue of representation. Virginia's existing constitution used a system of apportionment based on counties and election districts, which favored the planters of the tidewater. (Their counties and districts might be as populous as those in the mountains of western Virginia, but since so many easterners were slaves, eastern masters wielded disproportionate political power.) Western Virginia wanted apportionment based on white population. This was a racial yardstick, but it would diminish the clout of slave owners.

Madison offered a compromise—representation based, at least in part, on population, counting every slave as three-fifths of a person. "It is due," he said, "to justice; due to humanity; due to truth [and] to the sympathies of our nature" that slaves be considered "a part, though a degraded part, of the families to which they belong." Madison's concern for keeping slaves in the family recognized their personhood, but a three-fifths rule in the Virginia constitution—like the three-fifths rule in the U.S. Constitution—would be a political gift to slave owners, smaller perhaps than district-based suffrage but still a structural benefit. Madison's fellow delegates crowded around to hear the great man speak—then took up their former arguments, unmoved. In the constitution that was finished in January 1830, the eastern planters were able to keep a district-based system. When the faithful Lafayette wrote from France to ask whether his favorite Americans had managed to curtail slavery, Madison had to tell him no. "Any allusion . . . to the subject you have so much at heart would have been a spark to a mass of gunpowder."

Madison had lived among, and off of, slaves all his long life. What did he think about the institution? About slaves? What were the sympathies of his nature? There is with him little of the emotional grist we find in Jefferson—no acting out, no agony, no craziness. No one ever imagined, much less charged, that Madison had a slave mistress, and his writings are free from visions of divine punishment and crackpot racial theories alike.

Sometime about 1821 he tried his hand at a new genre for him—a parable of north and south, in which the two sections were called Jonathan and Mary Bull, descendants of John Bull (Britain), now married. He never published it, and happily for his reputation it is little known. Mary, it seems, has a black left arm, stained by a "certain African dye" when a ship "enter[ed] a river running through her estate" and unloaded "the noxious cargo." The stain makes Jonathan, for no good reason, turn against her. The story is a wallow of self-pity and blame-shifting: Mary denies that she "brought the misfortune on myself," and says she is "as anxious" as Jonathan to get rid of it and has done "everything I could" to lessen the evil. Everything except anything. At story's end, Jonathan is "touched" by Mary's protests, and their "bickering . . . ended as the quarrels of lovers *always*, and of married folks *sometimes* do, in increased affection." Madison says nothing more about the black arm or the noxious cargo, for they are not the point of his story; Jonathan and Mary's little spat is. Freeing slaves is not on his agenda, only keeping the peace between north and south.

But as the years passed, his thoughts could not pass over the subject. In 1835, he was visited by Harriet Martineau, a young English Unitarian making an American tour (a fashionable activity for English writers: Mrs. Trollope had already logged her miles, and Charles Dickens would follow). Martineau found Madison "lively—often playful," but one subject depressed him. "With regard to slavery he owned himself to be almost in despair." He talked more about it than anything else, "acknowledging without limit or hesitation all the evils with which it has ever been charged." He pitied white mistresses, forced to preside over untrustworthy servants; he pitied slave girls, pregnant at age fifteen. "He observed that the whole Bible is against negro slavery; but the clergy do not preach this."

His only hope was Liberia. Martineau did not share it. In almost twenty years, the American Colonization Society had resettled fewer than 3,000 people; America's slave population, meanwhile, had increased by 60,000 a year. "How such a mind as his," Martineau observed, "could derive any alleviation to its anxiety from that source is surprising."

On the question of slavery, all Madison's intelligence and political skills amounted to nothing. His statesmanship failed, and in failing he typified the founding generation, instead of leading it. Some founders made local contributions—Jay, George Clinton, Alexander Hamilton, and the other founders of the New-York Manumission Society began a forty-two-year march toward emancipation in their state. A handful made personal contributions—Washington freed his slaves in his will. Even Jefferson left rhetoric. But too many founders, like Madison, ignored slavery, hoped it would go away, or toyed with impossible solutions.

M adison faced another great issue in his retirement years: disunion. When he was young, he had helped to form a more perfect union, but now that he was old, it looked as if the country might fly apart. His thoughts on union were much more focused and forceful than his thoughts on slavery.

Broadly speaking, the younger cohort of founders, to which Madison belonged, valued union as much as liberty; in their minds, union was the necessary condition of American freedom, national and personal. In *The Federalist*, Madison and Hamilton had unreeled variation after variation on this belief.

Yet the United States was a new, large country in a wild continent with weak communication and strong local cultures. Centrifugal forces were powerful. Timothy Pickering and his die-hard friends chewed at secession from the election of 1804 until the Battle of New Orleans.

In 1819, sectional strife took a new and lurid shape when Missouri applied for statehood. It would be the second state carved out of the Louisiana Territory, after Louisiana itself, and compared to Louisiana, it seemed almost a blank slate, with a thin history of pre-American settlement. What kind of a state it became—slaveholding or free—would be a portent for the development of the west. The House passed a bill for Missouri's admission with a requirement that it be a free state; the Senate rejected the requirement.

Two years of controversy erupted. Slavery, the issue Madison had tried all his life to keep off the table, now filled the table, and it took a starkly sectional form. Thanks to northern prosperity and fecundity, the House had a free-state majority, but the Senate was evenly balanced, eleven free states versus eleven slave (after Madison's retirement, Mississippi, Illinois, and Alabama had joined the Union). Even more than politics or the development of the west seemed to be at stake: the nature of the country appeared to be up for grabs.

Two of Madison's colleagues from the Constitutional Convention were sitting in Congress when the controversy blew up. Charles Pinckney was a representative from South Carolina (not Charles Coatesworth Pinckney, the Federalist also-ran, but his younger Republican cousin who had helped tip the 1800 election to Jefferson and Burr). Some founders liked slavery just fine; Pinckney was a vehement and openly racist supporter. He denied that blacks could ever be citizens anywhere, because they were savages, and he said they were savages because they were stupid. "The African man . . . is as unchanged as the lion or tiger which roams in the same forests with himself."

The other veteran of Philadelphia in Congress was Rufus King, who still sat in the Senate for New York. Federalism was moribund, but feuding Republicans in King's state kept him in Washington as a neutral placeholder. He accepted slavery where it already was as a fait accompli but fervently opposed extending it. "All laws and compacts imposing [slavery] upon any human being are absolutely void, because contrary to the law of nature, which is the law of God."

What did the Father of the Constitution think? As a supporter of diffusion, Madison did not want to see slavery ruled out of Missouri. He also thought Congress had no power to make such a condition: they could not place a new state "above or below the equal rank and rights possessed by the others." What most worried him about Missouri, however, was the politics of the clash, which, as he put it in his letter to Robert Walsh, "fills me with no slight anxiety." When Jefferson was worried, he pulled out the *vox humana*. When Madison was worried, he hunkered in understatement. He now wrote Walsh a structural analysis of political parties. "Parties . . . must always be expected in a government as free as ours. When the individuals belonging to them are intermingled in every part of the whole country, they strengthen the union of the whole, while they divide every part." This was the doctrine of the Virginia Plan—unity through diversity. Now, however, the Missouri question seemed to have generated parties "founded on geographical boundaries. . . . What is to control those great repulsive masses from awful shocks against each other?"

Compromise buffered the masses for the time being—Congress admitted Missouri as a slave state and the Maine district of Massachusetts as a free state, and forbade slavery in most of the remainder of the Louisiana Territory—and time quickly gave politicians other things to quarrel about. But at decade's end, the threat of disunion reappeared.

In 1828, Congress passed a tariff designed to protect manufacturing, though one critic called it "a machine for manufacturing presidents." Andrew Jackson's supporters in Congress hoped the Tariff of 1828 would gain him the votes of northern manufacturers and workers in that year's election (they assumed he had the south and west locked up). Jackson won handily, sweeping the south and west, as well as Pennsylvania and more than half of New York's electoral votes. But John Calhoun, now vice president, had ambitions of his own; the former nationalist, who had once proposed a federal road and canal bill to combat sectionalism, had concluded that his only hopes for advancement lay in carving out a southern base for himself.

The tool Calhoun chose was a report written anonymously by him and issued by the South Carolina legislature, attacking the tariff as a burden on slave-owning agricultural states: since they bought their manufactured goods from the north, or abroad, under a high tariff their costs would rise. That complaint was ordinary interest-group politics, but Calhoun raised the temperature by attacking the tariff as unconstitutional— tariffs, he claimed, could be levied only to raise revenue, not to support manufactures—and asserting South Carolina's right to "interpose" against enforcing it. For justification he cited Hamilton in *The Federalist*, and the Virginia and Kentucky Resolutions of Madison and Jefferson. But since the *Federalist* paper he cited was #51, one of Madison's, he was relying entirely on Virginians. Madison was thus drawn into the fight as an oracle.

Madison was sure that tariffs to support manufacturers were constitutional. As he told Joseph Cabell, a Virginia state senator, protective tariffs had been proposed and passed in the First Congress, and many congresses since—an "unbroken current" of "prolonged and universal practice."

The threat of interposition represented a more personal challenge, since Calhoun presented it as his (and Jefferson's) brainchild. New England Federalists at Hartford had invoked interposition in 1814. Madison had ignored them then, not because they had no right to invoke it, but because they invoked it in a bad cause (he had a war to win and they wanted to end it). Now Calhoun was claiming the same right.

But was he really? Madison wrote a long letter of reproof to Calhoun's mouthpiece in the Senate, Robert Hayne of South Carolina. Hayne never answered; evidently he was too flummoxed by Madison's attack. When Edward Everett, a Massachusetts congressman, learned of the letter and asked if he could print it in the *North American Review*, a Boston journal, Madison agreed. His letter, addressed now to Everett, appeared in October 1830.

Madison tried to take control of what he had written in the Virginia Resolutions, and in the Report on the Alien and Sedition Acts. The doctrine of interposition he had outlined called on the states, plural, "to *concur* in declaring . . . acts to be unconstitutional, and to *co-operate* in . . . necessary and proper measures" to maintain their rights (Madison's italics). The measures he had in mind were the counterthrusts of politics—rallying the public, winning elections—and "as the event showed," they were "equal to the occasion" (i.e., Jefferson and Madison threw the bums out in 1800). He never imagined that a state acting alone could void a federal law.

In the worst case—repeated abuses and no possibility of political relief—there remained the right of revolution. But that was "an extra- and ultra-constitutional right." It could not be smuggled into the Constitution by halves in the form of nullification.

The effect of Madison's letter was dramatic. His three predecessors as ex-presidents either published nothing in their retirement (Washington, Jefferson) or published too much (John Adams defended his diplomatic career in a series of articles for a Boston newspaper that dragged on for three years and that bores even his admirers). Madison's appearance in the *North American Review* was strategic and forceful. It received praise from an unexpected source. "Madison," wrote Chief Justice Marshall, "is himself again."

Madison also worked behind the scenes. In 1831, Nicholas Trist, a young man who was both a Charlottesville native and a grandson of Madison's old Philadelphia landlady, became President Jackson's private secretary. Jackson was determined to enforce the laws and to keep Calhoun in his place, and through Trist Madison had a pipeline to him. The following year Jackson, running for reelection, paid a courtesy call at Montpelier.

Jackson won, and South Carolina decided to execute its four-year-old threat. At the end of 1832, a state convention voted "to NULLIFY certain Acts of the Congress of the United States, purporting to be laws" that taxed imports. If Washington tried to enforce the tariff, South Carolina would "organize a separate government." Secession was the logical consequence of nullification; both assumed that state sovereignty was undiminished by the Constitution and that the United States was a league. If a state could veto laws all by itself, it could take itself out of the Union.

South Carolina was not acting in a void; willing to go it alone, it nevertheless invited other southern states to join in endorsing its doctrines. South Carolina's challenge provoked a debate in the Virginia legislature. Supporters of South Carolina moved to reprint Madison's Report on the Alien and Sedition Acts, as if it were a pro-nullification document. Opponents of South Carolina moved to reprint Madison's *North American*

Review letter, which explained that it was not pro-nullification. The nullifiers replied that the *North American Review* letter was "trash" and that the aged Madison who wrote it was "enfeebled." They wanted Madison when he agreed with them, or not at all.

Madison could not be split in two, especially when he was still alive to assert his own wholeness. But Jefferson was more easy to kidnap. By 1832, he was dead and so unable to explain himself. Moreover, the Kentucky Resolutions he had written really did fit the nullifiers' program. South Carolina had quoted a ringing line from the first paragraph: "whensoever the General Government assumes undelegated powers, its acts are unauthoritative, void, and of no force." In his draft of the Kentucky Resolutions, Jefferson had even written that "every state has a natural right . . . to nullify of [its] own authority all assumptions of power by others." The Kentucky legislature had struck out that language, but Jefferson's draft had leaked in the years since.

As he had promised, Madison took care of his friend. In two 1832 letters to Trist, he laid out the case for Jefferson (*his* Jefferson). He urged contemporary Americans to look at the whole record: the collected works of long-lived men "would without a *single exception*" show "apparent if not real inconsistencies" (Madison's emphasis). He stressed all the times when Jefferson had called for reining the states in, especially when he was a member of the Continental Congress. "It is remarkable how closely the nullifiers . . . shut their eyes and lips, whenever his authority is ever so clearly and emphatically against them." He pointed, finally, with the insight of a great biographer, to an aspect of Jefferson's nature, which had made him so thrilling to live with, and so in need of Madison's ears and advice: "Allowances also ought to be made for a habit in Mr. Jefferson as in others of great genius of expressing in strong and round terms, impressions of the moment." Jefferson wrote memorably, like Homer. But before you take Homer for a guide to living, consult a scholar. Like Madison.

The nullifiers had gone too far—for the present. Virginia and other southern states would not follow their lead, and South Carolina backed down in the face of threats and blandishments: Jackson and Congress declared that the law would be enforced, and Congress also agreed to lower the tariff. Madison was glad to have won, but he feared that permanent damage had been done. In April 1833, he wrote Henry Clay, who as a senator had helped defuse the crisis. South Carolina, he said, had bequeathed "the torch of discord" to its country. The phrase was from Pope's *Iliad*, where it describes the goddess of strife inspiring the Greeks to fight the Trojans.

> *. . . baleful Eris, sent by Jove's command*
> *The torch of discord blazing in her hand . . . (Book 11, l. 5–6)*

The "tendency" of Calhoun's efforts, Madison went on, "whatever be the intention, is to create a disgust with the union, and then to open the way out of it."

Behind the tariff battle crouched another: slavery. Calhoun himself acknowledged the "peculiar labor" on which South Carolina's agricultural economy rested. The tariff battle was Missouri all over again, somewhat more disguised. When Madison thought of slavery directly, the only solution he could see was Liberia. When he thought of slavery as a sectional issue, he looked to the Union as the bulwark against the conflicts it generated.

It is both foolish and irresistible to ask how a 109-year-old James Madison would have voted in the four-way election of 1860. Not for Abraham Lincoln: Lincoln wanted to keep slavery out of the west, and Madison would have tried to tie his constitutional arguments up in knots. Not for John Breckinridge, rule-or-ruin southerner and heir of Calhoun. Perhaps he would have voted for Stephen Douglas, latter-day Jacksonian; more likely for John Bell, the Tennessee Unionist whose platform was union and Constitution, with slavery off the table, and whose running mate was Edward Everett, publisher of the *North American Review* letter. Bell and Everett were not persuasive; they finished fourth in the popular vote and carried only three states (Virginia, Kentucky, and Tennessee). Madison's doctrines by themselves could not keep the country together. But when the crash came, postelection, it is impossible to imagine Madison deserting the Union.

In 1834, he wrote a short note, "Advice to My Country," which was his political last will and testament. He wanted it released posthumously, when it would have the seriousness of death. "The advice nearest to my heart" was that the Union "be cherished and perpetuated." His tale about John and Mary Bull had shown his limitations as a storyteller, so he relied on two stories that were already familiar. "Let the open enemy to it [the union] be regarded as a Pandora with her box opened; and the disguised one as the Serpent creeping with his deadly wiles into Paradise."

The end of such a long life must be a parade of deaths. Jefferson, as all the world learned, died on July 4, 1826. Two days later, Madison wrote Trist that for fifty years he and Jefferson had not experienced "an interruption or diminution of mutual confidence and cordial friendship, for a single moment in a single instance." Not one moment? Not one instance? Surely Madison idealized his dead brother and his own fidelity. But in a lifetime of collaborations, this was the most productive as well as the most gratifying.

His mother died in February 1829, a month after her ninety-seventh birthday. Before she passed, she told a visitor, "I have been a blest woman, blest all my life, and blest in this my old age. I have no sickness, no pain." Her face had fewer wrinkles than that of her famous son, who had been as dutiful to her as he had been devoted to his friend.

James Monroe died on July 4, 1831, in New York City, where he had gone to live with a daughter (his Virginia homes were lost to debt). Madison and Monroe had known several interruptions of confidence—when they ran against each other for Congress, when Madison set Monroe up to negotiate an impossible treaty, when Monroe tried to slip ahead of

Madison into the White House. Yet Madison had compensated Monroe for beating him by positioning him for ultimate victory. So friendship and party unity had been restored.

In the fall of 1832, he wrote a sweetly stoical letter thanking an in-law for a winter cap. Dolley had been knitting him socks. "I am thus equipped *cap-a-pie* [head-to-toe] for the campaign against Boreas and his allies the frosts and the snows. But there is another article of covering which I need most of all and which my best friends cannot supply. My bones have lost a sad portion of the flesh which clothed and protected them, and the digestive and nutritive organs which alone can replace it are too slothful in their functions." For a hypochondriac, Madison had had a good, long run, but the time comes when reality catches up with the anxieties of even the sturdiest.

One of our sources for his last days is Paul Jennings, the slave who as a teenager had helped Dolley evacuate the White House. He had become Madison's manservant in 1820, and shaved him every other day for the rest of his life. In 1836, Madison became unable to walk, but Jennings testified that his mind was "bright" and that he still loved to talk.

A morbid question of timing arose. Jefferson and Monroe had died on the nation's birthday; so had John Adams, who had died on the very same day as Jefferson. So far the only ex-president not to die on July 4 had been Washington, who had succumbed to an illness after being caught in a December snowstorm. As June crept on, doctors offered to keep ex-president Madison going until the Fourth with stimulants. He refused the medication and the melodrama, so that he could die "in the full possession of all his noble faculties," as a niece of Dolley's put it.

He died on June 28. Jennings was with him. At breakfast he could not swallow. "What is the matter, Uncle James?" a niece asked. "Nothing more than a change of mind, my dear," he answered. Intellectual to the end, and beyond: he was his mind, and he did not say it was ending but changing. "His head," wrote Jennings, "instantly dropped, and he ceased breathing as quietly as the snuff of a candle goes out."

EPILOGUE

Legacy

D olley Madison survived her husband by thirteen years (she lived into the era of daguerreotypes; hers show a plump old lady's face, though the smile still suggests the charm and the power of her sweetness). A few events of her widowhood shine a sideways light on Madison.

Dolley inherited Montpelier, a small brick house in Washington,* and a grim economic outlook. Madison had hoped that his precious notes on the Constitutional Convention would keep her comfortable. In his will he described them as "particularly gratifying . . . to all who take an interest in the progress of political science and the cause of true liberty," and he expected "considerable" profits from publishing them. But no commercial house would bite. Harper's in New York was willing to publish them but wanted Dolley to assume all the risks. She then offered the notes to Congress for $100,000. John Calhoun, who by that time was a senator, called them "invaluable" but denied that Congress had the power to buy them, citing Madison's Report on the Alien and Sedition Acts as justification. There, he said, Madison had proved "beyond all controversy" that Congress had "no more than specific powers." Congress ignored

---

* Which still stands, with an added third story and a porch on H Street, at the northwest corner of Lafayette Square.

Calhoun but also shortchanged Dolley, buying the notes for $30,000. They were published in 1840.

Madison had freed no slaves in his will. Edward Coles, his idealistic former secretary, was disappointed. He described slave traders descending on Montpelier, looking for merchandise. "It was like the hawk among the pigeons. The poor creatures would run to the house and protest against being sold." Dolley sold a few slaves to neighbors and relatives, and tried other expedients, including yet another mortgage, to keep Montpelier afloat; in 1844, she finally sold the remainder of the estate and its inhabitants (to a single buyer, so there was at least a chance that everyone would be kept together).

Paul Jennings fared better. After Madison died, he continued to serve Dolley at Montpelier and in the brick house in Washington. Dolley sold him to a man who sold him to Sen. Daniel Webster of Massachusetts for $120; Jennings then went to work, for wages, for Webster and purchased his freedom. One of his jobs was to take provisions to his former mistress, who lived down the block. Webster "told me," Jennings recalled, "whenever I saw anything in the house that I thought she was in need of, to take it to her. I often did this, and occasionally gave her small sums from my own pocket." Love grew even among the rocks.

Dolley became a kind of Washington monument. In 1848, a year before she died, she attended the laying of the cornerstone of the actual Washington Monument, along with Alexander Hamilton's widow, Eliza. The presence of the two old ladies on the reviewing stand represented a posthumous fusion, in honor and forgetfulness, of their husbands, friends, then enemies, and of the man they had both served.

Madison lies in the family cemetery, a five-minute walk from the front door of Montpelier; the graveyard was more convenient to the original house on the property, which the Madisons vacated when he was a boy. His grave is in a corner of the plot, marked by an obelisk;

the shaft surmounts a blocky base, simply inscribed MADISON, along with his dates.

When it was first shown to me, I learned that the stone was not contemporary with his burial, but had been put up in 1857, twenty-one years later. What was his original marker, I asked. There was none, I was told; your marker was your family plot. Your dead relatives indicated who you were, and your living ones would remember where you were.

It is impossible not to think, one more time, of Thomas Jefferson, and of the care he took over his gravestone: sketching the design, providing the dimensions, specifying the deeds he wanted inscribed. He took care of himself when dead. Madison was content to return his body to the family that (especially his parents) had taken such good care of him, and where he had first learned how to live and work with others.

Madison took care of his reputation in other ways (think of his convention notes), but his real monument is not them, or any other item or thing—not even originals of the Constitution or Bill of Rights, or first editions of *The Federalist*. The English architect Sir Christopher Wren was buried in one of his creations, St. Paul's Cathedral, where he has a famous epitaph: if you seek his monument, look about you. Madison's circumambient monument is American constitutionalism—the laws of doing and not doing, and all the debate and revisions they have generated (debating and revising are among the laws; some of the most important ongoing debates—over the power of the federal government, and of the courts; over free speech and freedom of religion—go back to Madison's lifetime). Many other people helped build constitutionalism, including enemies of his, and he would be the last person to deny his collaborators. But he played a major role.

His other monument, coequal if not greater, is American politics, the behavior that makes constitutionalism work: the ways and means of acquiring, conferring, and rebuking power, the party organizations and partisan media that are the vehicles of interest, ambition, and thought. He was at the birth of the American political system, and he understood it better than almost all his great peers. Like the Constitution, politics has changed since he died, but not in ways that would make it unrecognizable to him, or that make him foreign to us. It is all around us, in election years, and every day between elections as well.

Politics can be low, sometimes sordid. Much of that has to be endured, because that is the way men are. "If men were angels," as Madison wrote, "no government would be necessary." But some of the shortcomings of politics may be capable of improvement. So say why and do better. As Madison also wrote, "The censorial power is in the people over the government, and not in the government over the people." Both of those remarks were addressed to government, but they also apply to politics.

Madison at his best, and worst, belongs not just to his family, but to every citizen. We have been working together for a long time.

NOTES

The letters of James Madison, Thomas Jefferson, and George Washington are all online, readable at websites maintained by the Library of Congress. Fortunately, most of the founders and their correspondents wrote legibly, Albert Gallatin excepted. Letters are identified here with obvious abbreviations of the most famous names (JM, TJ, etc.) and dates. All of Madison's are cross-referenced to the most common one-volume edition of his *Writings* (M) whenever they are also found there.

Many public documents, from the Magna Carta to the South Carolina Ordinance of Nullification, are readily available online. They are simply named.

The Constitution and the King James Bible are not footnoted.

Debates	McClellan, James, and M. E. Bradford, eds. *Debates in the Federal Convention of 1787 as Reported by James Madison*. Richmond, VA: James River Press, 1989.
FP	*The Federalist* (cross-referenced to H and M).
H	Hamilton, Alexander. *Writings*. New York: Library of America, 2001.
J	Jefferson, Thomas. *The Life and Selected Writings of Thomas Jefferson*. New York: Modern Library, 1944.
M	Madison, James. *Writings*. New York: Library of America, 1999.
W	Washington, George. *Writings*. New York: Library of America, 1997.

INTRODUCTION

1 **heat and humidity**: Gleig, 61; **"pelt[ing] the enemy"**: Brant V, 291
1 **"what the devil"**: Brant V, 290; **"The enemy are"**: ibid., 297
3 **"The innumerably"**: Adams (*Madison*), 1002
3 **"the former"**: "Memorandum on the Battle of Bladensburg,": M, 700
4 **"[I] expressed"**: ibid., 701; **"attacks resembling"**: Ketcham, 51

4 "a little round": Adams (*Madison*), 452; "**commanding talents**": Ketcham, 532

5 "I remarked": "Memorandum on the Battle of Bladensburg,": M, 702

5 "the arrangements": ibid.

6 **during his lifetime:** Ketcham, 669; "*answer its national*": JM to TJ, 9/6/87, M, 136

6 "a better choice": JM to Sparks, 4/8/31, M, 855

7 "He always": Farrand III, 94

7 "In this favorable": "A Sketch Never Finished Nor Applied," M, 840

8 "the happiness": ibid.

8 "fullest toleration": ibid., 925

8 "I flatter myself": JM to TJ 1/22/86

9 "with a holy zeal": M, 504

10 "could not be distinctly": ibid., 387

12 "the great little": Allgor, 28

CHAPTER I: YOUTH, REVOLUTION

16 "the addition": JM to Bradford 11/9/72, M, 5

16 "the young colonel": Ketcham, 389

17 "my brothers": JM to Bradford 11/9/72, M, 4

18 "If you meet": JM to TJ 8/12/86, M, 57; "**The talent**": Ketcham, 39

18 "never knew": ibid., 35

19 "**Come, noble Whigs**": Brant I, 87; "[He is] full": Ketcham, 428

19 "miscellaneous studies": Brant I, 111; "a long": JM to Bradford 11/9/72, M, 3; "**You hurt**": Brant I, 105

20 "I am too dull": JM to Bradford 11/9/72, M, 3

20 "that diabolical": JM to Bradford 1/24/74, M, 7; "**When I have been**": Harper and Jacumin, 127

20 "I have neither": JM to Bradford 1/24/74, M, 7; "**Religious bondage**": ibid., 9

21 "the mind prefers": JM to Frederick Beasley 11/20/25

22 "There is something": Ketcham, 61; "a hostile attack": ibid., 64

23 "useless members": Broadwater, 80; "all men": ibid., 82–83

23 "the fullest toleration": M, 925

23 "All men": ibid., 10

24 "No man": ibid.

24 "all men": ibid., 10, 925

24 **"were in the practice"**: "Detached Memoranda—Popular Elections," ibid., 767
25 **silent for two years**: Ketcham, 89
26 **"They say"**: ibid., 107
26 **missed only seven**: ibid., 82; **missed hardly any**: ibid., 101
26 **"the venerable"**: ibid., 93
27 **"clear indications"**: ibid., 96
27 **"perpetual union"**: Rossiter, 351
28 **"arm[ed] with coercive"**: JM to TJ 4/16/81, M, 13
29 **"The God"**: J, 311
30 **Madison measured**: Ketcham, 151
30 **"It would give me"**: ibid., 109; **"Firmness"**: ibid., 110
31 **"There is not"**: Brookhiser (*Founding Father*), 114; **"the great fatigues"**: Leibiger, 16; **"As for our"**: ibid., 21
31 **"The story"**: ibid., 6
32 **"father of his country"**: Brookhiser (*Founding Father*), 159
32 **"Mr. Hamilton"**: Hamilton (*Intimate Life*), 35
33 **"pernicious to leave"**: Meyerson, 19; **"the most intelligent"**: ibid.; **"contains both"**: ibid., 38
33 **"We have borne"**: ibid., 20; **"general funds"**: ibid., 23
34 **"imprudent and injurious"**: ibid., 24; **"the energy"**: H, 121
34 **"Mr. Hamilton"**: Meyerson, 24; **"guide the torrent"**: H, 122
34 **"You will give"**: W, 500
35 **"rigid adherence"**: Meyerson, 32

CHAPTER 2: THE CONSTITUTION

38 **"I began"**: JM to TJ 6/19/86; **"Seven o'clock"**: TJ to JM 10/28/85, J, 388–389
39 **"a valuable lesson"**: JM to TJ 6/19/86
40 **"I set out"**: TJ to JM 9/6/89, J, 488–493
41 **"many interesting"**: JM to TJ 2/4/90, M, 473–477
42 **"that no man"**: J, 313
42 **"disavows a dependence"**: M, 30–34
42 **"produced all"**: JM to TJ 1/22/86; **"Well aware"**: J, 311
43 **"the state senate objected"**: Malone I, 279; **"They did not"**: JM to TJ 1/22/86
43 **"his unremitted"**: Leibiger, 34
44 **"Nature has given"**: JM to Lafayette 3/20/85, M, 25; **"Your own"**: Leibiger, 42

45 **"if anything"**: Leibiger, 53
45 **"fresh and endearing"**: ibid., 57
46 **"measures to cement"**: Meyerson, 58; **"render the constitution"**: ibid., 59
47 **"literary cargo"**: Ketcham, 183
47 **"of subjection"**: JM, "Of Ancient and Modern Confederacies"
48 **"common interest"**: M, 71; **"what probability"**: M, 73
48 **"I smelt"**: Grigsby, 32
49 **"It was"**: JM to GW 12/7/86, M, 59–60
49 **"except Maryland"**: JM to GW 2/21/87; **"have come into"**: JM to GW 3/18/87
50 **"I will hope"**: GW to Edmund Randolph 4/9/87, W, 650
50 **"these delays"**: Brookhiser (*Founding Father*), 57
51 **"licentious publications"**: *Debates*, 29, 5/28/87; **"opened the main"**: ibid., 30, 5/29/87; **"the Articles"**: M, 89, 5/29/87
51 **"in all cases"**: M, 89–91, 5/29/87
52 **"whether he meant"**: *Debates*, 35, 5/30/87; **"absolutely necessary"**: JM to GW 4/16/87, M, 81
52 **"The majority"**: M, 75; **"consistent with"**: ibid., 92, 6/6/87; **"justice and"**: ibid., 120, 7/5/87
53 **"enlarge the sphere"**: ibid., 92, 6/6/87; **"control the centrifugal"**: M, 99–100, 6/8/87
53 **"the intrigues"**: ibid., 105, 6/19/87
54 **"Passing over"**: ibid., 117, 6/30/87; **"we were now"**: ibid., 111, 6/26/87
54 **"a spirit"**: Farrand III, 94–95; **"able and close"**: M, 117, 6/30/87
55 **"Every species"**: Farrand III, 92; **"fickle and inconstant"**: ibid.; **"pork still"**: Elliot, *Debates* I, 423
55 **"I am sorry"**: GW to AH 7/10/87, W, 653; **"No man"**: Farrand III, 92
56 **"sustains the sovereignty"**: *Debates*, 119, 6/16/87; **"You see"**: ibid., 116, 6/15/87
56 **"cunning"**: Rossiter, 91–92; **"the proudest"**: ibid., 130
56 **"the great division"**: M, 118, 6/30/87
57 **"he had rarely"**: *Debates*, 228, 7/2/87
57 **"The time"**: ibid., 289, 7/16/87 (actually 7/17)
58 **"the *plan*"**: JM to TJ 9/6/87, M, 136
58 **"The people"**: *Debates*, 534, 8/31/87
58 **"The curiosity"**: "A Sketch Never Finished Nor Applied," M, 840
59 **"In this favorable"**: ibid.

59 "very extravagant": Brookhiser (*Gentleman Revolutionary*), 83
60 "A better choice": JM to Jared Sparks 4/8/31, M, 855; "No man's": *Debates*, 621, 9/17/87

CHAPTER 3: *THE FEDERALIST,* THE BILL OF RIGHTS

61 "laid before": Rossiter, 130; "when altered": JM to GW 9/30/87, M, 138
62 "would sooner": *Debates*, 536, 8/31/87; "now under": JM to TJ 10/24/87, M, 153
62 "There are subjects": JM to Edmund Randolph 1/10/88, M, 191
63 "A free republic": Brutus, #1, 10/18/87
64 "The people": FP 1, H, 171, 174
64 as had happened: Meyerson, 88; "In the beginning": "Detached Memoranda, The 'Federalist,'" M, 768–769
65 "A patient": FP 38, M, 204–205
66 "that the great": FP 40, M, 222
66 "one of our": FP 54, M, 310–314
66 "A nation": FP 49, M, 287–288; "If men": FP 51, M, 295
67 "In all": FP 55, M, 316
67 "Why is the": FP 14, M, 172
67 "Extend[ing] the sphere": FP 10, 165–167
68 "The proposed": FP 39, M, 217; "parchment barriers": FP 48, M, 281–283
68 "The interior structure": FP 51, M, 294–296
68 "Energy": FP 70, H, 274; "the veins": FP 11, H, 206–207
69 "a known difference": "Detached Memoranda, 'The Federalist,'" M, 769
69 "agitated": FP 19, M, 182
70 "You will be": Labunski, 44
70 "I think": ibid., 45; "The consciousness": GW to JM 3/9/88
70 "a few hours": *Debates*, 597, 9/12/87; "remains in the people": Elliot, *Debates* II, 435
71 "what propriety": Brutus, #2, 11/1/87; "A bill of rights": TJ to JM 12/20/87, J, 438
71 "For the first": JM to Elizabeth House Trist 3/25/88, M, 353
72 "as Homer wrote": J, 6
72 David Robertson: M, 931–932; "he spoke": M, 354; "here Mr. Madison": M, 390
73 "I hope": M, 354–355; "Madison among": Leibiger, 94

73 "an illustrious": Labunski, 97–98; "Is it come": M, 381
74 "If there were": M, 381; "If an enumeration": M, 405
74 "bill of rights": Labunski, 105; "You agree": ibid., 66
75 "can produce": M, 407; "A storm": Ketcham, 263
75 "Moderate exercise": GW to JM 6/23/88
75 *"extravagant self-importance"*: JM to TJ 10/17/88, M, 419
76 "I could . . . lay": TJ to JM 2/20/84
77 "he resisted": Labunski, 153; "The secret wish": JM to Edmund
     Randolph 11/2/88, M, 424
77 "I sincerely": TJ to JM 7/31/88, J, 450; "anxiously desired": JM
     to TJ 10/17/88, M, 420–422
78 "A brace": TJ to JM 3/15/89, J, 463; "despised": JM to Edmund
     Randolph 11/23/88, M, 425
78 "extreme distaste": JM to GW 12/2/88; "seemed to consider":
     Labunski, 166
78 "essential rights": JM to George Eve 1/29/89, M, 428; "the many
     important": Labunski, 167
79 "unsuccessful advocate": JM to Thomas Mann Randolph 1/13/89
79 "the smallest": JM to TJ 3/29/89
80 "deep": Maclay, 121
80 "the security": M, 440
81 "the most": Labunski, 227
81 "they have": M, 446–447; "spirit of deference": M, 439; "frothy":
     Labunski, 226
81 "the political thermometer": ibid., 231; "They were treated":
     Maclay, 133; "injure the beauty": Labunski, 221
82 "kill the opposition": JM to Richard Peters 8/19/89, M, 471; "Vir-
     ginia has been": Labunski, 251
83 "pensive": Reif
83 "an ingenious": FP 37, M, 200, FP 10, M, 164, FP 53, M, 308
83 "practical attention": FP 53, M, 308

CHAPTER 4: THE FIRST POLITICAL PARTY

85 "a man": Ames I, 569; "the drudgery": JM to Edmund Randolph
     3/1/89, M, 429; "His Highness": Maclay, 29
85 "splendid tinsel": M, 434
86 "destroy": ibid., 436
86 "talk together": Elkins and McKitrick, 114
86 *"Hamilton . . . is"*: JM to TJ 5/27/89; "personal goodwill": H, 736

88 **"too voluminous"**: JM to TJ 1/24/90
88 **"collision"**: Brookhiser (*Hamilton*), 85
89 **"I call not"**: Maclay, 183–185; **"exploring the interior"**: JM to TJ 1/24/90
89 **"We must go"**: *Debates and Proceedings*, 1st Cong., 2nd Session, 1387, 2/24/90
90 **"hangs heavy"**: Ames I, 729
90 **"somber, haggard"**: Elkins and McKitrick, 155–156
91 **its war debts**: McDonald, 181–187, 404–405
92 **"a little in advance"**: M, 488; **"the diffuse"**: ibid., 485
92 **"whenever the end"**: FP 44, M, 256; **Rep. Elias Boudinot**: Elkins and McKitrick, 231–232
93 **"Mark the reasoning"**: M, 486
93 **"listen[ing] favorably"**: ibid., 749
94 **"unnatural"**: Ketcham, 281–282
94 **"other powers"**: Elkins and McKitrick, 67; **"greatly the advantage"**: JM to Comte de Moustier 10/30/88
95 **"advantages are"**: Ketcham, 281; **"Mr. Madison"**: H, 527
95 **"We think"**: H, 523
95 **"has been treated"**: TJ to JM 8/28/89
96 **"the vehement"**: H, 521; **"want an American"**: Brookhiser (*Gentleman Revolutionary*), 166
96 **"may [you] enjoy"**: Paine, 433
96 **"fewer evils"**: Brookhiser (*America's First*), 95
97 **"political heresies"**: O'Brien, 103; **"Nothing was"**: ibid., 108
97 **"Mr. Adams"**: JM to TJ 5/12/91, M, 491
98 **"the latent"**: FP 10, M, 161–162
98 **"[I would] quarrel"**: Brookhiser (*America's First*), 48; **"Let me"**: W, 969; **"I never"**: J, 460
99 **"There was every"**: Malone II, 362
100 **"Delenda est"**: ibid.
100 **"more conspicuous"**: Pasley, 541; **"Beckley Clerk"**: JM to Edmund Randolph 4/12/89
101 **"From hints dropped"**: Cunningham (*Beckley*), 42
101 **"The following"**: ibid., 43; **"It would be"**: Marsh, 58
101 **"possess[ing] the confidence"**: Cunningham (*Beckley*), 44; **"A second Pope"**: Leary, 36
102 **"a moderate knowledge"**: ibid., 186; **"antidote"**: ibid., 188
102 **"all my letters"**: ibid., 190–191; **"With Mr. Freneau"**: Cunningham (*Republicans*), 17

103 **"the little task"**: Sheehan, 156; **"'Tis not"**: M, 512
103 **"the consumption"**: M, 514; **making exports**: ibid., 495; **"The spirit"**: H, 664
104 **"progress of reason"**: ibid., 506–508
104 **"Are not"**: FP 6, H, 179–181; **"cords of affection"**: FP 14, M, 172
105 **"a general intercourse"**: M, 501; **"Let it be"**: ibid., 500; **"every good citizen"**: ibid., 502; **"Every citizen"**: ibid., 504
105 **"the real domination"**: ibid., 510–511
105 **"new vices"**: ibid., 504–505; **"one party"**: M, 504–505

CHAPTER 5: LEADING AN OPPOSITION

109 **"Republican party"**: Cunningham (*Republicans*), 33–49; **"The Republican party, as it"**: M, 532
109 **"Having thus"**: JM to GW 6/20/92, M, 526
110 **Jefferson warned Washington**: TJ to GW 5/23/92, The Anas of Thomas Jefferson, 10/1/92
110 **"Mr. Madison cooperating"**: H, 738; **"a man"**: ibid., 751; **"peculiarly artificial"**: ibid., 741
111 **"the union"**: ibid., 738
111 **fingering Madison's role**: Leibiger, 163; **"Could no"**: H, 756; **"injurious"**: Leary, 202; **"mutual forbearances"**: W, 817, 819; **"not a syllable"**: J, 521
111 **"some instrumentality"**: H, 789; **election of 1792**: Cunningham (*Republicans*), 45–49
112 **"artificial boundaries"**: JM to Roland 4/93
112 **"Curious example"**: Brookhiser (*Hamilton*), 113; **"The French"**: O'Brien, 141
113 **"deeply wounded"**: J, 522
113 **"blasphemer"**: M, 534; **"heretical"**: JM to TJ 6/13/93, M, 534–536; **"a womanish"**: H, 745
113 **"look of an upstart"**: Brookhiser (*Gentleman Revolutionary*), 140
114 **"I live here"**: Elkins and McKitrick, 343; **"more affectionate"**: ibid., 342
114 **"for us"**: ibid., 344; **"the executive power"**: H, 805; **"For God's sake"**: Elkins and McKitrick, 362
114 **"foreigners"**: M, 537
115 **"much inflamed"**: Brookhiser (*Leadership*), 220
115 **"It is not thus"**: Elkins and McKitrick, 348
115 **"quitting a wreck"**: ibid., 364; **"to avoid"**: Ketcham, 345

116   "his farm": M, 522
116   "obnoxious": JM to Edmund Pendleton 1/2/91; "impracticable": H, 210; "ardent spirits": H, 563; "of any consequence": H, 767–768
117   "the advantage": FP 46, M, 271; "resistance": JM to Monroe 12/4/94
118   "a standing army": JM to Monroe 12/4/94
118   "The real authors": ibid.; **Madison thought:** JM to TJ 12/21/94
118   "the cradle": Elkins and McKitrick, 462; "certain self-created": W 888, 893
119   "An action": M, 551–552
119   "The game": JM to Monroe 12/2/94
120   "I should be": W, 886
120   "the gayeties": Allgor, 20
121   "*grosse*": Adams (*Madison*), 112; "the most beautiful": Allgor, 249; "Thou must": ibid., 28; "the great little Madison": ibid.
121   **American leadership class:** Wood, 78; "I cannot express": M, 550
122   **"Dolley" was no nickname:** Allgor, 416
122   "Mrs. Madison": Morris II, 417; "Everybody loves": Allgor, 232
123   "it flew": JM to Monroe 12/20/95, M, 554
124   "the *British party*": ibid., M, 555
124   "really a colossus": TJ to JM 9/21/95
125   **rejected the idea:** *Debates*, 495, 565; "The situation": JM to TJ 12/27/95
125   "The nature": W, 930–932
126   "hereditary prerogatives": M, 568; "high authority": M, 580; "oracular guide": M, 574
127   "great fault[s]": Ketcham, 360
127   "the people of Maryland": Elkins and McKitrick, 447
127   "Mr. Madison looks worried": ibid., 846

CHAPTER 6: WILDERNESS YEARS

129   "inflexible": JM to JM Sr. 3/16/97
129   "passionate attachments": W, 973
130   **potential successors:** M, 522–523
131   "*I* have not seen": JM to Monroe 9/29/96; "to plant": Cunningham (*Republicans*), 108
132   "The public": TJ to JA 12/28/96
132   "I have felt": JM to TJ 1/15/97, M, 582–583
134   "a foot": Green et al., 21–22

135 "**a real treasure**": Ketcham, 359

135 "**You are right**": Stevens, 23

136 "**van of every**": Durey, 31; **work as a schoolteacher:** James Callender to JM 5/28/96

137 "**A curious specimen**": Brookhiser (*Hamilton*), 134

137 "**a man of genius**": Brodie, 422

138 "**something**": Elkins and McKitrick, 571; "**No, no**": ibid., 573

138 "**kindl[e] a flame**": JM to TJ 5/13/98, M, 588

139 "**false, scandalous**": Elkins and McKitrick, 591–592

140 "**in case**": Virginia Resolutions Against the Alien and Sedition Acts, M, 589–591

141 "**Confidence**": see the discussion of the Kentucky Resolutions of 1798 in *The Papers of Thomas Jefferson*, Vol. 30, 529–556. Compare Jefferson's drafts, written before October, with the version finally passed in November.

141 **did not expect or want it:** Brookhiser (*Adamses*), 46

142 "**inflammatory**": Elliot, *Debates* IV, 537

142 "**A sergeant**": Elkins and McKitrick, 698

143 "**grasp[ed] for power**": ibid., 710

143 "**hideous**": Brodie, 424

143 "**Death**" he said, "**has robbed**": Leibiger, 221

144 **to the courts:** see the replies of Rhode Island, New York, New Hampshire, and Vermont in Elliot, *Debates* IV, 533–539; "**the Judicial**": M, 613

144 "**pave the way**": Report on the Alien and Sedition Acts, M, 619–620, 647–652

146 "**We have beat you**": Miller, 513

146 "**Rather suddenly**": JM to TJ 2/28/01

CHAPTER 7: IN POWER

147 "**we want**": Sparks III, 130

149 "**a Hamiltonian**": Ketcham, 410

150 "**I was extremely**": James Callender to JM 4/27/01

150 **conveyed to him by Madison:** Lomask I, 303

150 **Davis was so zealous:** Cunningham (*Republicans*), 183; "**be found**": Lomask I, 302

151 "**expedient**": Adams (*Jefferson*), 207

152 "**the passing wind**": The Anas of Thomas Jefferson, 1/26/04

152 "What is the spirit": Adams (*Randolph*), 92
153 "It is well known": Brodie, 464
153 Madison thought: JM to TJ 2/18/98, M, 585
154 Jefferson wondered: J, 557
156 "We must marry": Adams (*Jefferson*), 277
157 division of powers: AH to Pickering 2/21/99
157 "It is possible": Sparks III, 180. See also H, 1001, and Morris II, 444
158 "Gentlemen": W, 763
159 "the pageantry": M, 531
159 "The wine": Adams (*Jefferson*), 549
159 hangovers the next day: Allgor, 73–74; "the principle": Adams (*Jefferson*), 549
160 "plain, unassuming": Adams (*Jefferson*), 546
160 "Mobs of boys": Ketcham, 431–432
161 "has furnished": Adams (*Jefferson*), 555
161 "Quite pretty": Allgor, 103
162 "stability": *Debates*, 108, 6/13/87
162 "If there be": H, 972; "Is it a recommendation": H, 979
162 "the adventure": Chernow, 714
163 "That [Mr. Hamilton]": JM to James K. Paulding 4/31
164 "respectable retirement": Lomask I, 332

CHAPTER 8: PROBLEMS OF POWER

165 "maps are not": Adams (*Jefferson*), 486
166 "I considered it": ibid., 695
167 American vessels overall: Wood, 642
168 "The progress": Ketcham, 443
168 John Quincy Adams . . . approved: ibid., 444
168 "clear, calm": Adams (*Jefferson*), 679
170 Jefferson developed a migraine: Ketcham, 451
170 "to a power": Adams (*Jefferson*), 887. Monroe was writing some years after the fact.
170 John Randolph . . . proposed: Adams (*Randolph*), 150
171 Jefferson's character: see Adams (*Jefferson*), 1021–1022; "retaliating regulations": JM to Monroe 8/7/85
171 "of absolute": *Debates*, 475, 8/21/87; he had calculated: M, 495; "force all": JM to TJ 9/14/05; "mak[e] it to": Malone V, 488; Dooley, 207–208

172 **"Governmental prohibitions"**: Adams (*Jefferson*), 1043–1044
172 **"Congress must"**: Wood, 653–656; McDonald, 271–273; Cornog, 86
173 **His enemies said so**: Adams (*Jefferson*), 1172; **"dear"**: ibid., 1056; **"a spectator"**: ibid., 1171; **"continues to take"**: Ketcham, 458–461
173 **"Mr. Madison is"**: Adams (*Jefferson*), 1181
174 **Washington's example**: see TJ to John Taylor 1/6/05
174 **"I came here"**: Adams (*Jefferson*), 716; **"accidental miscarriage"**: Cunningham (*Beckley*), 52
176 **"It has been"**: JM to Monroe 5/25/07
176 **spoke slightingly of Monroe**: Allgor, 133; **"unfortunate"**: ibid.
177 **"gives dinners"**: Allgor, 122
177 **"personal attachment"**: Ketcham, 484
177 **"We ask"**: Adams (*Jefferson*), 1083
179 **"interpose"**: ibid., 1251; **"to my family"**: TJ to David B. Warden 2/25/09

CHAPTER 9: PRESIDENT

181 **"difficulties"**: M, 680–682
182 **"woebegone"**: Ketcham, 475
182 **"I emerged"**: Irving, 24
183 **"he can spell"**: Ketcham, 482
183 **the Invisibles**: Henry Adams attributed the nickname to Rep. Nathaniel Macon of North Carolina. Adams (*Gallatin*), 427
185 **"fraud and folly"**: JM to TJ 8/3/09
186 **"a plain"**: Adams (*Madison*), 87; **"a mob"**: ibid., 110; **"*une bonne, grosse*"**: ibid., 112; **"detestable"**: ibid.; **a swell of Anglophobia**: see ibid., 152–154; Ketcham, 497.
186 **"Too late"**: JM to TJ 4/23/10; **"loves"**: Adams (*Madison*), 181
187 **"understood"**: Adams (*Madison*), 180; **"we commit"**: ibid., 181; **"It is a bargain"**: ibid., 239
187 **Jefferson . . . labored**: see TJ to JM 3/30/09
187 **"with great kindness"**: Monroe to John Taylor 5/9/10; **"Differences of opinion"**: JM to Monroe 3/26/11
188 **"a remedy"**: JM "Memorandum as to Robert Smith," 4/11
189 **Washington handled**: see Brookhiser (*Founding Father*), 97–98; Brookhiser (*Leadership*), 129–132; **Adams fired**: see Elkins and McKitrick, 735–736; Brookhiser (*Leadership*), 222–223
190 **"Energy"**: FP 70, H, 423

190 **"a mere expedient"**: JM "Memorandum as to Robert Smith," 4/11
190 **fed dirt to allies**: see Ketcham, 490
191 **"I have found"**: Chernow, 647
191 **"under the varied"**: JM to Charles Ingersoll 6/25/31
191 **"made his opinion"**: Brant V, 137
192 **a rumor**: see ibid., 268; **inconsistent**: Irving Brant, his admiring biographer, writes of "Madison's lifelong unwillingness to make a public display of political inconsistency." Brant V, 269
192 **"the power"**: Adams (*Jefferson*), 234
193 **"The withered arm"**: ibid., 134
195 **"violating"**: war message to Congress, 6/1/12, M, 685–690
196 **"stimulating everything"**: Hickey, 75; **"The old officers"**: Scott, 31–36
196 **"consumed his time"**: Ketcham, 522; **a drunk**: Hickey, 90
197 **"It was a fair"**: JM to Henry Wheaton 2/26/27
198 **top legal minds**: Hickey, 70
198 **"seasonable antidote"**: ibid., 67, 69; **"a mere matter"**: TJ to William Duane 8/4/12
199 **shot**: TJ to JM 11/4/12
199 **"an unprincipled fellow"**: Morris II, 539
200 **"vigor in war"**: Cornog, 99; **Historians scoff**: see Adams (*Madison*), 581, parroted by almost everyone ever since

CHAPTER 10: WAR LEADER

202 **Monroe disliked Armstrong**: see Monroe to JM 12/27/13; **"a proper mixture"**: "Review of a Statement Attributed to Gen. John Armstrong . . . ," 2/24.
202 **"national sovereignty"**: M, 693–696
203 **"did not like"**: Ketcham, 560
204 **"We have met"**: Hickey, 133; ***"Ripsi, Rantsi"***: Anderson, 279
204 **"Don't give up"**: Hickey, 156
205 **"The committee"**: Adams (*Madison*), 661
206 **"Those are regulars"**: Hickey, 187
207 **a letter**: JM to JA 8/13/14, M, 697–700
207 **harassed only by the humidity**: see Gleig, 54; **"good spirits"**: Ketcham, 576
208 **Self-hating wits**: Hickey, 198; **"it would be proper"**: Memorandum on the Battle of Bladensburg 8/24/14, M, 702
209 **"clear out!"**: Jennings, 9

209 **"Jemmy's health"**: Ketcham, 579; **"seat"**: Allgor, 361; **"I never saw"**: Adams (*Madison*), 1013–1014

210 **"tear off"**: Memorandum on Armstrong's Resignation 8/29/14, M, 703–706

211 **"No, no!"**: Brant V, 290

213 **"a right"**: Adams (*Madison*), 1093

213 **"Such a bargain"**: Ingersoll II, 294;

214 **Madison lobbied against**: ibid., 264

214 **Gallatin had warned**: Adams (*Madison*), 1190

214 **"Mr. Clay"**: Nevins, 129

215 **"I feel no"**: Lodge, 28–31

216 **"[I have] been told"**: Morris II, 548; **"[Shall] the slave holding"**: ibid., 543

216 **"I hear"**: ibid., 559

216 **"in case"**: M, 589; **"in cases"**: Dwight, 361

217 **"a crisis so momentous"**: ibid., 378

218 **"Mr. Madison"**: Ingersoll II, 340

218 **The man who had called**: M, 617; **"preserve and promote"**: M, 709; **"universal peace"**: M, 505–508; **"Experience has taught"**: M, 708

219 **"the wisdom"**: M, 707

219 **"contemptible little"**: Hickey, 279; **"Madison's wrinkled"**: Ingersoll II, 348

220 **"Let us forget"**: Sparks III, 361

221 **"with a laudable"**: M, 716–717

221 **"a low, sordid"**: Adams (*Madison*), 1283; **"by any just"**: M, 719–720

222 **"a school boy"**: Ketcham, 612

CHAPTER 11: RETIREMENT, DEATH

223 **"The truth is"**: Allgor, 363

224 **$40,000**: see Allgor, 351

225 **"It is said"**: JM to TJ 9/2/93, M, 549

226 **"If the end"**: *McCulloch v. Maryland*. See also H, 621

226 **"the general and abstract"**: JM to Spencer Roane 9/2/19, M, 733–734

226 **"hang . . . inference"**: TJ to Justice William Johnson 6/12/23

227 **"troublesome"**: JM to TJ 6/27/83, M, 800–802

227 **"egregious"**: McCoy, 85–86

228 **"on the democracy"**: Robert Yates Notes, 6/12/87; **"the popular branch"**: *Debates*, 108

228 **"the older"**: McCoy, 164

229 **"As the scheme"**: Ketcham, 651

229 **"There is one"**: TJ to JM 2/1/25

230 **"But why"**: TJ to JM 2/17/26, J, 728

230 **"You cannot"**: JM to TJ 2/24/26, M, 811

231 **"Have they not"**: Elliot, *Debates* III, 590

231 **"Such an idea"**: M, 406; **his last journalistic hoax**: Van Doren, 775; **"proceed with"**: JM to Edmund Randolph 3/21/90

231 **"the rights"**: Ketcham, 627. Italics in original; **"whipping negroes"**: see "War Leader," above

232 **"better the condition"**: JM to Robert Walsh 11/27/19, M, 743

232 **"permanently removed"**: JM to Robert J. Evans 6/15/19, M, 728–730

233 **$109 million**: Hickey, 303

233 **"gangs of negroes"**: McCoy, 311–312

233 **"Not believing"**: Washburne, 47

234 **"You are pursuing"**: McCoy, 313–314

234 **"abundant stock"**: Ketcham, 636

235 **"It is due"**: M, 825

235 **"Any allusion"**: JM to Lafayette 2/1/30

235 **"certain African dye"**: M, 781, 786

236 **"lively—often playful"**: Martineau I, 190–192

238 **"The African man"**: Benton VII, 110; **"All laws"**: King VI, 276

238 **"above or below"**: JM to Robert Walsh 11/27/19, M, 741

239 **"founded on"**: ibid., M, 744; **"a machine"**: Remini, 329

239 **"interpose"**: South Carolina Exposition and Protest

240 **"unbroken current"**: JM to Joseph Cabell 9/18/28

240 **too flummoxed**: see McCoy, 140; **"to *concur*"**: JM to Edward Everett 8/28/30, M, 851

241 **"an extra-"**: ibid., M, 848; **"Madison"**: Brant VI, 484

241 **"to NULLIFY"**: South Carolina Ordinance of Nullification

242 **"trash"**: McCoy, 154

242 **"whensoever"**: *Journals*, 34; **"every state"**: see Jefferson, *The Papers*, Vol. 30, 529–556, first two drafts

242 **"would without"**: JM to Nicholas Trist 5/32, M, 860; **"It is remarkable"**: JM to Nicholas Trist 12/23/32, ibid., 862–863; **"Allowances"**: JM to Trist 5/32, ibid., 860

243 The **"tendency"**: JM to Henry Clay 4/2/33; **"peculiar labor"**: South Carolina Exposition and Protest

244 **"The advice"**: M, 866
244 **"an interruption"**: JM to Nicholas Trist 7/6/26, M, 812
244 **"I have been"**: Hunt, 236
245 **"I am thus"**: JM to Andrew Stevenson 11/20/32, M, 861
245 **"bright"**: Jennings, 18; **"in the full"**: Allgor, 376; **"What is the"**: Jennings, 18–19

EPILOGUE: LEGACY

247 **"particularly gratifying"**: McCoy, 164
247 **"invaluable"**: *Register*, 24th Cong., 2nd Session, Senate, 858–859
248 **"It was"**: McCoy, 320
248 **"told me"**: Jennings, 14–15; **she attended**: Harvey, 46
250 **"If men"**: FP 51, M, 295; **"The censorial"**: M, 552

BIBLIOGRAPHY

Adams, Henry. *History of the United States of America During the Administrations of Thomas Jefferson.* New York: Library of America, 1986.
———. *History of the United States of America During the Administrations of James Madison.* New York: Library of America, 1986.
———. *John Randolph.* Armonk, NY: M. E. Sharpe, 1996.
———. *Life of Albert Gallatin.* Philadelphia: J. B. Lippincott & Co., 1879.
Allgor, Catherine. *A Perfect Union.* New York: Henry Holt and Company, 2006.
Ames, Fisher. *Works of Fisher Ames,* 2 vols. Indianapolis: Liberty Classics, 1983.
Anderson, David Rollin, ed. *Anthology of Western Reserve Literature.* Kent, OH: Kent State University Press, 1992.
Benton, Thomas Hart. *Abridgement of the Debates of Congress . . . ,* 7 vols. New York: D. Appleton & Company, 1858.
Brant, Irving. *James Madison,* 6 vols. Indianapolis: Bobbs-Merrill, 1941–1961.
Broadwater, Jeff. *George Mason, Forgotten Founder.* Chapel Hill: University of North Carolina Press, 2006.
Brodie, Fawn M. *Thomas Jefferson: An Intimate History.* New York: Bantam Books, 1975.
Brookhiser, Richard. *Alexander Hamilton, American.* New York: Free Press, 1999.
———. *America's First Dynasty: The Adamses, 1735–1918.* New York: Free Press, 2002.
———. *Founding Father: Rediscovering George Washington.* New York: Free Press, 1996.
———. *Gentleman Revolutionary: Gouverneur Morris, the Rake Who Wrote the Constitution.* New York: Free Press, 2003.
———. *George Washington on Leadership.* New York: Basic Books, 2008.
Chernow, Ron. *Alexander Hamilton.* New York: Penguin Press, 2004.
Cornog, Evan. *The Birth of Empire.* New York: Oxford University Press, 1998.
Cunningham, Noble E. Jr. *The Jeffersonian Republicans.* Chapel Hill: University of North Carolina Press, 1957.

————. "John Beckley: An Early American Party Manager." *William and Mary Quarterly*, Third Series, Vol. 13, no. 1 (January 1956).

Debates and Proceedings in the Congress of the United States . . . Washington, DC: Gales and Seaton, 1834.

Dooley, Patricia L., ed. *The Early Republic: Primary Documents on Events from 1799 to 1820*. Westport, CT: Greenwood Press, 2004.

Durey, Michael. *With the Hammer of Truth: James Thomson Callender and America's Early National Heroes*. Charlottesville: University Press of Virginia, 1990.

Dwight, Theodore. *History of the Hartford Convention*. Freeport, NY: Books for Libraries Press, 1970.

Elkins, Stanley, and Eric McKitrick. *The Age of Federalism*. New York: Oxford University Press, 1993.

Elliot, Jonathan, ed. *The Debates in the Several State Conventions . . .* , 4 vols. Washington, DC: Printed for the editor, 1836.

Farrand, Max. *The Records of the Federal Convention of 1787*, 3 vols. New Haven, CT: Yale University Press, 1911.

Gleig, George Robert. *The Campaigns of the British Army at Washington and New Orleans, 1814–1815*. London: John Murray, Albermarle Street, 1879.

Green, Bryan Clark, and Ann L. Miller with Conover Hunt. *Building a President's House*. Orange, VA: Montpelier Foundation, 2007.

Grigsby, Hugh Blair. *The History of the Virginia Federal Convention of 1788*. Richmond: Virginia Historical Society, 1890.

Hamilton, Allan McLane. *The Intimate Life of Alexander Hamilton*. New York: Charles Scribner's Sons, 1911.

Harper, Keith, and C. Martin Jacumin, eds. *Esteemed Reproach: The Lives of Rev. James Ireland and Rev. Joseph Craig*. Macon, GA: Mercer University Press, 2005.

Hickey, Donald R. *The War of 1812*. Urbana and Chicago: University of Illinois Press, 1989.

Hunt, Galliard, ed. *The First Forty Years of Washington Society . . .* New York: Charles Scribner's Sons, 1906.

Ingersoll, Charles J. *History of the Second War Between the United States of America and Great Britain . . .* , 2 vols. Philadelphia: Lippincott, Grambo & Co., 1852.

Irving, Washington. *Letters of Washington Irving to Henry Brevoort*. New York: G. P. Putnam's Sons, 1918.

Jefferson, Thomas. *The Writings of Thomas Jefferson*, 19 vols. Washington, DC: Thomas Jefferson Memorial Association, 1907.

————. *The Papers of Thomas Jefferson*. Princeton, NJ: Princeton University Press, 1950–.

Jennings, Paul. *A Colored Man's Reminiscences of James Madison*. Orange, VA: Montpelier Foundation, 2009.

Ketcham, Ralph. *James Madison, a Biography*. Charlottesville: University of Virginia Press, 1990.

King, Charles R. *The Life and Correspondence of Rufus King*, 6 vols. New York: G. P. Putnam's Sons, 1894–1900.

Labunski, Richard. *James Madison and the Struggle for the Bill of Rights*. New York: Oxford University Press, 2006.

Leary, Lewis. *That Rascal Freneau*. New York: Octagon Books, 1964.

Leibiger, Stuart. *Founding Friendship*. Charlottesville: University of Virginia Press, 1999.

Lodge, Henry Cabot. *One Hundred Years of Peace*. New York: Macmillan Company, 1913.

Lomask, Milton. *Aaron Burr*, 2 vols. New York: Farrar, Strauss, Giroux, 1979.

Maclay, William. *The Diary of William Maclay and Other Notes on Senate Debates*. Baltimore: Johns Hopkins University Press, 1988.

Malone, Dumas. *Jefferson and His Time*, 6 vols. Boston: Little Brown and Company, 1948–1981.

Marsh, Philip M. "John Beckley, Mystery Man of the Early Jeffersonians." *Pennsylvania Magazine of History and Biography* 72, no. 1 (January 1948).

Martineau, Harriet. *Retrospect of Western Travel*, 2 vols. London: Saunders and Otley, 1838.

McCoy, Drew R. *The Last of the Founders*. New York: Cambridge University Press, 1989.

McDonald, Forrest. *Alexander Hamilton: A Biography*. New York: W. W. Norton & Company, 1979.

Meyerson, Michael I. *Liberty's Blueprint*. New York: Basic Books, 2008.

Miller, John C. *Alexander Hamilton: Portrait in Paradox*. New York: Harper & Brothers, 1959.

Morris, Anne Cary. *The Diary and Letters of Gouverneur Morris*, 2 vols. New York: Charles Scribner's Sons, 1888.

Nevins, Alan, ed. *The Diary of John Quincy Adams, 1794–1845*. New York: Longmans, Green, and Co., 1928.

O'Brien, Conor Cruise. *The Long Affair*. Chicago: University of Chicago Press, 1996.

Paine, Thomas. *Collected Writings*. New York: Library of America, 1995.

Pasley, Jeffrey L. "'A Journeyman Either in Law or Politics': John Beckley and the Social Origins of Political Campaigning." *Journal of the Early Republic* 16, no. 4 (Winter 1996).

Reif, Rita. "Founding Fathers, Large as Life." *New York Times*, November 24, 2002.

Rossiter, Clinton. *1787, the Grand Convention*. New York: Macmillan Company, 1966.

Scott, Winfield. *Memoirs of Lieut.-General Scott*. New York: Sloan & Company, 1864.

Sheehan, Colleen A. *James Madison and the Spirit of Republican Government*. New York: Cambridge University Press, 2009.

Sparks, Jared. *The Life of Gouverneur Morris, with Selections from His Correspondence* . . . , 3 vols. Boston: Gray & Bowen, 1832.

Stevens, John Austin. *Albert Gallatin*. Boston and New York: Houghton, Mifflin, and Co., 1883.

Van Doren, Carl. *Benjamin Franklin*. New York: Viking Press, 1938.

Washburne, E. B. *Sketch of Edward Coles*. Chicago: Jansen, McClurg & Company, 1888.

Wood, Gordon S. *Empire of Liberty*. New York: Oxford University Press, 2009.

INDEX

Note: References to James Madison in subheadings are shown with the initials JM.